BRAND STORY®

*How to Launch Your Shoestring
Start-up Like a National Brand*

BRAND STORY

How to Launch Your Shoestring Start-up
Like a National Brand

BRUCE MILLER

Miller eMedia
Decatur, Georgia

Miller eMedia LLC

615 Sycamore Street

Decatur, GA 30030

www.milleremedia.com

bruce@milleremedia.com

BRAND STORY | Contents

00 **INTRODUCTION** 9
The author's improbable journey to become a brand strategist.

01 **IN THE MOOD FOR COFFEE?** 21
Why successful brands pull you off the freeway.

02 **BRAND POSITIONING: A BRIEF HISTORY** 41
A door-to-door stove salesman changes the industry.

03 **REVERSING SPACE: How to connect to your customers** 55
We can still learn from Steve Jobs on how to put the customer experience first.

04 **THE BRAND WORKSHOP** 69
You know your customer; now it's time to position your brand.

05 **THE NAME GAME** 83
Why naming your business is more consequential than naming your child.

06 **ON YOUR MARKS, TRADEMARK!** 101
Why you should file a trademark, and how to do it without a lawyer.

07 **CREATE A LOVE RELATIONSHIP WITH CUSTOMERS** 113
A hip new food truck roaming LA can teach us how to connect with customers.

08 **THE ELEVATOR PITCH** 127
How a game-changing pitch in the men's room launched a career in clean technology.

09 **LOOK AND FEEL** 135
Successful movies explain why it's the story that drives the look and feel.

10 **POSITIONING NON-PROFITS** 149
Pitching to major donors? Ultimately, everyone is a consumer.

11 **TOUCHPOINTS** 161
How to build a universe of touchpoints that point to your brand story.

12 **BRAND STORIES** 185
The personal stories behind the brands: Thrive Farmers | Sara Anderson | Form Yoga | Klickly

13 **THE ROLLERCOASTER OF RISK** 227
How to stay on top of the journey when, suddenly, "The Thrill is Gone."

ACKNOWLEDGEMENTS, CREDITS, and AUTHOR BIO 240

BRAND STORY
How to Position Your Shoestring Startup Like a National Brand

INTRODUCTION

The Panda Express lady teased me with a skewer of Kung Pao chicken.

"Taste?"

As Michael and I walked through the mall – past *Cinnabon, Sbarro, Orange Julius, Jamba Juice* and the other markers of American food court culture – I wondered what an archaeologist would think, a thousand years from now, digging through the ancient strata buried at Atlanta's Perimeter Mall, trying to discern the difference between *Famous Amos* and *Mrs. Field's.*

My business partner, Michael Higgins, and I were there to meet Mark Kaplan, the CEO of *Great Wraps* — America's original fast food wraps chain.

Mark grinned to us like Br'er Rabbit from the fast-food patch, "Hey, guys. Welcome to *Great Wraps!*"

Mark was hiring us to facelift the *Great Wraps* brand. For branding guys like Michael and me, a rebrand was our dream job.

"Mark, this is very cool," I fibbed as I surveyed The *Great Wraps* brand experience.

"Try some of these," Mark beamed as he handed me a tray of *Kurly Fries*. I sighed in relief that Mark didn't ask me to sample the "Ultimate" — a slab of curly fries topped with cheese, bacon, and Ranch Dressing — a vascular bomb that delivered a payload of 790 calories and 59 grams of fat. Mark directed me to the "Flavor Bar."

"Can you believe it?" Mark exclaimed. "After sixty years of fast food, ketchup and salt are still the only major flavors for fries in this country!"

I had never considered the limitations of ketchup, but Mark continued.

"People want choices. *Great Wraps* has eight proprietary spice blends. Go ahead and mix and match."

I sprinkled "*Hellacious Jalapeño*" on my Kurlies, and prepared to hallucinate.

The first step in brand strategy is to determine if the product line tells a cohesive story. I perused the offerings: *Gyro Wrap, Santa Fe Wrap, Spicy Chipotle Wrap, Falafel Wrap, Hummus Veggie Wrap, Buffalo Wrap, California Wrap...*

"These all make sense," I said approvingly. "People are moving away from bread." I learned to patronize clients from my mom, so I added, "Mark, this is *Great Wraps'* moment."

"And we have bowls," Mark continued, "for those who want to go completely bread-free. And smoothies."

"*Eat Great. Feel Great.*™ I like the tag line," I said to keep the compliments flowing. "*Great Wraps* are, umm, the healthy alternative."

Mark beamed with pride.

I walked the length of the counter until a promotional sign stopped my tracks. Michael also saw the sign, but cautioned me with a look: "Don't go there."

"Mark, tell me about the Philly Cheesesteak," I inquired with devious curiosity.

I sprinkled "Hellacious Jalapeño" on my Kurlies, and prepared to hallucinate.

"Isn't that great?" Mark boasted. "No one's got a cheesesteak in the food court, so we added it to the menu."

SPECIAL
SMALL
PHILLY CHEESESTEAK
WITH FRIES
$4.99
GRILLED SIRLOIN STEAK,
WHITE AMERICAN CHEESE,
GRILLED ONIONS, MUSHROOMS
& GREEN PEPPERS
NOT VALID WITH ANY OTHER
DISCOUNT OR COUPON

"But aren't wraps, you know, great wraps... the world's greatest wraps, isn't that the Big Idea?" I asked gently.

"The way I see it," Mark explained with perfect business logic, "if someone's in the mood for a cheesesteak, we get that sale."

"Sure, sure," I agreed, "*But Eat Great, Feel Great...* Doesn't a cheesesteak negate the whole, healthy wrap thing – the brand concept?" I couldn't help myself.

Michael glared at me. His blood pressure was rising.

"In the mall, it's all about incremental revenue," Mark explained. "Imagine a guy and a girl in the food court. She wants something light, say Chinese, but he doesn't. That's my opening... to pull them away from *Panda*. They come here; he gets a cheesesteak and she gets a bowl. It's a zero-sum game in the food court. You're competing for a small universe of hungry customers."

"What if *Chick-Fil-A* added a burger to their menu," I countered? "The cows on the billboard..."

Michael quickly interrupted. "We'll put together some logo ideas to get the ball rolling."

"What if Chick-Fil-A added a burger to their menu?"

EAT MOR CHIKIN'
Chick-fil-A

"Good deal," Mark replied. I quietly fumed that the cheesesteak had sabotaged my vision of Mark as the King of Wraps.

As it turned out, Mark let his son design the new logo, and we didn't get the job. Soon after, two more cheesesteaks appeared on the menu: *Chicken Philly* and *Chipotle Philly*. Brand purity it ain't, but in the zero-sum world of food courts, a sale is a sale.

I don't want to disparage *Great Wraps*. With over 50 stores and more coming, Mark knows his customer. But, *Great Wraps* illustrates the core conflict all businesses face: "Brand versus Product."

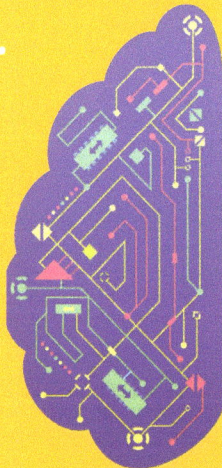

Visit any corporate marketing department, and you will find a fundamental tension between marketing people and product people. The cognitive product side of our brain believes that customers seek the best products. In this way, customers compare features, functionality, and price to make an informed buying decision.

The brand side of our brain draws from the subconscious — a pastiche of desires and associations delivers an unspoken feeling: *This brand is for me.* Sure, I can practice yoga in $9 *Hanes EcoSmart* sweatpants, but what I really want are the $79 yoga pants from *Prana*.

The thesis of this book builds on an idea outlined in 1971 by advertising legend, David Ogilvy, which is:

- *People don't buy products; they buy brands — or more accurately, they respond to brand positions.*

Brands are like love affairs. Inexplicable chemistry sends a signal to our limbic brain: *"This brand is for me."* As anyone wearing overpriced jeans will testify: A brand is a badge of identity.

"This brand is for me."

Brands explain why you might prefer a grungy neighborhood coffee bar over *Starbucks* or *Great Wraps* over *Chipotle* — or vice versa.

Mark got into the wrap business 30 years ago. He bought the original wrap concept — the Greek-themed *Gyro Wrap* and rebranded the chain as *Great Wraps. Great Wraps* launched at a time when nobody was serving wraps.

Today everyone has wraps — *McDonald's, Chick-fil-A, Chipotle*, even the mecca of bread, *Panera*, has wraps. I wish Mark had seized command of the wrap concept and cemented a dominant position: *"Home of the Original Wrap."*

If my mom, PR legend Nann Miller, had Mark as a client, she would have established a National Wrap Day with a music tie-in. I can see her celebrating with "Wrap" music, Celebrity Wrap Recipes, a wrap for Tu Pac, and a monster-sized wrap — aka the Notorious B.I.G Wrap. Mark could have followed the genius of *7-Up* and position *Great Wraps* as *"The Un-Sandwich."* Ahh, if only it weren't for those concept-killing cheesesteaks served on white bread hoagie rolls.

Brand positioning is more art than science, but, after two decades of positioning brands, I have discovered that even the most shoestringy of startups can follow three basic steps:

The three basic steps to branding your shoestring start-up:

Shoestring Brand Positioning:

1. *Align your brand to the needs of your target customer,*

2. *Establish a differentiator or secret sauce that solves those needs, and*

3. *Take one step at a time to build out your brand and prove that it works.*

If you want to savor brand positioning at its essence, order a hot dog from James Hammerl, a super-friendly guy in our neighborhood who opened a hot dog shack called *DoggyDogg*.

James started with a hot dog cart, then moved up to selling artisan dogs from a cinder block hut — a building around the corner from me that has served as our neighborhood's launch-pad for startups.

For decades, the tiny hut housed a taxi dispatch transmitter until cell phones killed radio dispatching. After sitting vacant for years, Rita King, a delightful, chain-smoking artist from Germany started a tiny picture framing business. Rita's husky Marlene Dietrich voice, drooping cigarette ash, and passion for framing formed an authentic brand experience.

Las Brasas, a rotisserie chicken takeout business , next managed to squeeze into the hut.

As the neighborhood's brand strategist, I convinced the *Las Brasas* owners, John and Maria Koechlin from Lima Peru, to build their brand around their authentic Peruvian recipes (including their trademark tangy green sauce made from zingy peppers and huacatay leaves). Since the average American has no concept of Peru, their cuisine was positioned as the authentic alternative to grocery store rotisserie chicken. *Las Brasas* was a big success, so much so, they moved to take over a large sit-down restaurant around the corner.

The cinder block brand incubator was bequeathed to the hot dog guy, James Hammerl. As James explains in his brand story:

"I was in Bavaria, coming out of a Christmas mass and walking towards the town square. Amid the fog and snow, I noticed a gentleman selling tasty sausages from a cart. From that moment, I knew I wanted to take hot dogs to another level in Atlanta."

Doggy Dogg raises the foodie factor on the humble wiener. James takes a locally-sourced sausage, slathers it in farm-to-table kimchi or homemade kraut, and wraps it in a fresh bun from a local pastry chef. Doggy Dogg's tag line captures the "Big Idea" of his brand:

> *Bringing cultural ingredients to an American classic: the hot dog.*

By elevating ballpark fare to foodie sophistication, *Doggy Dogg* created a new brand category: late-night, hipster hot dogs. More importantly, James affirms the shoestring thesis of this book:

A guy with a hot dog cart and a dose of customer sense can successfully position a brand.

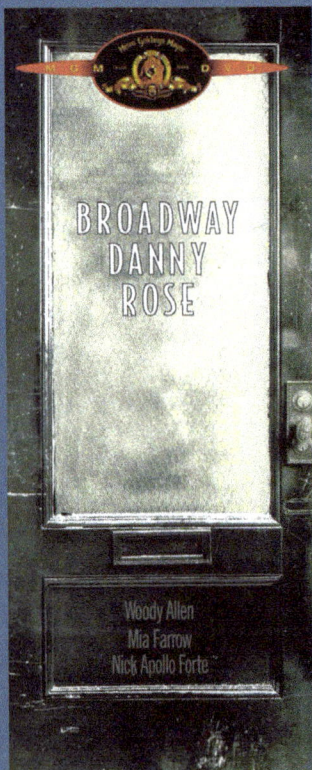

A guy with a hot dog cart can position a successful brand story.

A little bit about my background: Twenty years ago, Michael and I ran the creative department at *CheckFree Corp.*, a bank technology company in Atlanta. We won the Max Award for Georgia's marketing campaign of the year, and installed the trophy in the president's office. In gratitude, *CheckFree's* management fired our entire department the next day. The geniuses wanted to clear the deck and bring in an outside agency, so, Michael and I went off to start *Design Coup,* a scrappy, young branding agency.

Over the years, we helped an assortment of *"Broadway Danny Rose"*[1] types launch their business dreams. We scored some national brands that paid the bills, including lots of healthcare and tech, but we sharpened our branding chops by developing brands for shoestring startups.

We helped a Jewish woman launch her "Kippah Clip" to keep skull caps attached in prayer, and we branded a wall-patch compound made from old paint for a dad with seven home-schooled children. We also designed scores of cheap products for *Dollar General,* and we created a patriotic liquor brand, *SpiritsUSA,* for an Aussie bar owner whose efforts were stymied by Georgia's Prohibition-era laws which effectively mandated that he divorce his wife.[2]

My talent in brand positioning came from my mother, Nann Miller. Lauded as the *"PT Barnum of the PR Industry,"* my mom broke many glass ceilings by building one of the first woman-owned PR firms. She would be grinning in her grave to see how most PR firms today are owned or run by women. The joke in the family was that my mom was so savvy at positioning a story that she could get a news truck to pull up to a birthday party. She had a

_____

1 The movie, Broadway Danny Rose portrayed a tireless New York talent agent played by Woody Allen who promoted a roster of oddball acts.

psychic sense for the *"big idea"* – how to dramatize the brand story in a single compelling image through the power of contrast: *big/little, new/old, rich/poor* – and *camel/hotel.*

Here's the camel story: She famously rebuffed the Israeli Tourist Commission when they asked her to publicize a tourism banquet at the Los Angeles Hyatt Regency. "A bunch of people eating?" Nann scoffed, "That's not news!"

The Israelis persisted, so my mom zeroed in on the wacky idea of having a camel check into the hotel.

"That's crazy!" the client blurted. "There are no camels in Israel!"

"And you… you don't have a story," she countered, "So, we will have to make one. Camel, hotel — contrast."

When the news trucks rolled up to the hotel, the crews looked sheepishly at each other, "How did we fall for this?"

Rosie the Camel entered the hotel through the garage and into the freight elevator while the cameras waited in the lobby. The doors slid open to reveal an empty elevator.

"Where's Rosie?" my mom blurted, unwittingly becoming the focus of the story. "The camel's lost! Somewhere in the hotel!"

Suddenly a scene from the Marx Brothers, the police arrived to issue my mom a ticket for not having a filming permit for "livestock" on a city street. From there, the story grew. The camel story was picked up by the locals, the networks, and the *LA Times*. Two weeks later, the cameras returned to follow the saga to the courthouse when the "ship of the desert" made a second appearance to pay its fine.

Dramatize the brand story in a single compelling image through the power of contrast.

"The camel is lost! Somewhere in the hotel!"

Los Angeles Times

Another humdrum day at 7th and Hope Sts. as Rosie the camel is led through traffic to be registered at the Hyatt Regency.
Times photo by John Malmin

Ship of the Desert Invites Americans to Israel
Rosie the Camel Takes Room at L.A. Hotel to Promote Tourism

BY KATHY BURKE
Times Staff Writer

Rosie went downtown Tuesday morning. She was given a ride from San Bernardino and hung around the corner of 7th and Hope Sts. for almost half an hour in the 48-degree weather.

Her manager, Bob Holter, paraded her around a bit and everyone seemed to agree she was worth a second look. Then she and Bob went inside the Hyatt Regency Hotel and Rosie got a room.

By the time the morning was over, Rosie had earned every bit of the 35 pounds of hay

and five pounds of grain she eats each day.

Rosie is a camel, and Tuesday morning she was representing Israeli camels. All of Israel, in fact.

Pinned to the gold blanket thrown over her hump were T-shirts and buttons advertising the "California Visits Israel" display at the hotel.

Today, Mayor Tom Bradley will proclaim the week of Jan. 8-14 "California Visits Israel" week, seven days of festivities at the hotel designed to celebrate and stimulate Israel's "year of tourism," 1976.

For those who weren't quite awake at 9 a.m.

Tuesday at 7th and Hope, Rosie was as good as a cup of strong coffee.

Cars slowed, pedestrians stopped.

At the registration desk, where she was presented a hotel key, she began eating mums from the pots on the counter.

If nothing else, Rosie's presence alerted passersby to the fact that camels exist outside Egypt and the Sahara—although a few clung to the stereotype.

"Poor thing," said one elderly woman in a blue hat. "I bet it feels lost. I bet it's looking for a sand dune. Or a sphinx."

And that is how I grew up. One day, I would be shooting a radio DJ diving into the world's largest Hires Root Beer float, or filming diamond-clad bikini models stepping out from a Brinks truck into L.A.'s new Jewelry Center, or staging the world's longest ribbon cutting spanning the Long Beach harbor for the new Hyatt Long Beach, or recording Zsa Zsa Gabor promoting the Beverly Hilton as an homage to the second of her nine husbands, Conrad Hilton.

One night, as my mom drove home from her office, she stopped her car at a hillside overlooking the Harbor Freeway to marvel at the glowing skyline. From her weed-filled vantage point, Nann saw a huge crowd in her mind's eye – the perfect stunt to publicize her client, the Central City Association of Los Angeles.

Three month's later, Nann Miller's vision was realized: The world's largest group photo was staged to welcome global visitors to the 1984 Olympics on billboards throughout the area.

Positioning is not grandiose

A brand position communicates a simple idea to a target audience in a memorable way:

- *Hires Root beer is better with ice cream...*

- *The new Hyatt Regency offers a stunning view of Long Beach Harbor...*

- *The LA jewelry industry's scattered sales reps now can work from one centralized location.*

This book will encourage you to stop obsessing about your product or service and focus on your brand. Then you will understand the adage:

"People don't buy products; they buy brands." And more to the point, "They engage with brand positions."

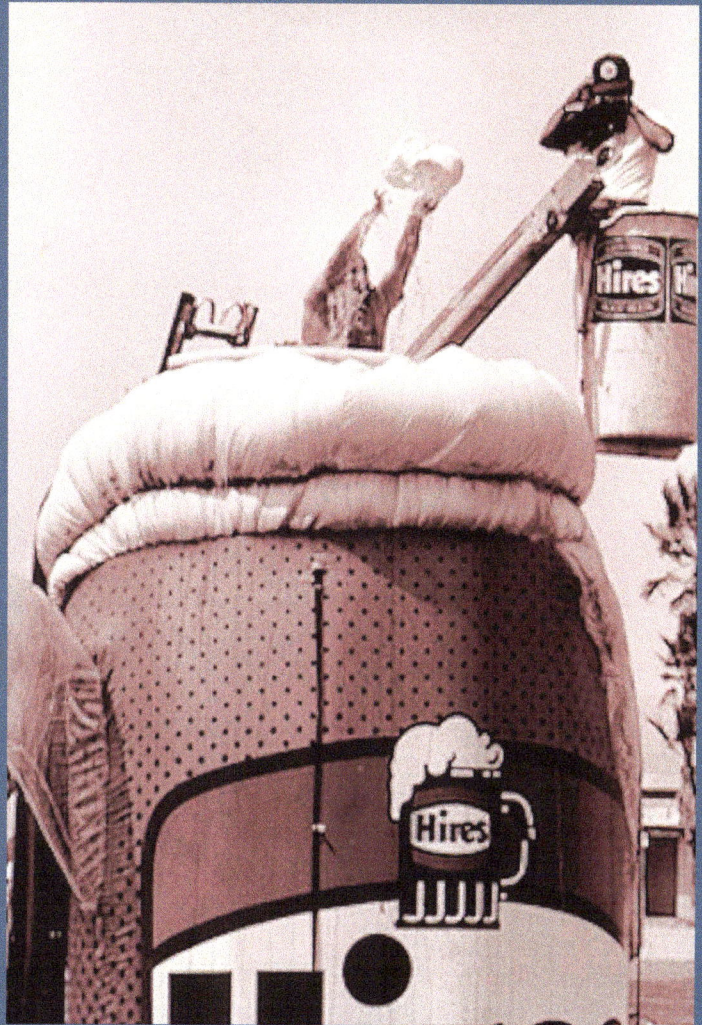

"People don't buy products; they buy brands."

Zsa Zsa Gabor with Nann Miller

IN THE MOOD FOR COFFEE?

If market researchers invented a Rorschach test for brand effectiveness, it might look like an interstate highway sign.

Six logos appear in a flash before you must act on your Pavlovian response: Get off the freeway — or not — before the exit zips past.

At 70 mph, a subconscious burst of bias pulls you to one brand over the others. A logo is not a brand, but a logo activates a reservoir of feelings and associations which taken together, is a Brand Story®.

Let's dig into the stories behind these brands:

Starbucks — In 1982, Howard Schultz made a business trip to Milan, Italy, where he noticed how the local coffee bars served as public spaces to hang out — all 200,000 of them. From this experience, Schultz focused the Starbucks concept on comfort, aesthetics, and a place to meet — wholly different from the greasy diner/coffee shop scene in the States. Today, Starbucks is still more about the place than the product — or as one snarky customer pointed out on Twitter:

"Gas station coffee beats Starbucks. The only thing that keeps Starbucks in business is indoor seating and free WiFi."

That's because Starbucks is selling ambiance, which takes us to Dunkin:

Dunkin Donuts — In 2008, Dunkin sponsored a blind taste test against Starbucks. With eyes closed, tasters preferred Dunkin 54% to 39%. As a result, Dunkin shifted its focus from donuts to coffee.

IHOP proudly ignores every coffee trend.

Today, the company has taken the next logical next step, dropping "Donuts" from the name altogether.

DUNKIN'

IHOP — *Dunkin* may have dropped Donuts, but *International House of Pancakes* will have set the precedent. In 1973, the acronym became the brand: *IHOP*.

As a coffee destination, *IHOP* proudly ignores every coffee trend by listing a total of two brews on its menu: Reg and Decaf. Your waitress is central to the *IHOP* brand experience, refilling your never-ending cup while she calls you *"hun."*

In 2008, IHOP took their acronym to the next level with a faux name change to *"IHOB."* The *B for Burger* campaign generated 20,000 stories and 36 billion earned media impressions. Burger sales rose (briefly), but as Brand Story people know, you can't transform *IHOP* into *Five Guy*s or *In-N-Out* by swapping a letter.

Biscuitville — This North Carolina chain prepares home-style biscuits, sweet tea, and coffee the way God intended. *Biscuitville* makes its biscuits in realtime behind a glass partition. Their "biscuit lab" is a fabulous concept – so much so, I wish they would leverage it as the "big idea" for a cool brand. Despite a recent rebrand, their aspirations remain small and un-cool, which is okay with me given my transplanted love of Southern culture. *Biscuitville* sources its coffee from a family-owned roaster in Concord, NC – proof that life doesn't need to be complicated.

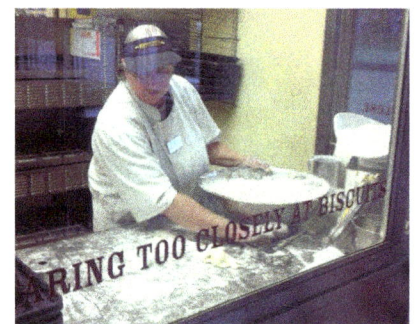

McDonald's — How do you pair a Big Mac® with a Machiatto? If you're *McDonald's*, nearly everything on the menu is a force fit. My guess is that they aimed their marketing analytic ray gun at the fastest-growing restaurant category (coffee) and determined that espresso fits fine with a Happy Meal®. *McDonald's* research likely identified two types of coffee drinkers: one in need of cheap coffee and the other looking for a cafe experience. It's not clear which crowd *McCafé* is targeting.

Yes, *McDonald's* beat the taste of *Starbucks* in a Consumer Reports test (everybody seems to), but did they expect coffee snobs to savor the aroma of Arabica mixed with fryer fat? Why not? Everything fits at *McDonald's*.[1]

Chick-fil-A — This never-on-Sunday chain built a passionate following for its chicken sandwiches — along with a sad reputation for blah coffee. I was part of their coffee-turnaround when we developed *Chick-fil-A's* new coffee brand: *Thrive Farmer's*. *Chick-fil-A* now serves great coffee that supports indigenous farmers, but unlike *McDonald's*, *Chick-fil-A* did little to position itself as a coffee destination except change the brew.

Take the 70 mph Rorschach test

Sense your feelings associated with each brand.
Which one pulls you off the highway, and why?

---

1 "McDonald's coffee beats Starbucks, says Consumer Reports," The Seattle Times, 2-2-2007.

"Pardon me, would you have any Grey Poupon?"

We feel good by the brands we keep.

300 Varieties

Everything is a commodity — A depressing thought if you are starting a business, but sorry, it's unlikely your great idea is unique. With commodity products (breakfast cereal, gasoline, cleaning products, fast food, etc.), the brand establishes the difference – not what's in the box. In most cases, the brand *is* the difference. On one level, we're we're all six years old and prefer our 99-cent commodity burger with a clown.

Moutarde gets fussy — Remember the boring yellow commodity from our hot dog youth, and how *Grey Poupon*, in its famous TV ads, reinvented mustard by serving it to a fussy aristocrat? *Grey Poupon* removed the yellow turmeric (healthful!), added a splash of white wine, and poured it into an iconic glass jar. *Voila, moutarde* that commands twice the price!

Brands 'R' Us — Upscale mustard, craft beers, sensual shampoos — the truth is, we feel good by the brands we keep — even if they are commodity products. Consider yogurt — a new idea back in Mesopotamia, 5000 BC

When I was in college, we made our yogurt like the Mesopotamians: Heat some milk, whisk in some yogurt, and let it sit. The live-cultured *probiotics* that foodies crave today came basic with the homemade stuff, but without a brand position.

Cottage cheese gets a facelift — With yogurt spawning endless varieties (there are now more than 300 different types of yogurt at the average grocery store), cottage cheese wasn't getting the love.[2] A cheeky BuzzFeed article expressed this sentiment. Titled, *"Cottage Cheese Is Fucking Disgusting"* the article blurted:

---

2 "Yogurt Sales Sour as Options Proliferate," Wall Street Journal, April 9, 2019

"Cottage cheese is not good. It looks like white diarrhea and tastes like absolutely nothing. Please eat some yogurt instead. No more of this cheese pretending to be cheese. Banish it forever."[3]

As a cottage cheese lover, I took offense, but it's true – the brand experience for cottage cheese remained untouched for decades.

Enter two entrepreneurs looking for a niche: Jesse Merrill and Anders Eisner (son of Disney CEO, Michael Eisner). They realized that cottage cheese was the last product in the store to forgo a trendy brand position. Even salt now comes in a pink hue from the Himalayas. Merrill and Eisner roamed the aisles looking for an un-gentrified grocery niche:

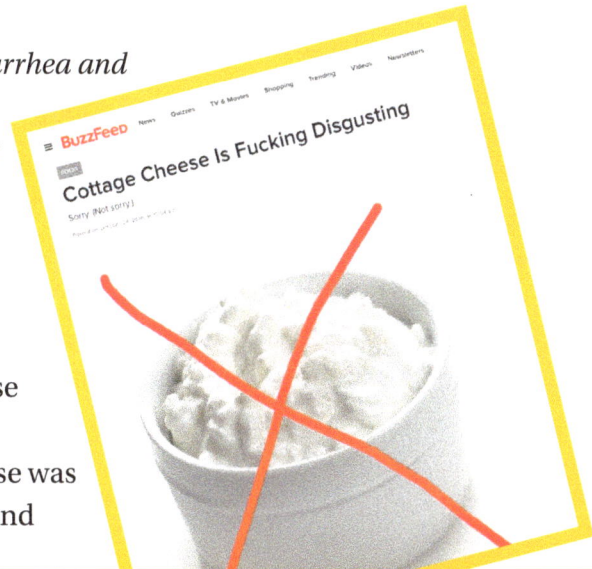

"We decided we wanted to be the Greek yogurt of cottage cheese."

"We decided we wanted to be the Greek yogurt of cottage cheese," says Merrill."[4]

The result: *Good Culture Organic Cottage Cheese* with pineapple, strawberry chia, blueberry acai, mango, and Kalamata olive flavors. Like with *Grey Poupon, Good Culture* effectively doubled the price of conventional cottage cheese. And just like that, cottage cheese was feeling the love.

Engaging customer desire — In 1991, advertising legend, Patrick Scullin conceived the "Swedish Bikini Team" to sell an admittingly bland lager, *Old Milwaukee Beer.*

---

3 https://www.buzzfeed.com/laraparker/listen-we-all-need-to-accept-that-cottage-cheese-is-fucking. October 26, 2016

4 Raphael, Rina. "Can Cottage Cheese Become The Next Greek Yogurt?" Fast Company 6-21-17

The bikini team planted a deep association in your lizard brain...

"It was fully intended to be satire," Scullin confessed, "a tongue-in-cheek send-up of typical beer commercials." Despite feminists protesting *Old Milwaukee's* over-the-top sexual objectification, according to Adweek, the campaign "helped make Old Milwaukee great again."[5]

Whatever you think of bikinis selling beer, Scullin ignited the propulsive force behind all selling: *Desire*. Desire doesn't require bikinis, but the bikini team planted a deep association in your lizard brain: beaches, blonds, bikinis, and beer — *Old Milwaukee beer*.

Even probate lawyers engage desire — Consider these headlines for *probate lawyers* and the deep feelings they elicit during a sensitive time:

- *"In difficult times, work with someone you trust."*

- *"Don't face probate alone."*

- *"You can't pick your family, but you can pick your attorneys."*

- *"Prevent the death of a loved one from becoming the death of a family."*

You versus your competitors — To make a sale, a customer must *desire* your product or service. That's obvious, but the customer must also desire your product over a competitive product — a challenge if your competitor has more money than your shoestring brand. And the greatest challenge? Since most products and services are commodities, *features and benefits* won't win the day. All that's left is brand.

In the beer market, mass-market lagers like *Old Milwaukee* represent the ultimate commodity — undifferentiated by taste, price, fizz, or color. Cultivating brand loyalty for commodity products is difficult, but also crucial.

---

5 Coffee, Patrick. "Chief Creative Officer Patrick Scullin Talks Selling His Agency," AdWeek, 4-17-18.

26

Consider Coors Beer — In the 1970s, *Coors* was a regional beer limited to eleven Western states. Since the beer was unpasteurized, contained no preservatives, and had to be kept cold, distant shipping wasn't a possibility. For people outside those eleven states (I lived in Illinois), the beer's cult status prompted long-distance beer runs and even bootlegging.

The 1977 hit film, *Smokey and the Bandit* celebrated a bootleg shipment of *Coors* from Texas to Georgia. Even Paul Newman's contract stipulated *Coors* on ice to be available on all his movie sets. In 1970s California, this cult following gave *Coors* an astonishing 43 percent of the market. By comparison today, *Anheuser-Busch Inbev* commands 40 percent of the global market – but divvied among 500+ brands!

Coors understood that the *mystique*, not its light taste, fueled the *desire* for its beer, so the company fueled that desire by keeping a tight rein on distribution.

Eventually, the Federal Trade Commission found *Coors* to be guilty of restraint of trade, a beer case that went to the Supreme Court — no Kavanaugh jokes, please.

Successful brands tell compelling stories (until they don't) – In 2005, *Coors* merged into a multinational entity and lost whatever shreds remained of its origin story.

"Double Aged" ON COORS LABELS

Means a Lot To Those Who Relish a Truly Fine Beer

The term "Double Aged" as it appears on Coors Beer labels is not merely an advertising expedient. It means just this: The Coors people *make their own Malt* from the choice of Colorado's finest barley crop. Then, this private brand malt is *thoroly aged* before the extract is taken off. This is ageing process No. 1. Then, after the brew is fermented the beer is again thoroly aged in modern glass lined lager casks. This is ageing process No. 2. So you see "Double Aged" describes the process which accounts for the smooth, mellow softness of Coors Export Lager and gives it that fine *finished* flavor which means so much to those who relish a truly fine Beer.

KEGLINED CANS
STUBBY BOTTLES
ON DRAUGHT

The most succcessful brands grow from their founders' personal stories:

Compare that to Samuel Adams, possibly the first independent craft beer in the United States. I interviewed founder Jim Koch early in his career, not long after he quit his job at *Boston Consulting Group* to turn his grandfather's beer recipe into a business. Koch went from bar to bar, offering samples from his consultant briefcase while his former secretary, Rhonda Kallman, placed *Samuel Adams* cards on the tables. Koch and Kallman risked it all to launch today's craft beer revolution – an achievment today's beer snobs often overlook.

The *Samuel Adams* brand story still gets mileage from Koch's entrepreneurial dream 35 years ago. The company's *"Brewing the American Dream"* program mentors young entrepreneurs and celebrates the brand's origin story.

Samuel Adams demonstrates how the most successful brands grow from their founders' personal stories:

Patagonia — In the 1960s, Founder and outdoor climbing enthusiast, Yvon Chouinard, championed environmentally-friendly methods of climbing which also pioneered a new breed of outdoor wear. Today, *Patagonia* supports grassroots activists working to find solutions to the environmental crisis.

TOMS — In 2006, Blake Mycoskie was traveling in Argentina, playing polo and drinking wine, when he met a woman who was collecting shoes for the poor. She made such a strong impression that Mycoskie launched *Toms Shoes*, a company with a unique business model: *One for One*®. The company matches every pair of shoes customers purchase with a new pair for a child in need. The company has given out more than 50 million pairs of shoes this way. Fueling Blake's philanthropy is a brand story that builds affinity with customers who share his values.

Toms Shoes has become *TOMS*®. Enshrined on Blake's memoir, and on a wall of the company headquarters, is his brand motto:
Start Something That Matters.

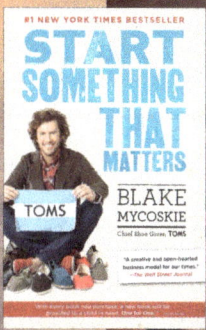

Bombas — Following a similar path as *TOMS*, in 2013, Randy Goldberg and David Heath saw a Facebook post that mentioned the need for socks at homeless shelters. They solicited $145,000 through the crowd-source site Indiegogo. Next, they raised $1 million in angel investment, and a year later, they appeared on *Shark Tank*.

Their brand concept, *One Pair Purchased = One Pair Donated*, was built from their story. *Bombas*, derived from the Latin word for bumblebee, boasts $50 million in annual sales and gives customers a reason to believe, having donated more than 20 million items.

One Pair Purchased = One Pair Donated

KANE11

Kane11 - Since we're talking about socks, Pete Hunsinger sought to capitalize on the stylish-socks-for-men craze with a completely different brand concept: *"You'll never go back to multi-size socks again."* Hunsinger and his partner asked hundreds of men, "What size do you wear?" If they knew at all, most men agreed their socks didn't fit well, so Hunsinger created a precise-size system from 7 to 17 displaying the sock size as a big woven brand statement.

I don't mind my cheap multi-size *Adidas* socks (fits 6-12!), so *Kane11* isn't solving my top-of-mind problem. But, Kane11 shows how to create a new category that "solves" a problem and commands that brand position.

Spanx — Possibly, the most celebrated startup tale of all time belongs to a one-time fax machine salesperson, Sara Blakely, who wanted a smooth, sleek look in her white pants. "I cut the feet out of a pair of pantyhose and substituted them for my underwear," she recounted. "The moment I saw how good my butt looked, I was like, 'Thank you, God, this is my opportunity!'"

Nieman Marcus placed her first order and today, Sara is a billionaire. The original snipped pantyhose is enshrined at company headquarters – a celebrationt of the power of Sara's brand story.

The original panty hose is enshrined as an acknowledgement of the power of Sara's brand story.

SPANX®
BY SARA BLAKELY®

Jacob the Pressure Washer — Now, for some shoestring nitty-gritty. Each of these big, successful brands have compelling origin stories, but what about your startup? You may want to *walk dogs, tutor high school students, or offer Brazilian waxes* and feel you don't need a brand story. Sorry, you do. Here's proof:

When my son, Jacob, was in high school, he needed money, so I suggested pressure washing. We found a used Honda pressure washer on Craigslist, printed some cards, then launched a profoundly simple marketing plan by way of a compelling "brand story" (below).

Sounds straightforward, but after we posted to Decatur Metro, our community blog, a rush of dads responded with an immediate felt connection. They remembered the sinking teen feeling when their first four-wheel junker needed an infusion of cash.

Two Guys and a Pressure Washer

- Driveways
- Sidewalks
- Decks and more

Great work & low prices from two Decatur High School students

Jacob Miller
404 555-1212

decatur metro

"16-year-old Jacob purchased a 1990 BMW that suddenly needs parts — and they're expensive. Jacob will gladly pressure wash your walkway, porch, or exterior to get his wheels rolling again."

Jacob's brand story illustrates a principle:

A story is the smallest unit of emotional transformation.

Whether it's a novel, a sit-com, or a joke, all stories work the same way. At it's most basic, a story has a:

1. *Set-up*
2. *Complications,* and a
3. *Resolution.* Yeah, just like a Seinfeld episode.

Brand stories *emotionally transform* prospects to become customers.

Brand Stories are real stories:

Jacob the Pressure Washer

Jacob's old BMW, broke down and needs expensive parts. Will kindly pressure wash to get rolling again.

Tom's Shoes

Tom traveled to Argentina, saw kids without shoes, so, created a way to share the wealth. Kids now have shoes again.

Spanx

Sara needed a quick fix to make her butt look good. After a quick snip of her pantyhose – *presto* – a $1 billion enterprise.

Later, when you build your Brand Positioning Statement, you'll see how a brand position works like a story:

1. **Set-up:** *Identify* Your *Target Customer,*
2. **Complications:** *What is their Problem or Need?*
3. **Resolution:** *Your Unique Solution,* and
4. **Proof that it Works:** *Bombas donated 23 million pairs of socks!*

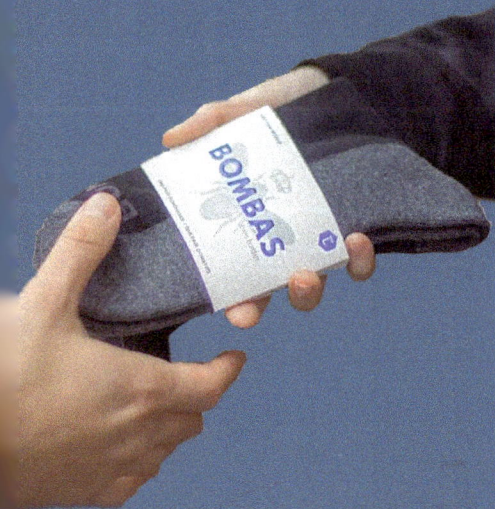

23,725,494
ITEMS DONATED

Every brand offers a solution to a problem:

Starbucks

"I want a pumpkin latte, a relaxing atmosphere, and free WiFi."

Dunkin Donuts

"I don't need a freakin' couch, just good-tasting coffee... fast!"

Biscuitville

"I'm looking for Southern comfort food and fresh home-made biscuits."

Chick-fil-A

"Farmer-direct coffee combined with great customer service aligns with my values."

IHOP

"A cozy booth, all-American fare, and a waitress who calls me *hun* – that's my kind of comfort."

McDonald's

"I'm not looking to change my routine. I want fast, easy, predictable, and clean."

What is a brand position?

When you respond to a highway sign or any brand proposition, you are seeking a solution to a problem: *I need coffee now.* Pretty simple.

Each of these brands may be high or low in terms of price, quality, and experience compared to the other brands. In this way, the brand holds a *position* in the marketplace — and a position in the customer's mind.

A brand holds a position in the marketplace — and a position in the customer's mind.

Let's take another brand Rorschach test:

Toyota Avalon

MSRP: From $35,650

Lexus ES 350

MSRP: From $39,750

What's your preference? Toyota Avalon or Lexus ES 350?

They share the same chassis, engine, drivetrain, and suspension. Except for the badge, they are practically the same car. Their brand positions, though, are miles apart. In some configurations, the *Toyota* is more luxurious than the *Lexus* (who knew?), but for the status-seeker, the extra $4,000 for the *Lexus* badge buys a lot of self-esteem.

Remember peak GM? For Baby Boomers, the brand differentiation between *Chevy, Olds, Buick,* and *Pontiac* boiled down to: *"Our family always drove a __."*

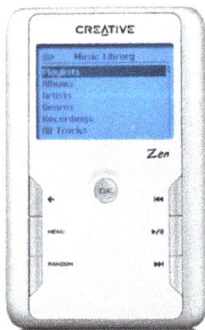

iPod versus Zen — Consider the original *Apple iPod* versus the *Creative Zen* mp3 player. In 2005, the *Zen Touch* offered twice the storage, a more durable case, and dramatically more battery life for less money than an *iPod*. But, in the minds of consumers, it was a "faux-Pod." It could not unseat *Apple's* commanding position in the hearts of consumers.

Creative Zen Touch

The iPod was pricier than the Zen, so cost was not the deciding factor.

Consumers coveted the *Apple* brand for its cool factor, quality, ergonomics, and integration with the *Apple* ecosystem.

For the *Zen* to compete, it needed to carve out its own compelling argument. Here's an idea:

"Dude! If you had purchased a Zen, there would be money left over for actual music!"

Apple iPod Classic

Let's turn that Zen argument into a brand position:

> *"For digital music lovers with a limited budget, only the Creative Zen gives you a full-featured player <u>and</u> a music library for the price of an empty iPod."*

With this brand position, the *Zen* wouldn't try to compete on features, specs, quality, or cool factor.

Here's my mock ad that states the obvious: *An mp3 player without music is useless.*

Unfortunately for the *Zen*, they tried to compete on features and failed.

Mock advertisement

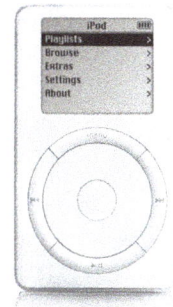

Got Music?

For the price of an empty iPod

Get a full-featured Zen Touch plus a library of music!

*Lorem ipsum dolor sit amet, consectetur adipiscing elit, sed do eiusmod tempor incididu ut labore et dolore magna aliqua. Ut enim ad minim veniam, quis nostrud exercitation u llamco laboris nisi ut aliquip ex ea commodo consequat.

CREATIVE

For the Zen to compete, it needed to carve out its own compelling argument.

When you think about a brand, it's a safe bet that its position is the first thought or feeling that comes into your mind. Most products are commodities, so this top-of-mind feeling results from money the creative types invested into the brands. As the brand strategist for your startup, your job is to identify your brand position and plant it like a seed so it will always sprout top-of-mind.

The Zen Touch illustrates a common positioning challenge: If it was your product, what would be your preferred position: 1) *superior features,* 2) *better price,* 3) *save your money for music,* or 4) like the Un-Cola of mp3 – the *un-Pod alternative*?

Alas. You can't be all things to all people. Your brand position needs to be unique and boldly expressed as a big idea – like this gasoline offer you can't resist.

Your customers have no incentive to choose your business unless you spell it out. Here are some examples:

Panera Bread has long pushed its *"100% clean ingredients"* brand position (no artificial preservatives, sweeteners, flavors, and no colors from artificial sources). It's a clever bit of positioning because to the uninformed, *100% clean* implies that *Panera's* menu is organic (free from pesticides, synthetic fertilizers, GMOs, etc.) — **which it is not.** Despite this fuzzy distinction, Panera has successfully associated its brand with wholesomeness, hence its tag line: *Food as it should be*™.

Food as it should be.

Jimmy John's built its sandwich brand on *"Freaky Fast"* delivery with an implied

promise that Jimmy will deliver your sub in under 20 minutes during non-peak hours. It worked. The young designers in our agency clicked their lunch orders at noon and scarfed bicycle-delivered sandwiches 20 minutes later. *Jimmy John's* wasn't about *Boar's Head* meat, wasabi mayo, or artisan bread — just fast-delivery. So why is *Jimmy John's* moving its brand position to *"Freaky Fresh?"* Do they expect to knock *Panera* from its commanding position for wholesomeness?

Volvo is another distinctive brand that evolved from a commanding brand position. In our workshops, we would take an instant poll, *"When you think of Volvo, what is the first word that comes to mind?"* Invariably, people would respond, "Safety." *Volvo's* association with safety was so deep and long-standing that the brand has long been synonymous with crash-test dummies and soccer moms transporting their kids to activities.

Volvo's brand position began to change after the company sold the division to *Ford* in 1999. In 2010, *Volvo* was sold again, this time to the Chinese company, *Geely*. For a while, if you went to the *Volvo* home page, you couldn't find the word, "*safety*" — not even in small print. After the 2008 recession, *Volvo* moved up-market (pretending to be a Swedish BMW?) Or perhaps Volvo realized that middle-class soccer moms couldn't justify hauling kids with cleats in a $50,000 SUV. Today, the brand is evolving again as it moves toward an all-electric brand position.

Shoes.com demonstrated how a compelling brand position will ultimately make or break a company. This dot-com company launched in 1996 during the great Internet "land rush" — a time when companies were launching ill-fated brands like *Pets.com, Webvan, eToys, and Kozmo.com.*

"We let our customers do the marketing for us through word of mouth."

Enter Zappos. Three years later, in 1999, a competitor entered the e-shoes market: *ShoeSite.com*. Almost immediately, the new company changed its name to *Zappos* after "*zapatos*," the Spanish word for "shoes." *Zappos* was snappier than *Shoes.com*, but that's not why *Shoes.com* went bankrupt in 2017, while *Zappos* was raking in over $1 billion in revenue.

The *Zappos* magic began in 2001 when Tony Hsieh came on board. He realized that *Zappos* wasn't selling shoes; it was selling a brand experience: *Powered by Service.*™

Hsieh explained:

"The number one driver of our growth at Zappos has been repeat customers and word of mouth. Our philosophy has been to take most of the money we would have spent on paid advertising and invest it into customer service and the customer experience instead, letting our customers do the marketing for us through word of mouth."[6]

Customer service is the brand. On one level, perks like free delivery and free returns built the foundation for *Zappos'* legendary customer service. If you don't like the shoes, you can box them up and send them back for no charge. *Zappos* might even ship them to you overnight if you have an important job interview. But that's not their secret sauce. The core of the *Zappos* brand is the emotional connection its people make with their customers. Their reps radiate high energy and personality.

6 "Delivering Happiness: A Path to Profits, Passion, and Purpose". Book by Tony Hsieh, 2010.

How do you find folks to evangelize a brand?
After a week of training, *Zappos* makes "The Offer." The infamous pitch goes like this: "If you quit today, we will pay you for the time you've worked, plus a $1,000 bonus." That's right, a bribe to quit!

By weeding out folks who don't share the excitement and commitment (for what's frankly a phone job in a cubicle), *Zappos* maintains its high-energy culture. In this way, *Zappos* follows the first rule of brand positioning: Align your brand to the needs of your target customer. The *Zappos* customer is not "someone who needs shoes," but "someone who wants a fantastic customer experience." In this way, *Zappos* is not an online shoe store, but rather, a *customer service platform* that happens to sell shoes.

Could you work in a gung-ho workplace like *Zappos* with its silly stunts and whoop-it-up culture? Maybe not?

What about your business? Do you have the *chutzpah* to become the ambassador for your brand? Can you embody your brand so that people take notice? What if you're a quiet type who wants the quality of your work to do the talking? In that case, "quiet-type" is your brand. Own it, live it, and identify the customer who is looking for you.

Do you have the *chutzpah* to become your own brand ambassador?

Align your brand to the needs of your target customer.

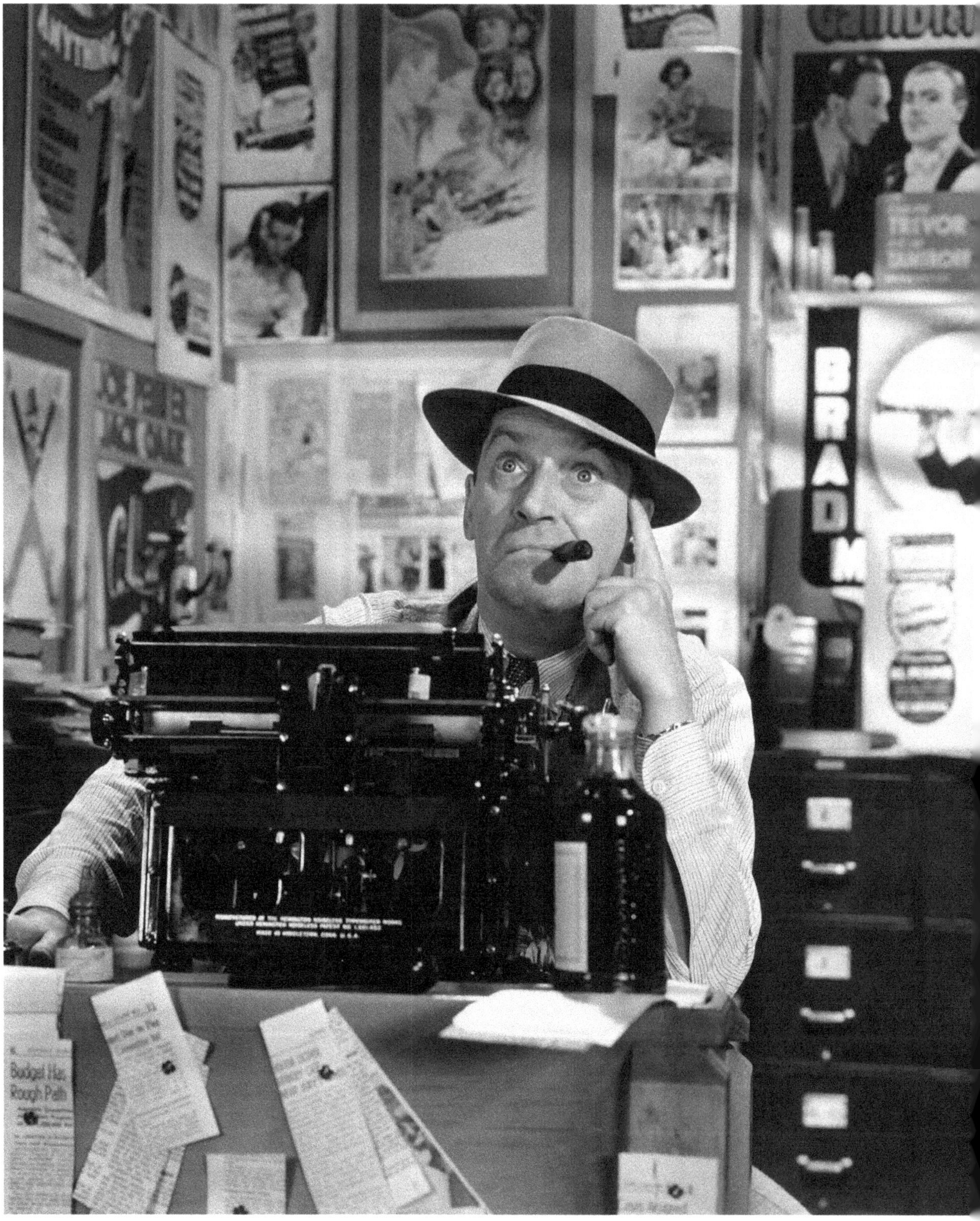
JOE PENNER
JACK OAKIE
Budget Has Rough Path

BRAND POSITIONING: A BRIEF HISTORY.

If you want to become a lawyer, you start with the Magna Carta. As a budding brand guru, it helps to know your history.

The AMC television series, *"Mad Men,"* captured a pivotal period in the advertising business — the Sixties — when creative execs ran the ad industry and the "Pepsi Generation" emerged to steer the culture toward youth-oriented consumerism. It was a time when brand stories first emerged. Instead of an *Alka Seltzer* puppet singing, *"Relief is just a swallow away,"* brands began to develop more complex personalities:

- **Avis** confessed to being a runner-up: *"Avis is only No. 2. But we try harder."*

- **Volkswagen** embraced full-on self-deprecation with: *"If you run out of gas, it's easy to push."*

- **Levy's** brought cultural diversity into advertising with the iconic Doyle Dane Bernbach campaign for their rye bread: *"You don't have to be Jewish to love Levy's."*

- **By the seventies**, some brands began to push blatantly sexual personas, including the notorious *"Fly Me"* campaign for *National Airlines*:

The Father of Advertising – These breakthroughs emerged, in part, through the groundbreaking work of David Ogilvy, founder of *Ogilvy & Mather* – work he began decades earlier. Ogilvy's unlikely career path hit all the right notes for him to become known as *"the Father of Advertising."*

In the 1930s, David Ogilvy started selling stoves door-to-door in England. His boss asked him to write a sales manual, *The Theory and Practice of Selling the AGA Cooker,* in which Ogilvy concluded:

- *"A successful salesman needs the tenacity of the bulldog and the manners of the spaniel. If you have any charm, ooze it."*

Ogilvy's selling skills landed him a job at a London ad agency. To this day, Ogilvy's sales manual still stands as a seminal piece on sales theory.

In 1938, Ogilvy persuaded his London boss to send him to America to work with the Gallup research organization. His work at Gallup gave Ogilvy a deep understanding of consumer behavior.

Counter-Espionage – After Gallup, Ogilvy worked for British Intelligence during World War II where he applied his new behavioral insights into writing compelling wartime propaganda. His new boss, Sir William Stephenson, was the inspiration for the Ian Fleming character, James Bond 007.

Ogilvy & Mather – After the War, Ogilvy moved to the States, where he built his namesake agency on two core principles:

- *The function of advertising is to sell, and*

- *Advertising success derives from customer knowledge.*

David Ogilvy: The father of advertising

At a time when advertising was loud, preachy, and prone to simplistic jingles, Ogilvy felt that customers should be approached with intelligence, stating: *"The customer is not a moron; she's your wife."*[1]

"The customer is not a moron; she's your wife."

By the 1960s, a creative revolution was sweeping through art, music, film, sexuality, and politics. Ogilvy thrust this cultural shift into the world of advertising. Rather than discussing his theories in stuffy trade publications and industry speeches, Ogilvy published his thoughts as provocative full-page consumer ads. In 1971 he challenged the industry by running a legendary ad in the New York Times, titled: *"How to create advertising that sells."*

How to create advertising that sells

by David Ogilvy

Ogilvy & Mather has created over $1,480,000,000 worth of advertising, and spent $4,900,000 tracking the results.

Here, with all the dogmatism of brevity, are 38 of the things we have learned.

1. The most important decision. We have learned that the effect of your advertising on your sales depends more on this decision than on any other: *How should you position your product?*

Should you position SCHWEPPES as a soft drink—or as a mixer?

Should you position DOVE as a product for dry skin or as a product which gets hands really clean?

The results of your campaign depend less on how we write your advertising than on how your product is positioned. It follows that positioning should be decided before the advertising is created.

Research can help. Look before you leap.

2. Large promise. The second most important decision is this: what should you promise the customer? A promise is not a claim, or a theme, or a slogan. It is a *benefit for the consumer.*

It pays to promise a benefit which is unique and competitive. And the product must *deliver* the benefit you promise.

Most advertising promises *nothing.* It is doomed to fail in the marketplace.

"Promise, large promise, is the soul of an advertisement"—said Samuel Johnson.

3. Brand image. Every advertisement should contribute to the complex symbol which is the brand image. Ninety-five percent of all advertising is created *ad hoc.* Most products lack any consistent image from one year to another.

The manufacturer who dedicates his advertising to building the most sharply defined personality for his brand gets the largest share of the market.

4. Big ideas. Unless your advertising is built on a BIG IDEA it will pass like a ship in the night.

It takes a BIG IDEA to jolt the consumer out of his indifference—to make him *notice* your advertising, *remember* it and *take action.*

Big ideas are usually *simple* ideas. Said Charles Kettering, the great General Motors inventor: "This problem, when solved, will be simple."

BIG SIMPLE IDEAS are not easy to come by. They require genius—and midnight oil. A truly big one can be continued for twenty years—like our Eyepatch for Hathaway shirts.

5. A first-class ticket. It pays to give most products an image of quality—a first-class ticket.

Ogilvy & Mather has been conspicuously successful in doing this—for Pepperidge, Hathaway, Mercedes-Benz, Schweppes, Dove and others.

If your advertising looks ugly, consumers will conclude that your product is shoddy, and they will be less likely to buy it.

6. Don't be a bore. Nobody was ever *bored* into buying a product. Yet most advertising is impersonal, detached, cold—and dull.

It pays to *involve* the customer.

Talk to her like a human being. Charm her. Make her hungry. Get her to participate.

7. Innovate. Start trends—instead of following them. Advertising which follows a fashionable fad, or is imitative, is seldom successful.

It pays to *innovate,* to blaze new trails.

But innovation is risky unless you pretest your innovation with consumers. Look before you leap.

8. Be suspicious of awards. The pursuit of creative awards seduces creative people from the pursuit of sales.

We have been unable to establish any correlation whatever between awards and sales.

At Ogilvy & Mather we now give an annual award for the campaign which contributes the most to *sales.*

Successful advertising sells the product without drawing attention to itself. It rivets the consumer's attention on the *product.*

Make the product the hero of your advertising.

9. Psychological segmentation. Any good agency knows how to position products for *demographic* segments of the market—for men, for young children, for farmers in the South, etc.

But Ogilvy & Mather has learned that it often pays to position products for *psychological* segments of the market.

Our Mercedes-Benz advertising is positioned to fit nonconformists who scoff at "status symbols" and reject flimflam appeals to snobbery.

10. Don't bury news. It is easier to interest the consumer in a product when it is *new* than at any other point in its life. Many copywriters have a fatal instinct for burying news. This is why most advertising for new products fails to exploit the opportunity that genuine news provides.

It pays to launch your new product with a loud BOOM-BOOM.

11. Go the whole hog. Most advertising campaigns are too complicated. They reflect a long list of marketing objectives. They embrace the divergent views of too many executives. By attempting too many things, they achieve nothing.

It pays to boil down your strategy to one simple promise—and go the whole hog in delivering that promise.

What works best in television

12. Testimonials: Avoid irrelevant celebrities. Testimonial commercials are almost always successful—if you make them credible.

Either celebrities or real people can be effective. But avoid *irrelevant* celebrities whose fame has no natural connection with your product or your customers. Irrelevant celebrities steal attention from your product.

13. Problem-solution (don't cheat!) You set up a problem that the consumer recognizes.

Then you show how your product can solve that problem.

And you prove the solution.

This technique has always been above average in sales results, and it still is. But don't use it unless you can do so *without cheating;* the consumer isn't a moron, she is your wife.

14. Visual demonstrations. If they are honest, visual demonstrations are generally effective in the marketplace.

It pays to *visualize your promise.* It saves time. It drives the promise home. It is memorable.

15. Slice of life. These playlets are corny, and most copywriters detest them. But they have sold a lot of merchandise, and are still selling.

16. Avoid logorrhea. Make your *pictures* tell the story. What you show is more important than what you say.

Many commercials drown the viewer in a torrent of words. We call that logorrhea (rhymes with diarrhea).

We have created some great commercials *without* words.

17. On-camera voice. Commercials using on-camera voice do significantly better than commercials using voice-over.

18. Musical backgrounds. Most commercials use musical backgrounds. However, on the average, musical backgrounds reduce recall of your commercial. Very few creative people accept this. But we never heard of an agency using musical background under a new business presentation.

19. Stand-ups. The stand-up pitch can be effective, if it is delivered with straightforward honesty.

20. Burr of singularity. The average consumer now sees 20,000 commercials a year, poor dear.

Most of them slide off her memory like water off a duck's back.

Give your commercials a flourish of singularity, a burr that will stick in the consumer's mind. One such burr is the MNEMONIC DEVICE, or relevant symbol—like the crowns in our commercials for Imperial Margarine.

21. Animation & cartoons. Less than five percent of television commercials use cartoons or animation. They are less persuasive than live commercials.

The consumer cannot identify herself with the character in the cartoon. And cartoons do not invite belief.

However, Carson/Roberts, our partners in Los Angeles, tell us that animation can be helpful when you are talking to children.

They should know—they have addressed more than six hundred commercials to children.

22. Salvage commercials. Many commercials which test poorly can be salvaged.

The faults revealed by the test can be corrected. We have *doubled* the effectiveness of a commercial simply by re-editing it.

23. Factual vs. emotional. Factual commercials tend to be more effective than emotional commercials.

However, Ogilvy & Mather has made some emotional commercials which have been successful in the marketplace. Among these are our campaigns for Maxwell House Coffee and Hershey's Milk Chocolate.

24. Grabbers. We have found that commercials with an exciting opening hold their audience at a higher level than commercials which begin quietly.

What works best in print

25. Headlines. On the average, five times as many people read the headline as read the body copy.

It follows that, if you don't sell the product in your headline, you have wasted 80 percent of your money. That is why most Ogilvy & Mather headlines include the brand name and the promise.

26. Benefit in headlines. Headlines that promise a benefit sell more than those that don't.

27. News in headlines. Time after time, we have found that it pays to inject genuine *news* into headlines.

The consumer is always on the lookout for new products, or new improvements in an old product, or new ways to use an old product.

Economists—even Russian economists—approve of this. They call it "informative" advertising. So do consumers.

28. Simple headlines. Your headline should *telegraph* what you want to say—in simple language. Readers do not stop to decipher the meaning of obscure headlines.

29. How many words in a headline? In headline tests conducted with the cooperation of a big department store, it was found that headlines of ten words or longer sold more goods than short headlines.

In terms of *recall,* headlines between eight and ten words are most effective.

In *mail-order* advertising, headlines between six and twelve words get the most coupon returns.

On the average, long headlines sell more merchandise than short ones—headlines like our "At 60 miles an hour, the loudest noise in this new Rolls-Royce comes from the electric clock."

30. Localize headlines. In local advertising it pays to include the name of the city in your headline.

31. Select your prospects. When you advertise a product which is consumed only by a special group, it pays to "flag" that group in your headline—MOTHERS, BED-WETTERS, GOING TO EUROPE?

32. Yes, people read long copy. Readership falls off rapidly up to fifty words, but drops very little between fifty and five hundred words. (This page contains 1909 words, and *you* are reading it.)

Ogilvy & Mather has used long copy—with notable success—for Mercedes-Benz, Cessna Citation, Merrill Lynch and Shell gasoline.

"The more you tell, the more you sell."

33. Story appeal in picture. Ogilvy & Mather has gotten notable results with photographs which suggest a story. The reader glances at the photograph and asks himself, "What goes on here?" Then he reads the copy to find out.

Harold Rudolph called this magic element "story appeal." The more of it you inject into your photograph, the more people look at your advertisement.

It is easier said than done.

34. Before & after. Before and After advertisements are somewhat above average in attention value.

Any form of "visualized contrast" seems to work well.

35. Photographs vs. artwork. Ogilvy & Mather has found that photographs work better than drawings—almost invariably.

They attract more readers, generate more appetite appeal, are more believable, are better remembered, pull more coupons, and sell more merchandise.

36. Use captions to sell. On the average, twice as many people read the captions under photographs as read the body copy.

It follows that you should never use a photograph without putting a caption under it; and each caption should be a miniature advertisement for the product—complete with brand name and promise.

37. Editorial layouts. Ogilvy & Mather has had more success with editorial layouts than with "addy" layouts.

Editorial layouts get higher readership than conventional advertisements.

38. Repeat your winners. Scores of great advertisements have been discarded before they have begun to pay off.

Readership can actually *increase* with repetition—up to five repetitions.

Is this all we know?

These findings apply to most categories of products. But not to all.

Ogilvy & Mather has developed a separate and specialized body of knowledge on what makes for success in advertising *food products, tourist destinations, proprietary medicines, children's products*—and other classifications.

But this special information is revealed only to the clients of Ogilvy & Mather.

Ogilvy & Mather

2 East 48th Street, New York, N.Y. 10017

In a dense, full-page didactic, Ogilvy shared his thirty-eight proprietary secrets with the world. Fifty years later, Ogilvy's maxims still pass the test of time.

Here are seven Ogilvy precepts your shoestring startup can draw from:

1. **The most important decision:** *We have learned that the effect of your advertising on your sales depends more on this decision than on any other:* ***How should you position your product?***

---

1 Cracknell, Andrew. "Ads From The Real Mad Men." The Huffington Post. May 3, 2012.

Should you position Schweppes as a soft drink — or as a mixer?

Should you position Dove as a product for dry skin or as a product that gets hands really clean? The results of your advertising depend less on how we write your advertising than on how your product is positioned.

THE POSITIONING ERA COMETH

The product era.

In the 50's, hard-sell ads predominated.

The image era.

In the 60's, creativity came into vogue.

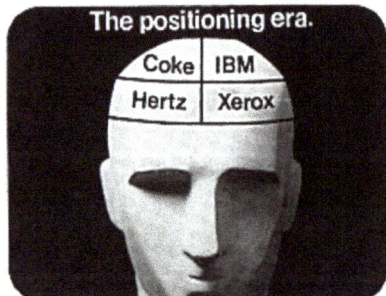

The positioning era.

| Coke | IBM |
| Hertz | Xerox |

In the 70's, strategy will be king.[2]

Thoughts: When you pull a bottle of *Schweppes* off the shelf for a gin and tonic, there is no calculation to your purchase. As the leading mixer, *Schweppes'* position makes the purchase automatic.

Ironically, the brand got its start in 1783 as a soft drink — the original soft drink. Ogilvy understood that *Schweppes* would get lost in back of the pack – after *Coke, Pepsi, Seven-Up, RC,* and *Orange Crush* – if he positioned it as a soft drink. By positioning *Schweppes* as a mixer, *Schweppes* became the category leader. Today, *Schweppes* holds a top-of-mind position instead of being lost in a sea of soft drinks.

In 1972, legendary ad men, Jack Trout and Al Ries drove this point home, announcing: *"The Positioning Era Cometh."* They demonstrated the folly of *RCA* and *GE* attempting to compete head-on against *IBM*, the category leader:

"[RCA and GE] have no hope to make progress head on against the position that IBM has established... While it's possible to compete successfully with a market leader, the rules of positioning say it can't be done 'head on.'"

Trout explained that psychologists determined that the human mind cannot juggle more than seven units at a time. This applies to high-interest categories like auto brands or soft drinks. *"The eighth company in a given field is out of luck. For low-interest product [categories], the average consumer can usually name no more than one or two brands."*[2]

---

2 Jack Trout and Al Ries, "The positioning era cometh," Advertising Age, April 1972.

Five days after Ogilvy's ad appeared, a second Madison Avenue agency, Rosenfeld, Sirowitz & Lawson, published its guiding principles. Number one, you guessed it: "

- *Accurate positioning is the most important step in effective selling.*"[3]

Brand positioning carves a top-of-mind category in which you can lead (example: mini TVs). More than a historical footnote, the purpose of this book is to help you apply the groundbreaking work of these celebrated branding gurus to your shoestring start-up.

PRESS BUTTON TO END WAR

On Oct.15th, students and faculty all over America will leave their classes for 1 day to ring doorbells and talk to their fellow Americans about the madness of Vietnam.

Fresh-killed chicken.

Mobil
We want you to live.

Will we ever kill the bug?

Len Sirowitz, chosen by Ad Weekly as "The Number One Art Director in America" in 1968 and 1970 was then Senior Vice President at Doyle Dane Bernbach. His work distilled brand positions into blunt, thought-provoking headlines.

---

3 Ries, Laura. "The Positioning Era Cometh," June 14, 2017, https://www.linkedin.com/pulse/positioning-era-cometh-laura-ries.

INTRODUCING:
Donnie

Even a teenager can position a brand.

Introducing the shoestring startup who will guide your branding journey: Donnie is 18 years old and launching a seriously-underfunded landscaping business.

He's got a pick-up truck, lots of enthusiasm, and lives in a hip part of town where Craftsman-style bungalows scrunch side-by-side on postage stamp lots.

Donnie has no funding, so he can't compete with the crews who service suburban lawns with motorized equipment. He finds an old-fashioned reel mower at the curb and positions his business: *"Lilliputian Lawn Care — The Tiny Yard Specialist."*

The in-town hipsters are intrigued by his truck. He preaches the merits of the push reel mower: It's better for the health of the grass, doesn't give off greenhouse gases, and reduces noise pollution.

More importantly, Donnie owns the category as the tiny yard specialist! This is positioning. Donnie is Schweppes, not Coke.

46

Back to Ogilvy:

2. **Large promise.** *The second most important decision is this: What should you promise the customer? A promise is not a claim, or a theme, or a slogan. It is a benefit for the consumer*

   It pays to promise a benefit which is unique and competitive. And the product must deliver the benefit you promise. Most advertising promises nothing. It is doomed to fail in the marketplace.

   "Promise, large promise, is the soul of an advertisement" — Samuel Johnson [1759].

How to create advertising that sells
by David Ogilvy

Thoughts: Your promise forms the core of your brand positioning statement. In a nutshell, unless your product or service fulfills a need or solves a customer problem, you don't have a viable business. Example: *Kane 11* targets men who feel ill-fit in their multi-size socks. Yes, it fills a niche.

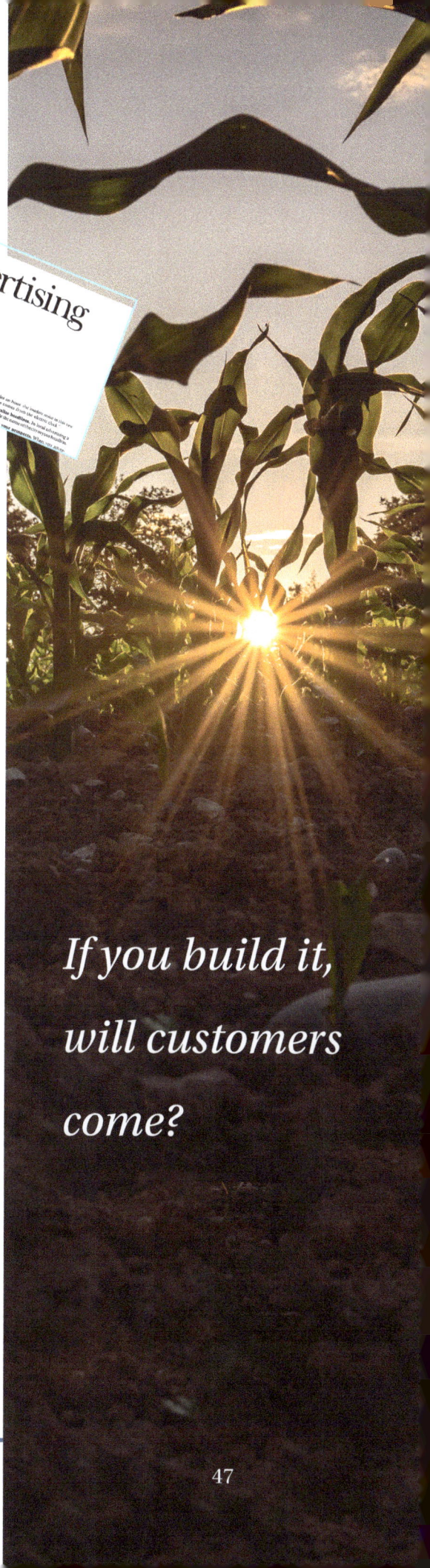

More than a finger-lickin' dinner, the Colonel promised to save your marriage with his take-home convenience.

So many startups believe the *Field of Dreams* trope: *"If you build it, [customers] will come."* The painful truth: Don't expect customers to come knocking just because you built a better mousetrap. In most big businesses, the Product Development folks (who design mousetraps) and the Marketing people (who build brands) work in separate silos. Both overlook the fundamental purpose of being in business: *To help the customer solve a problem.*

If you build it, will customers come?

> *"You must promise a benefit which is unique and competitive."*

**Brand Story:
A sharply defined
personality**

Solving a problem is the easy part. Ogilvy describes the harder part when he adds, *"You must promise a benefit which is unique and competitive."*

The kicker word is "unique." Since most businesses offer commodity products and services, being unique is the challenge: *" Kane 11 — The Leader in Exact-Sized Socks."*

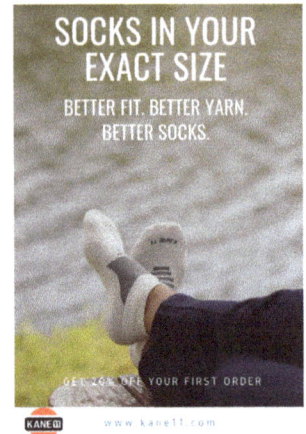

Ogilvy continues:

3. **Brand Image:** *Every advertisement should contribute to the complex symbol, which is the brand image. Ninety-five percent of all advertising is created ad hoc. Most products lack any consistent image from one year to another.*

   The manufacturer, who dedicates his advertising to building the most sharply-defined personality for his brand, gets the largest share of the market.

Thoughts: Ogilvy reminds us that customers respond to the brand image — what I call *Brand Story®*. These are the feelings, perceptions, and experiences associated with the brand. As a brand strategist, I'm also the "brand police," scrutinizing the ad hoc materials that emerge willy-nilly from various people and departments. I can tell if the marketing is "on-brand" (what Ogilvy calls a sharply defined personality) and not willy-nilly by testing it against the **4Cs**:

I.   **CLARITY** — Does it clearly express the brand position?

II. **CONSISTENCY** — Does it follow the brand look?

III. **CHARACTER** — Does it express the brand personality?

IV. **CUSTOMER** — Does it align to the needs of the target customer?

More from Ogilvy:

4. **Big ideas:** *Unless your advertising is built on a BIG IDEA, it will pass like a ship in the night. It takes a BIG IDEA to jolt the consumer out of his indifference – to make him notice your advertising, remember it, and take action.*

Big ideas are usually simple ideas. Said Charles Kettering, the great General Motors inventor: "This problem, when solved, will be simple." BIG SIMPLE IDEAS are not easy to come by. They require genius – and midnight oil. A truly big one can be continued for 20 years – like our Eyepatch for Hathaway shirts.

The man in the Hathaway shirt

Thoughts: I know, you just wanted to start a little dog-walking business called *Power Walk*, and now Ogilvy is demanding a Big Idea! Actually, he wants you to establish a Brand Concept – same as a Big Idea.

If you created a hierarchy of your message, from the central brand concept to the detailed marketing copy, it would have five levels, each with a different purpose:

We promise to poop out your pooch!

The Five Levels of Messaging

BRAND CONCEPT

TAG LINE

BRAND POSITIONING STATEMENT

ELEVATOR SPEECH

MARKETING COPY

"The Tiny Yard Specialist."

Brand Concept

Every effective brand is built around a central idea: The Brand Concept.

With just a few words, a Brand Concept defines: *"How we can help you and why we are different."*

The Brand Concept forms the DNA of the brand.

David Ogilvy talked about the *Big Idea*. More than big, the Brand Concept is the core idea of the brand position. Here are two examples:

- In the 1970s, *Southwest Airlines* brought a new concept to the market: *no-frills air travel*. This innovative, but simple concept grew a tiny airline with three planes in three Texas cities into the nation's leading domestic airline in market-share (a virtual tie with *American*).

  Southwest promoted its *no-frills* concept by serving 106 million packs of peanuts per year to passengers, a brand ritual abandoned in 2018 due to allergy concerns. Peanuts were out, but *Southwest* stood by its big idea, as they stated in the peanut obituary: *"Peanuts will forever be part of Southwest's history and DNA."*

- The Brand Daddy of Big Ideas is *Dollar Shave Club*. Launched in 2012 with a low-rent YouTube video that went viral (production cost $4500), founder Michael Dubin promised that his blades are *"F**king Great"* (currently at 26 million views). The brand name spells out Dubin's no-nonsense Brand Concept: *Subscription razor blades for just one dollar per month.*

With experience in improv, Dubin's in-your-face acting got your attention, but it was his disruptive business model that captivated investors. Four years later, *Unilever* bought *Dollar Shave Club* for $1 billion, one of the most successful exits ever for a VC-backed digital brand.

Can you distill your business idea down to a sentence?
10 Successful Direct-to-Consumer Brand Concepts:

BARK BOX	Spoil your pup with goodies delivered monthly in a box.
BONOBOS	Fit into a better pair of guy pants designed for the American butt.
chubbies ™	Attention-grabbing shorts for young guys who don't like pants.
soylent	Fuel up with engineered ready-to-drink meals sold like software.
WARBY PARKER	Save money with eyeglasses sold without the storefront.
Glossier.	Look good with beauty products inspired by real people.
Casper	Sleep well for 100-nights on a risk-free mattress shipped direct to your door.
allbirds	Walk with eco comfort in sustainable shoes made from New Zealand wool.
quip	Do good for your dentist with the iPhone of toothbrushes.
EVERLANE	Look chic in fashions made in ethical factories with "Radical Transparency"

To be true to the brand concept, *Gatorade* will always be associated with high-performance, thirsty athletes. And, family-focused *Disney* will never market R-rated movies (it uses the *Touchstone* brand for R). *Disney* and *Gatorade* hold such deeply ingrained positions in our DNA that we don't question their brand stories.[4]

_____

4 Okay, I take it back. Disney released R-rated *Stuber* in 2019.

"Finger Lickin' Good" *"Melts in Your Mouth, Not in Your Hands"* *"Just do it"* *"Because You're Worth It"*

"A Diamond Is Forever"

"Look Ma, No Cavities!"

"Got Milk?"

Tag Line

The tag line states your brand position with a concise, lyrical punch:

- Lilliputian Lawn Care: *"Manicuring our planet, one tiny yard at a time."*

- Casper Mattress: *"The Best Bed for Better Sleep."*

- Stitch Fix: *"Your partner in personal style."*

Let's discuss that Stitch Fix tag line. They send you a selection of new clothes, and you keep what you like and send back the rest without paying for shipping. Nice.

And the tag line: *"Your partner in personal style."*

Hmm. Does that capture the concept? How about... *"Your personal boutique in a box."*

And that takes us to the longest-running, most successful tag line of all time – credited with inventing the modern engagement ring:

- *"A Diamond is Forever"*

Brand Positioning Statement & Elevator Pitch

The Brand Positioning Statement works like a one-sentence business plan. It's an internal statement to guide your marketing efforts. For example:

- *For hip, young city dwellers who care about sustainability, only Lilliputian Lawn Care maintains in-town lawns without inflicting noise on the neighbors or adding carbon to the atmosphere. Our beautifully-clipped tiny lawns attest to the eco-advantage of manual mowing.*

You will craft your own Brand Positioning Statement in chapter 4.

The Elevator Pitch is a 3-5 paragraph sales pitch. You will build one in chapter 8.

To finish Ogilvy:

5. **A first-class ticket**. *It pays to give most products an image of quality – a first-class ticket… If your advertising looks ugly, consumers will conclude that your product is shoddy, and they will be less likely to buy it.*

Thoughts: My yoga teacher friend, Mandy Roberts, transformed a failing yoga business into Atlanta's leading yoga studio, in part, by pushing its brand aesthetic. Every piece of messaging — even the directional signs — carries the spirit of her brand. Mandy even brings a professional photographer to every yoga retreat to capture her brand story.

Design adds value to a brand — tangible financial value — because customers desire products that project sophistication, wholesomeness, durability, or innovation.

The High Line in New York City shows how design delivers dollars.

In 1980, a rusting elevated railway spur in the run-down Chelsea meatpacking district was abandoned from lack of use. A group of adjacent property owners sought to demolish the 1.5-mile eyesore.

Some neighborhood residents advocated preserving the derelict structure. Where others saw rusted steel, the visionary neighbors saw open space. They garnered support from the city, business moguls, leading architects, ecologists, and designers.

Forty years later, the elevated park stands as an icon of contemporary landscape architecture and a quilt of tranquil spaces in a harsh urban setting. More importantly, the High Line revitalized the neighborhood with sophisticated apartments now fetching into the millions. With the inflow of hotels, restaurants, and public art, in 2015, the Whitney Museum built a new home designed by Renzo Piano with its front door on the High Line.

REVERSING SPACE.

How to connect to your customers

In 1997, Steve Jobs returned to Apple as a consultant after being forced out twelve years earlier.

Having watched his brainchild suffer through near bankruptcy, poor management, and a lack of innovation, the prodigal CEO made his turnaround appearance at the Worldwide Developers Conference in San Jose, CA. His Q&A came to a sudden halt when someone in the audience snarkily questioned his technical approach. Jobs paused, thought about it, then deftly used the jab to deliver a strategic insight into the most critical branding question:

"The hardest thing is," Jobs calmly explained, *"How does that fit into a cohesive, larger vision that's going to allow you to sell $8 billion, $10 billion of product a year? And one of the things I've always found is that you've got to start with the customer experience and work backwards to the technology. You can't start with the technology and try to figure out where you're going to try to sell it."*

But "starting with the technology" was exactly Apple's strategy during Jobs' absence. The company lost a decade of innovation, having licensed its system software to 75 companies in the US, Taiwan, and Japan to build Mac clones – including the *Motorola StarMax* (rhymes with Star Macs). How's that for a clony brand position? Restating Jobs' words:

"You can't start with the technology and try to figure out where you're going to try to sell it."

If there's one mistake all companies make, it's this: *Build a better mousetrap and hope a market exists to buy it.* Steve Jobs' defining gift was his ability to "reverse space" and start with the customer experience.

Reverse Space with your Customers – *Reversing space* allows you to view the world through your customers' eyes. I learned this practice — not from my brand strategy work — but from Reshad Feild, an English author/healer I befriended in my twenties.[1] As a healer, Reshad had the uncanny ability to know a person's history just from listening to the sound of their voice. I watched him on the phone, talking to a person he had never met, and sensing and describing their mother-father issues in detail.

"How does he do that?" I wondered.

As his student, Reshad taught me to *reverse space*. The easiest way to start is with a tree. You barely notice the tree when you seek its shade, but when the tree rips out your gutters, you curse it out. That is *reacting* to the tree.

Reversing Space starts with curiosity about the tree: What is it about? Why does it reach to the sky? Why does it work so generously to clean the air?

What is it about?

Why does it reach to the sky?

Why does it work so hard to clean the air?

---

1 Reshad Feild authored twelve new age books, performed with Dusty Springfield, and was the black-sheep scion of his aristocratic mother's Bentley Brewing fortune.

Reversing space captures the innocence of a six-year-old, lying in the grass watching the insects, birds, and trees. You let the world speak to you, seeing things, non-critically, as they are — including your customers.

In contrast, the market researcher puts the tree under the microscope — measuring the xylem, phloem, cambium, etc. As a shoestring brand strategist, you can't afford to buy fancy data, so you learn to observe and think like your customer. You must cast your customer as the protagonist in your Brand Story. You ask questions:

Why would someone pay $2.00 for a Kind Bar?

Because it tastes good, has less sugar, and more protein? Or, because you feel the need for some kindness? Maybe, no one loved you today. A Kind Bar feels your pain.

Who's the protagonist? – When you work for a corporation, you're the protagonist – the *we* in the story. *"Onward corporate soldiers! Let's conquer new markets!"* So, you build a better mousetrap. You forget the fact that if no one wants your product, there's nothing to conquer. When you *reverse space*, you realize that the customer has the lead role in your story. Customers have all the power.

Brand people use segmentation to understand their customers. They look at demographics, purchasing power, gender, socio-economic indicators, etc. They segment the people who buy their products into customer-types called *personas*. If you're selling financial services, you might identify *Aisha, the Stay-at-Home Mom* who handles the family finances.

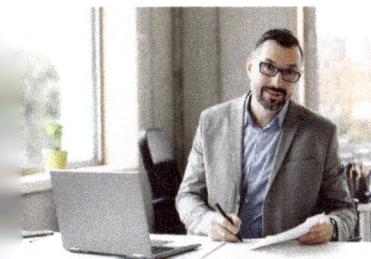

If you're selling cloud-based solutions, you might target *Tom, the Technical Decision-Maker* who rigorously compares specifications from each company.

Reversing space captures the innocence of a six-year-old.

> To build the characters in your Brand Story, *think like a novelist.*

Avoiding Stereotypes – I prefer to think like a novelist and build the characters in my Brand Story around the problems they are trying to solve in life. The challenge is to avoid stereotypes, for example: *"We're targeting Joe Lunch-Bucket with our all-American beer."* When you dig more deeply, you discover that Joe Lunch-Bucket is more likely named Jose, who works hard, loves his family, and prefers *Negra Modelo.* You can uncover this fact through market research, but by *reversing space*, you notice the world around you.

Reversing Space: My Characters

Start by Noticing — By *reversing space*, you see demographics changing, tastes shifting, and stereotypes falling away: Millennials aren't interested in automobiles; *Burger King* is pushing plant-based burgers; people aren't using desktop computers; Wall Street workers are wearing *Patagonia* instead of *Brooks Brothers*; Brooklyn hipsters are drinking low-carb hard seltzers instead of craft beers; and the smartest college kids dumpster-dive on move-out day.[2]

Even basic sundries like napkins and soap, physical destinations like banks and department stores, and all-American sports like football and golf are losing favor among millennials. Pro soccer is in.

---

2 Side note: My son's Ivy League girlfriend surfaced from a dumpster at Brown University with some Cartier earrings and a like-new Marmot down coat.

When you reverse space, you notice deeper emotional motives in the buying decision. Suppose you've invented a high-tech baby stroller and want to research the market. You head to an affluent hipster neighborhood on a Saturday morning to observe young couples getting coffee with sleek-wheeled baby contraptions that cost more than I paid for my first car – a 1965 Volkswagen bus.

You notice the shock-mounted wheels, the UPF 50+ canopy, the five-point harness, leatherette push-bar, phone charger, one-touch brakes, and the reversible seat. The baby seems comfortable, but she'd probably be just as happy in a $14.00 sling. Why did these couples pay $1200 for a *Bugaboo* stroller? You dig deeper and recognize that their big stroller investment cements their commitment as a couple. The baby is their first big project as a couple, and they want to do it right. Then comes the aha *reversing-space* moment. Drum roll:

- *The stroller has nothing to do with the baby!*

Beyond Meat – Suppose you're a vegan named Ethan Brown. You invent a convincing plant-based meat substitute because meat production takes a toll on human

Vegan fare for carnivores

health, the climate, our natural resources, and animal welfare. Your business becomes so successful, you get *Whole Foods* to carry it. Next comes your moment in the spotlight: you want to take the company public to expand your facilities, finance research, and dominate in an emerging global market. So, who is your target customer?

Vegans? Wrong.

Eco-progressives? Wrong again.

Meat eaters? Yup.

Beyond Meat enjoyed one of the most successful IPOs in Wall Street history, trading at 163% above its IPO price, making it the best performing first-day IPO in nearly two decades. From the *Beyond Meat* prospectus:

*Our brand commitment, "Eat What You Love," represents our strong belief that by eating our plant-based meats, consumers can enjoy more, not less, of their favorite meals, and by doing so, help address concerns related to human health, climate change, resource conservation and animal welfare. The success of our breakthrough innovation model and products has allowed us to appeal to a broad range of consumers, **including those who typically eat animal-based meats...**

Wow... Wall Street is subverting carnivores. The *Beyond Meat* prospectus is backed by a long list of research (take note, shoestringers, the research was free), but the central question is still one of *reversing space*.

Can you visualize your Uncle Cal eating a *Beyond Meat* burger at the family cookout? What if Joe's cardiologist told him to cut out meat? Can you *reverse space* and see Cal pressure-cooking beans for dinner? Nada. Suddenly, a vast market emerges (hard-core vegans, climate-conscious consumers, health-conscious moms, global countries without ranch lands, and *drum roll,* Uncle Cal). Or in the prospectus' words:

- *Beyond Meat is positioned to "compete directly in the $1.4 trillion global meat industry."*

Suddenly, the characters in your Brand Story aren't looking like vegans. Here's the casting call:

Brand Story Casting Call: *"Beyond Meat"*

Cardiac Cal

Gunner the Mechanic

Vegan Vicki

Mary the Mommy

Yolanda the Yogini

Climate Clint

If you've been lying in the grass thinking about your customers – or like our stroller-guy, observing them "in the wild" – it's time to cast your Brand Story. This isn't rocket science, so don't over-think it. Come up with 3 to 5, or even more, characters (with nicknames) who are likely to buy your product.

- **Cardiac Cal** is a medical-device rep with rising blood pressure and an expanding gut. Cal has been sternly warned by his cardiologist to quit red meat.

- **Gunner the Mechanic** is a meat lover with zero interest in vegan diets. His wife is curious about eating healthier.

- **Vegan Vicki** as a hard-core vegan and PETA member who craves a burger but remains steadfast meat-free.

- **Mary the Mommy** has no diet ideology but seeks wholesome foods for her family.

- **Yolanda the Yogini** studies nutrition, drinks Kombucha, and practices yoga.

- **Climate Clint** lays awake at night thinking about cows destroying the planet.[1]

---

1 A cow releases between 70 and 120 kg of methane per year. Methane is a greenhouse gas like carbon dioxide (CO_2). But the negative effect on the climate from methane is 23 times higher than the effect of CO_2.

Beyond Meat | BRAND STORY CHARACTER | "Cardiac Cal"

	PROBLEM: • BMI, cholesterol, glucose, and blood pressure are up. • Warned to lose weight and change diet by his doctor for cardiac health.	**SEEKING:** • Transition to a more plant-based diet without major lifestyle changes.	**TARGET:** • Mainstream consumer who loves meat, but seeks a plant-based alternative for health.
BACKGROUND: • 54-year suburban dad • Sales rep for a medical device company • Comfortable salary • College degree in marketing	**INTERESTS:** • Watching sports • Coaching kids soccer • Grilling out with friends	**BRANDS/MEDIA:** • Ford SUV • Lands End • Marvel action movies • Nirvana, REM, Pearl Jam	**GOALS:** • Increasing his sales commission to save for retirement. • Save money for kid's college

Describe each Brand Character in your story:

- The problem they have,

- What they seek to solve it.

- **Fill Out Your Casting Cards** – You've *reversed space*; now get to work. Describe each Brand Character in your story (potential customer cagtegories) using the Casting Card form shown above.[3] Some pointers:

1. **Brand Story Character** – Create a nickname like "Cardiac Cal" that slots him into a category. Find an image on Google that portrays your brand character.

2. **Background** – List demographics that shed light on your character's interest in your brand. These might include: age, education, region, income, ethnicity, or politics.

3. **Interests** – Paint a cultural picture of your character's interests. Hunting, scrapbooking, yoga, and hip-hop each describe very different people.

4. **Brands/Media** – Same as above. If you're developing high-end fashion accessories, it helps to know they love *Versace*. If you're launching a progressive blog, you need to know whether they read *The Atlantic* or watch *MSNBC*.

---

3 The form is included in the Brand Story slide deck that can be downloaded at milleremedia.com.

What does your character want from life?

5. **Goals** – Are they building a career? Hoping to save the planet? Wanting the best for their children?

The top row boxes address your brand position:

6. **Problem** – Describe your character's problem (and not that they hate their boss) – just the problem or need your product or service addresses. Examples:

   - Ice cream provides an inexpensive frozen treat, but my doctor tells me to cut back on sugar. The 20g of sugar in my beloved *Ben & Jerry's* has suddenly become a *problem*.

   - I sit at a computer all day. Repetitive stress injuries have become a *problem*.

   - We just got a super cute Russell Terrier, but training our high-energy, barky dog has become a *problem*.

   - We're looking for a family vacation, but the high cost of airfare, hotels, and eating out is a real *problem*.

7. **Seeking** – Restate your character's problem to describe the solution they are seeking. Examples:

   - *Seeking* a gourmet ice cream with half the sugar.

   - *Seeking* an ergonomic chair with highly-adjustable armrests.

   - *Seeking* a "dog whisperer" trainer with the experience to work with difficult breeds.

   - *Seeking* a drivable vacation resort with efficiency kitchens where we can cook our own meals.

8. **Target** — Use your responses above to describe your target customer (See next page: *Describe Your Targets*).

My Brand Storyboard

Create Your Story Board — You've always wanted to hang in the writer's room for *Seinfeld* or *Friends*; here's your chance. A TV writer's room is adorned with a wall of index cards for episodes, acts, scenes, and characters. Your Brand Story Board wall will just pin Character Cards.

1. ***Create your board by pinning your cards to the wall.***

2. ***Next step: Do nothing.***

That's right. Simply *reverse space*. For the next day or week or month, let your characters speak to you. What do they want from your brand? What turns them on, and off? Does your product connect to Yolanda's health fanatic needs? Does it meet Mary's motherly instincts? Or relieve Cal's health anxieties? Will your brand make Clint feel better about his impact to the planet? Will Gunner even dare to try it?

3. **Describe your customers** —Create a one-sentence description for each target customer in broad brushstrokes and enter it into the blue box on their card.

4. **Choose your targets** – Write a summary that lumps your chosen targets together. See Examples below:

Imagine you are filming a video for your product or service. Select the casting cards you want to to appear in the spot. These are your most likely target customers.

- **Example 1**– *Mainstream consumers who love meat, but seek a plant-based alternative for their health, the environment, and the welfare of animals.*

Does this statement address the needs of all of your chosen characters? If Cardiac Joe represents a key market, call it out:

- **Example 2** – *Mainstream consumers who love meat, but seek a plant-based alternative for their family's health, the environment, and the welfare of animals, <u>plus red-meat-lovers with cardiac concerns</u>.*

Target

Does that cover everyone? Since Climate Clint and Vegan Viki represent growing markets, let's add them to the mix:

- **Example 3** – *Meat-eaters who seek a plant-based alternative for their family's health or have cardiac concerns, <u>climate-aware consumers who seek to limit greenhouse gases</u>, and <u>veggie-lovers who support the welfare of animals</u>.*

Our target now includes mainstream eaters, cardiac folks, vegans, and climate-aware consumers.

A little research shows that 6-8 percent of men have heart disease, so not a huge market. Vegans represent just 1 percent (but seems to double every couple of years).

With its big IPO, *Beyond Meat* has big aims, so let's focus the brand solely on mainstream meat lovers. Cardiac Joe, Vegan Vicki, and Climate Clint will respond regardless. Let's go back and stick with Example 1:

- *Mainstream consumers who love meat, but seek a plant-based alternative for their health, the environment, and the welfare of animals.*

Your brand position needs to target your biggest market at the top of the bell curve. ***When you weigh all the factors, it's Mary the Mommy.***

Mainstream consumers who love meat, but seek an alternative...

Target customer: Who is the actual buyer? — Before you craft your brand positioning statement in chapter 4, make sure you have identified the *actual* buyer of your product or service. Here are examples where it can be confusing :

- **Wholesale Customers** – *McCain USA* provides frozen food to restaurants. Their sweet potato fries are not targeted to:

  · **Consumers** seeking a delicious and nutritious alternative to regular fries, but rather to:

  · **Restaurant owners** who want to: *"Bring excellence to every part of their menu all day long. Discover the sweet opportunity and profit potential of our sweet potatoes."* In other words, McCain's target customers (restaurateurs) don't consume the product.

- **Retailers** – My artist friend, *Sara Anderson,* sought to sell her artist-original silk scarves and kimonos directly to her target customer — the sophisticated woman who seeks a sensuous fashion accessory. When Sara's online store failed to gain traction, Sara realized that yoga studios and resort gift shops might be a better way to get her fashion line in front of consumers.

  By moving from retail to wholesale customers, Sara's new target customer became the gift shop manager or yoga studio owner. Unlike *McCain,* who targets the restaurant owner rather than the end consumer, Sara elected to focus her brand position on the end consumer because store managers would consider her product through the eyes of their customers. I talk to Sara in chapter 12.

- **Commodity Products** — If you sell a commodity product — one that everyone uses — identifying customer segments is more challenging. For example, with dish detergent, is there a *No-Scent-Sue* or an *Eco Eric?* If your dish soap avoids perfumes or uses plant-based cleaners, you can identify these specialized customers and their needs. But with most commodity products, global companies like *Proctor & Gamble* and *Unilever* spend millions to differentiate their detergents from nearly identical competitors.

- **Corporate Customers** — Selling to corporations makes identifying the target customer trickier. For one, the corporate sales cycle is longer with various selling stages, gatekeepers, and middle managers to get through before you reach the actual decision-maker. Secondly, the ultimate corporate customer is the shareholder. Shareholders have only one problem or need: *boosting earnings per share.*

Selling to corporations requires balancing three target customers:

1. First, you must identify the Gatekeeper. If you can't get a foot in the door, it's game over,

2. You must target the Decisionmaker who faces quarterly pressures to perform, and

3. You must address the the Corporation as a whole with its bottom-line mandate for shareholder earnings. Each person in the chain faces a different set of pressures and biases.

- **Non-Profits** — If you're a non-profit, it's tempting to see the recipients of your good work (i.e. poor people) as your target customers, but your actual customers are the donors. As a non-profit, you are in the business of soliciting funds by appealing to the conscience of your donors. That's straightforward, but it gets more complicated when you need to simultaneously "sell" to individuals for small donations and to foundations to get larger grants. I discuss this in Chapter 10.

Before you turn the page, take a moment to practice reversing space. Look at a chair in your room. See it as if you were visiting from another planet trying to make sense of the earthlings. Or study it through the eyes of your chiropractor. Suddenly, your benign chair becomes a lower-back torture device.

Try to look at the market for your new business through the eyes of Steve Jobs. How can you solve your customer's problem or improve their experience? This is why you are starting a business.

How can you solve your customer's problem or improve their experience? This is why you are starting a business.

For non-profits, your actual customer is the donor.

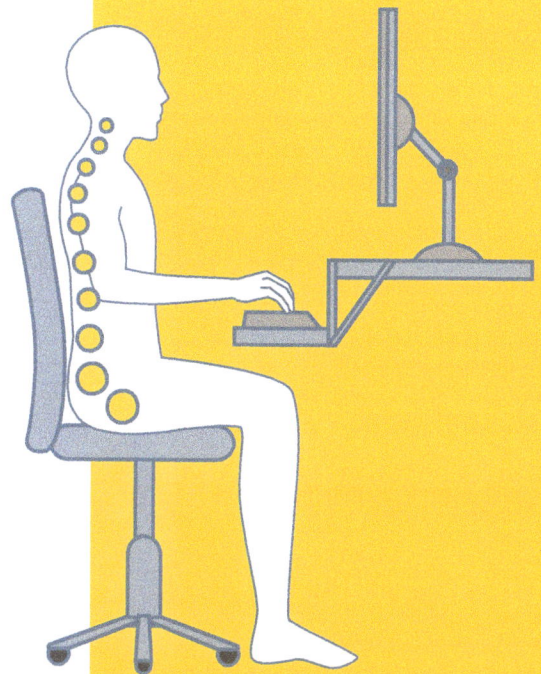

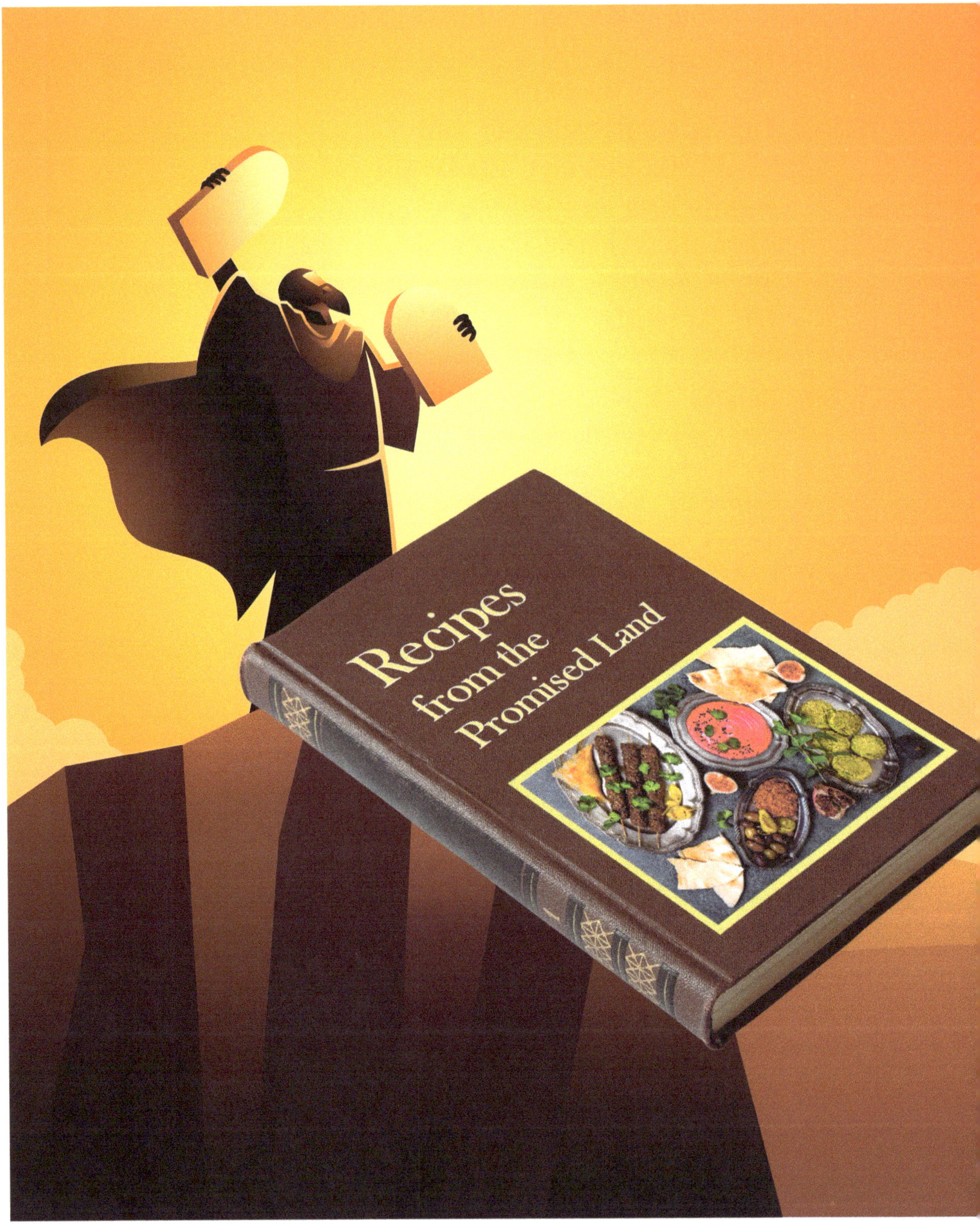
Recipes
from the
Promised Land

THE BRAND WORKSHOP.

You know your customer. Now, it's time to position your brand. The goal is for your customers to feel: *"This brand's for me."*

To summarize positioning, you want your customers to:

1. *Understand* what your business is about,

2. *Want* what you're selling, and

3. *Create* a positive associations for your brand in their minds.

Instead of selling with features and benefits, you are going to position your product to align with their needs and desires.

Positioning is like finding the right slot for a book on the bookshelf. Suppose you researched and wrote a book on "Biblical Recipes." There is a section in the library for Religion and a section for Cookbooks — but not for a book of Biblical Recipes. Where to put that book is a positioning problem. Amid the thousands of books, the religious reader won't find your book if it's in "Cooking," and the foodie won't find it if it's in "Religion."

- To position it correctly, you will need to know your target customer: Is she a *foodie* or a *Bible follower?*

The human mind screens and rejects information that goes against the slots on its mental shelf — data that doesn't fit with its beliefs and prior experiences (I'm a foodie, not a believer; I'm a believer, not a foodie). Researchers describe this as *confirmation bias*. We stop considering new information if the evidence we've already gathered confirms what we would like to be true.

Our screening nature also serves as a survival mechanism to manage information overload. If you made a note of every leaf in the forest, you might step on a snake. The mind screens out the canopy of green to recognize the diamondback poised on the trail.

Faced with a canopy of "leaves" (buying choices), the lawncare shopper doesn't have time to research every landscaping service to make a buying decision. Shoppers who prefer larger, well-established companies won't consider your startup, *Lilliputian Lawn Care.* By identifying your target customer, you can circumvent this disadvantage by aligning your brand to your target customer's needs. As the owner of *Lilliputian,* you recognize your strengths (small yards, no gas engines). As a result, you identify your target customer as someone deeply invested in a new slot on the shelf: *"Sustainable Lawn Care."* For this person, *sustainability* trumps *size.* So, let's position *Lilliputian Lawn Care* as *"The Sustainable Choice."*

For positioning to work, a market must exist of folks who care about pollution-free lawn care. Finding the right slot is like hitting the jackpot.

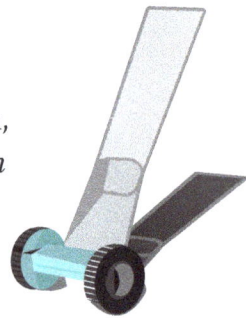

Here are nine famous examples where positioning hit it big (with much credit to Al Ries, whose book with Jack Trout, *Positioning, the Battle for your Mind,* is considered the most influential marketing book of all time).[1]

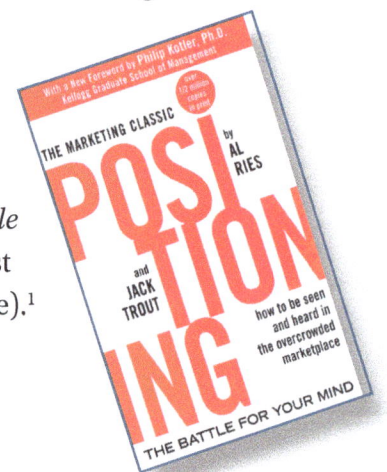

---

1 Ries, Al. "The battle over positioning still rages to this day," Ad Age, March 28, 2005

Nine brands that scored by successful positioning:

BRAND	POSITION	TARGET CUSTOMER	THE PAY-OFF
BMW	*The Ultimate Driving Machine*	High-performance luxury car aficionados.	By promoting high performance with smaller, more nimble vehicles, BMW now outsells Mercedes — the most famous luxury brand in the world.
Dyson	*The first vacuum cleaner that doesn't lose suction*	Gadget nerds with disposable income	After two years in the market, Dyson's high-tech vacuum captured the #2 position against Hoover, a 100-year old brand that, for decades, was synonymous with the word vacuum.
Barilla	*Italy's No. 1 pasta*	Italian food foodies who love Italy.	Barilla became the number 1 pasta in America after a mere three years in the U.S. market.
Grey Goose	*Rated the No. 1 tasting vodka in the world*	Status drinkers who want to flaunt their discerning palate	Seven years after its 1997 introduction, Grey Goose was purchased by Bacardi for more than $2 billion — all from good luck in a vodka competition plus a clever name.
Apple Computer	*Think Different*	Non-techies who prefer human-friendly computing devices	Apple positioned itself directly against IBM's "Think IBM" campaign. The Apple campaign included famous outside-the-box thinkers like Einstein, Hitchcock, and Picasso. By 2005, IBM was forced to abandon the personal computer industry it had started.
Max Factor	*The Makeup of Makeup Artists*	Women who follow celebrities and the world of Hollywood.	Max Factor was a tired old-school brand that repositioned itself as the professional standard by leveraging its Hollywood legacy.
HSBC	*The World's Local Bank*	Financial-savvy customers with a global mindset.	With operations around the globe, HSBC positioned itself as a friendly local bank you can trust.
Energizer	*It Keeps Going, and Going, and Going*	Value-driven shoppers who prefer name brands.	Does it actually last longer? That bunny certainly has your mind convinced — a strategic jab into the heart of Duracell, the durability king.
De Beers	*A Diamond is Forever*	Traditional couples with a materialist bent.	In the 1940s, when diamond sales were at an all-time low, the De Beers brand position solidified the link between eternal romance and diamonds. Three years later, 8 out of 10 brides received a diamond engagement ring.

Brand positioning is not just for big national brands. Here's my local all-female plumbing company:

BRAND	POSITION	TARGET CUSTOMER	RESULTS
M. Cary & Daughters Plumbing	*Armed, Licensed and Fabulous: The Old House Specialists.*	Progressive homeowners who live in restored old homes.	A strong tongue-in-cheek brand and a female crew command higher fees and loyal customers in our circa 1920s neighborhood.

A cautionary tale — Several years ago, Michael and I dreamed up a business idea that promised to become our ticket to wealth and success: *Magnatize.com.* Our target customer was the private-party car seller who customarily buys a "For Sale" sign at the hardware store, places it in his car window, and hopes for the best.

We created a high-tech alternative — Our car-selling kit offered an easy-peel vinyl window sign, stick-on numerals, seller forms to finalize the deal, and the ability to swipe a bar code on the sign with your phone. The buyer could instantly read an online ad, and contact the seller— *bzzt,* easy-peezy!

Our product went through several iterations until we scored the holy grail: Display space in Lowe's (2400 stores, $68 billion in revenue). We leveraged this coup to strike an even more lucrative deal with *AutoTrader.com* (8 million visitors per month who generate $90 billion in sales per year). We connected our humble product to both the world's biggest home improvement chain and the biggest car-selling platform. Even our worst-case scenarios projected six-figure revenues.

In the end, we lost our shirts. Yep, lost it all.

Where did we go wrong? We failed the first and most crucial test: *"Know thy customer."* In 2012, everyone was using smartphones — *hooray!* Except for one important group: *People who buy For Sale signs.* Whoops.

An additional problem: our product would require a *change in behavior.* (Note: If your business idea requires customers to change their behavior, make sure you think this through.) Yes, we developed a superior solution, but scrawling a phone number on a crappy window sign was cheaper and easier for our target customer. Defined loosely as:

Private-party car sellers who live mostly in the boonies, and who buy a For Sale sign at their local Ace Hardware, stick it in the window, and hope for the best.

If we had added *"low-tech"* to describe our target customer, we would have caught the disconnect and avoided a $250,000 loss, plus years of product development and persistant grief.

I'm not trying to scare you off with our sad tale, but...

...if M. Cary and Daughters can position a toilet float <u>and</u> position a successful brand at the same time — you can too with the Brand Story® Workshop approach.

We failed the first and most crucial test: "Know thy customer."

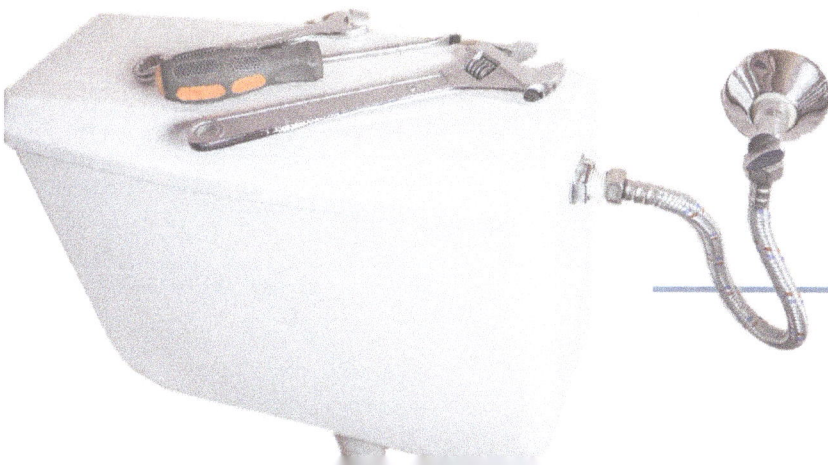

Brand Story Workshop

Brands live in the collective mind of the public, so it follows that a collective approach to brand positioning delivers the best results.

From experience, startups that huddle in a collaborative brand workshop are more likely to hit their mark. Here's why:

- **Bias** – If you market a product by following nothing but your instincts, you can become blinded by your dreams (e.g., Car-Selling Kit).

- **Points of view**– The Brand Story workshop throws analytical cold water on your expectations and channels creative energy from other peoples' points of view. You bring more data points into the decision process.

- **Cheap focus group** – I see this processused by my wife, Karen. When faced with a personal or professional problem, Karen will dial her network of friends and peers and talk it through. Football players huddle and marketers conduct focus groups.

- It never occurred to us, but Michael and I should have driven around town looking for *For Sale* signs, called the sellers, and pitched our Magnatize car-selling kit idea to to actual prospects:

"Are you selling the '73 Dodge Dart? I saw your sign and would like to get your feedback on a new product we're developing — an Internet-connected car-selling kit."

"Say what?"

Magnatize.com | BRAND STORY CHARACTER | "Analog Andy"

PROBLEM:
- Has a used car to sell.

SEEKING:
- Simplest and cheapest selling method is preferred.

TARGET:
- Buys and sells all of his cars second hand.

BACKGROUND:
- 71 years old, retired
- Rural resident
- Doesn't use computers very much

INTERESTS:
- Watching TV
- Works in his shop
- Hanging with grandkids

BRANDS/MEDIA
- Ford F150
- Milwaukee Tools
- Lands End

GOALS
- Saving money for trip to Gatlinburg
- House repairs

Prepare for battle

Think of your Brand Story Workshop as a war game — a chance to game out different scenarios. The *New Yorker* described the art of military decision-making the same way:

*Military planners use immersive war games, carried out in the field or around a table, **to bring more of the "decision map" into view**. In such games, our enemies discover possibilities that we can't foresee, ameliorating the poverty of our individual imaginations. And since the games can be played over and over, they allow decision-makers to "rewind the tape," exploring many branches of the "decision tree."[2]*

---

2 Rothman, Joshua, "The Art of Decision-Making," The New Yorker, 1-21-19.

Napoleon paid a terrible price for not gaming out his lofty goal to invade Moscow. After a long, bloody march, his armies entered the Russian capital and discovered a deserted city with no czarist officials to sue for peace, nor food and supplies to pillage. Russian patriots soon set fires across the city, leaving Napoleon's massive army without the means to survive the Russian winter.

Napolean's ambition blinded him from the flaws in his decision map. For Michael and me, a war game would have revealed the hard truth stated by "Analog Andy" with the Dodge Dart:

"Don't need a smartphone to sell a damn car."

THE GYM JOINT

Hi Jane,
I am launching a new business and need your help. Can I draw upon your experience in business and fitness to help me strategize the brand for the "The Gym Joint?"

Plan on 2-3 hours of brainstorming and strategy. Don't worry; it will be creative and fun.

Friday, March 23 from 2 pm.
Thanks for your much-appreciated support!
Lois

BRAND STORY WORKSHOP

- Participant 1
- Participant 2
- Participant 3
- Participant 4
- Participant 5

The Gym Joint

Month Day, Year

IMPORTANT: Open box carefully. DO NOT remove rock before reading instructions!

This box contains one genuine pedigreed

PET ROCK

Rock In The Box Productions 2010

Brand Positioning Steps

Step 1. Enlist Your Participants:

Enlist three to five people (plus you and your business partners) who can bring business experience, subject matter expertise, or an informed consumer perspective to your idea. It might be a business-savvy friend, a retiree from that line of work, or someone familiar with your product. If you have an existing business, invite the people who *touch* the brand: typically the CEO, sales and marketing people, customer service, or even key customers.

Step **2. Build Out Your Workshop Presentation:**

Use the Brand Story PowerPoint template to guide your workshop. The template follows the method described in this chapter. Fill out the blanks in advance using your work from this chapter to streamline the workshop. Plan on 2-3 hours for the workshop.

The opening section of the presentation — modeled on Chapter 1 of this book — explains how brands and brand positioning work. The purpose is to get your group quickly up to speed on brand positioning. A voice-over introduces each slide. *Download the file at Milleremedia.com.*

DISCUSSION:
Solving Your Target Customer's Needs:

Michael and I faced our moment of truth: Our car-selling kit didn't solve an actual problem for our target customer. We learned the hard way: Unless your business idea addresses a genuine customer need (including the need for a pet rock), your business is not viable. You don't want to be bleeding cash and accruing debt when you realize this.

The Workshop serves as a check that you will solve a real problem for real customers before you launch your business.

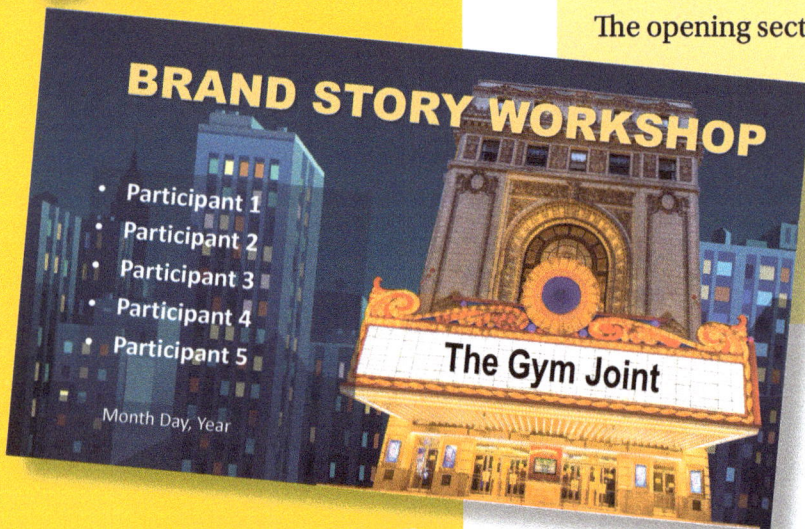

You identified your customer, their problem, and your solution. Now put it to the test with your Workshop group.

Consider *King of Pops*, a purveyor of expensive, gourmet "Popsicles" that sell for $3.00 each on the streets of Atlanta. Gourmet ice pops might seem like a cockamamie idea since you can buy original Popsicles for 25 cents each by the box at the store.

(Popsicle® is a Unilever brand used here generically.)

Question: What problem or need is solved by a $3.00 ice pop? Apparently, a real one:

- *King of Pops* started in 2010 with a single pushcart on a street corner in Atlanta. The company now sells 2-3 million ice pops per year, including wholesale to *Whole Foods,* major grocery chains, and big events.

The *King of Pops'* target customer seeks a spontaneous diversion, a foodie indulgence, and a guilt-free all-natural treat on a stick without breaking their pace. *King of Pops* wasn't the first. Consider the customer who buys a *Mrs. Fields* cookie at the mall for $2.00 compared to a pound of *Chips Ahoy* for roughly the same price – proof that a customer base exists for a $3.00 ice pop.

Customer needs aren't necessarily practical problems. Three-dollar Popsicles don't solve hunger. Your brand position can target a host of needs: practical, emotional, status, and more.

Unfortunately, our high-tech car-selling did not solve an obvious problem for Analog Andy.

Step 3. Circle your strengths. The problem you solve for your target customer will fall into one (or more) of these seven categories.

Circle each category where your product or service stands out.

✓ BETTER PRICE
✓ GREATER CONVENIENCE
✓ ENHANCED FUNCTIONALITY
✓ USER EXPERIENCE
✓ COMPANY EXPERTISE
✓ CONVEYS STATUS
✓ OTHER

The Big DIFFERENCE

Unless you stake a claim, you become a commodity.

Step 4. Describe Your Strengths — Describe what makes your product or service better or unique in each circled category. Here are two examples:

- COMPANY EXPERTISE — Lilliputian Lawn Care > *Small lawn sustainable expert. Grass is clipped instead of whacked. Providing sustainable lawn care without the pollution, noise, or hydrocarbons of conventional lawn care.*

- ENHANCED FUNCTIONALITY — Car-Selling Kit > Offers *seamless car-selling experience from end to end. Quicker to read, easier to contact the seller, gives the buyer all the information they need without having to call, and protects the buyer and seller with transaction forms.*

Write a short statement for each of your circled strengths.

Step 5. Determine Your Secret Sauce — Now comes the hard part: your differentiation, or "secret sauce." Study your circled categories and strength descriptions to see where you can stake a claim that matters to customers. Are you the fastest, most knowledgeable, more experienced, first with a function, most convenient, or user-friendliest? Do you offer a unique formulation or technology? Can you claim to install toilets with a female crew?

Discussion: Unless you stake a claim – a unique differentiator that sets your product or service apart – you become a *commodity*. Every product or service is a commodity at one level because there is nothing new under the sun. But, you don't want to appear to be a commodity. If you do, you'll have to compete on price or brand awareness without a differentiating position.

- Consider: *Kellogg's Frosted Mini Wheats* versus *Post Shredded Wheat* versus the *Great Value house brand*. When what's inside the box is all the same, you're forced to build a brand by promoting the outside of the box.

Gasoline is an obvious commodity – Refineries claim to add mysterious formulations to achieve brand differentiation. Example: *Chevron* with *Techron*, *Mobil* with *Synergy*, or *Shell* with *V12*. I doubt there's a driver on the planet who cares a wit about *Techron*, but the branded formulation creates the feeling that *Chevron's* secret sauce is better for your car.

Customers Want Proof

- Gasoline additives are simply detergents. Do they work?

- *Panera* claims "100% clean ingredients," but is *Panera's* menu free from pesticides?

- *Lilliputian Lawn Care* claims to be the only sustainable lawn service in town, but how does Donnie demonstrate no gas engines and no chemicals?

Step 6. Demonstrate Your Proof – Your customer wants faster, cheaper, better, the original, the newest, more features, or greater expertise. You need to prove it via happy customers, performance metrics, or proven results. Write down how you can prove your claim.

Examples of fact-based proof points:

- If you're opening a farm-to-table restaurant, your menu description would read: *"locally-sourced sausage from Ashwood Farms."*

- If your coffee claims: *"supporting farmers making a living wage,"* reveal how you source your beans and how farmers get paid.

- In 2008, *Dunkin' Donuts* reinvented its brand from a donut shop to a coffee destination by citing a blind taste test: 54.2 percent chose *Dunkin*, 39.3 percent chose *Starbucks*, and 6.3 percent had no preference. This is a provable metric.

- *Volvo* became synonymous with "safety" by citing NHTSA statistics with their crash test dummies.

- And *Jimmie John's* gave credence to their "Freaky Fast" brand position by comping free sandwiches to customers who suffered delays.

Jimmy John's ☑ @jimmyjohns · Jan 3, 2018
Replying to @
I hate messing up, but I love **making it right**. Thanks for giving me another chance!

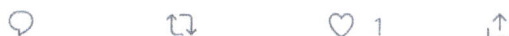

♡ 1

Proof Points:

54.2%

BRAND POSITIONING STATEMENT

You've done the heavy lifting. Now put it all together.

It's time to create your brand positioning statement. This internal statement guides how you present your business to the marketplace.

I've created a fictitious brand positioning statement for *Jimmy John's*:

Jimmy John's Brand Positioning Statement (fictitious)	
A. Target Customer: Describe your most likely customer(s).	*For twenty-something guys who live in dorms or work in cubicles…*
B. What are their needs? What is the problem they seek to solve?	*…and need to satisfy immediate hunger when there's little time to eat out and no inclination to cook…*
C. Secret Sauce: Beginning with "<u>only</u>," how do you uniquely solve their needs?	*…<u>only</u> Jimmy John's delivers subs so freaky fast, we start preparing your order before you're even off the phone.*
D. Proof: Give your customers a reason to believe!	*We are so committed to speedy delivery, if we can't get it to you in 15 to 20 minutes, we'll make it up to you.*

Brand positioning is like fishing. You don't blindly cast your hook in hopes of a fish — you select the correct tackle (your unique solution) and right bait (your secret sauce) for a specific fish (your target customer).

Jimmie John's does not advertise locally-sourced ingredients or *Boars Head* meat. They target college students and cubicle workers who won't take the time, nor afford the dollars for a restaurant meal. (Quick note: *Jimmie John's* has revised its brand position to tout speed and "fresh ingredients.")

Step 7. Fill out your Brand Positioning Statement

Okay, now it's your turn. This internal statement works like a chemical formula, so it doesn't need to be clever or catchy. Using your prepared customer description, secret sauce, and proof points, fill out your Brand Positioning Statement.

Your Brand Positioning Statement	
A. Target Customer: Describe your most likely customer(s).	
B. What are their needs? What is the problem they seek to solve?	
C. Secret Sauce: Beginning with "<u>only</u>," how do you uniquely solve their needs?	
D. Proof: Give your customers a reason to believe!	

So, what do I do with it? — First, congratulate yourself. Most businesses don't have a clearly-defined brand position. They operate in the *"if we build it, they will come"* territory.

In the chapters ahead, you will see how your brand position forms the foundation for your "Brand Platform" — the full recipe for how customers will experience your brand in the marketplace. With a Brand Platform, every sales pitch you make, Web site you build, and collateral piece you send out will be "on brand." Plus, you will attract the most-qualified prospects and make them customers for life.

But first, let's name your baby.

THE NAME GAME.

Banana fana fo-fana! Choosing a name that supports your brand story opens a big can of worms.

Your business name can draw on your vanity (a family name), pragmatism (the name explains what you do), or kismet (the name came to you in a dream). As any parent will attest, naming your offspring is usually a mix of serendipty and research.

Long before the Internet, my pregnant mom made it her practice to study movie credits as the names scrolled by. With the theater emptied, she scrutinized the screen, and considered names from the best boy, key grip, gaffer, and all. I'm named after – *drum roll* – *King Kong* supporting actor, Bruce Cabot.

Michael and I named our brand agency under different circumstances and with a different *Kong*:

As I explained in the Introduction, Michael and I met while running the creative department at *CheckFree Corporation*. We gave *CheckFree* the tagline: *"The Leader in Electronic Commerce,"* and to my absolute wonderment, the industry accepted this audacious claim as fact — my first eye-opener to the power of brand positioning.

Unfortunately, our burgeoning enthusiasm for brand strategy was routinely squelched by our *King Kong* boss, a CMO who would steal creative from trade magazine ads and direct us to copy it. Mr *Kong* would call us into his office at 2 pm, show us the ripped creative, and then send us back to our desks. "Oh, by the way," he'd announce. "Tight deadline; need it this afternoon."

It was a control tactic. Instead of grumbling, "*Eff* you and the horse you rode in on," we'd announce, "Time for a design coup!" and then do our own thing.

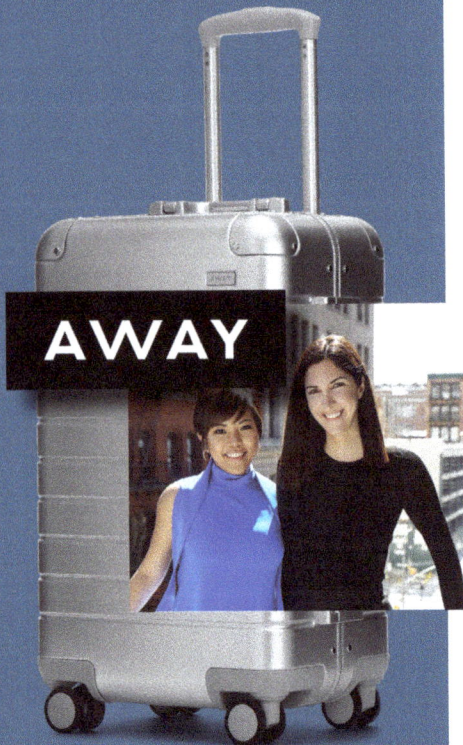

Eventually, *CheckFree* fired the department to bring in an outside agency. Michael and I launched our new agency, *Design Coup* – with *CheckFree* as our first big client. *Touché!*

We invested $250 each and set up our renegade-named business in back of my house – an experience that gives me undying enthusiasm for fortuitously-named startups like these:

Away – Jen Rubio, co-founder of *Away*, the luggage brand, described the fluke that named her company:

> » *"As I was doing my research, I tried to stay organized, so I made a folder on my computer named 'TBD Luggage Brand.' One day, I opened my computer and typed in "Away" as a placeholder – it just came to me. I thought, "There's no way we could use Away as a brand name. It's such a simple four-letter word and extremely common. We spent a lot of time brainstorming names but never came up with anything as good. My partner, Steph Korey asked a law firm if we could trademark Away. They laughed in our face, but she insisted. A week later, they called us, saying, 'You have been given a gift from the marketing gods.'"*[1]

Craigslist – In 1995, a streak of providence christened *Craigslist*. Craig Newmark remembered the moment:

> » *"When the mailing list I was running needed to have a name – (I'm very literal as a nerd and I was gonna call it 'San Francisco Events') – people around me told me they already called it Craigslist. I had inadvertently created a brand."*[2]

Airbnb – In 2007, Brian Cheske and Joe Gebbia, (recent grads from the Rhode Island School of Design), reached the pinnacle of brand serendipity while struggling to make their rent. A bunch of techies were coming to San Francisco's IDSA design

---

1 NPR, "How I Built This with Guy Raz," https://www.npr.org/2019/03/08/701651787/away-jen-rubio

2 The Guardian, July 14, 2019, https://www.theguardian.com/technology/2019/jul/14/craigslist-craig-newmark-outrage-is-profitable-most-online-outrage-is-faked-for-profit

conference but faced sold-out hotels. Brian and Joe bought inflatable air mattresses and rented floor space in their apartment to host visitors. Their ingenuity birthed the oddly-named *Air Bed and Breakfast,* which quickly became *Airbnb.* They later adorned the brand with "Bélo," the company's "universal symbol for belonging." Today, *Airbnb* is worth $31 billion.

The marketing gods will be kind to you too.

You've put in the hard work to identify your brand position, so let's play the Name Game by following the gold standard for company names and domains.

AirBed&Breakfast™

airbnb

The Bélo mark

The Gold Standard for Company Names

Names fall into three categories; decide where you want to be:

1. **Vanity Names** — Using your personal name for your business connects your enterprise to a real person. Freelancers, professionals, and one-person companies gain credibility when they proclaim: "I stake my reputation by branding my name."

   - Many of the most famous brands pay homage to their founders, (Conrad Hilton, Henry Ford, Bill Marriott), as do fashion brands like Tommy Hilfiger and Ralph Lauren. As a practical matter, if you want to attract talent and build your company, a vanity brand may limit your growth. Consider the difference in attracting talent between *Joe's Fresh Fish* and *Sustainable Seas Inc.*

2. **Descriptive Names** — This is the default choice for most new businesses, and it makes sense: *A-1 Driveway Replacement, Doggie Dips and Dos*, and *Perfect Wedding Cake* all tell customers exactly what the business offers. During the 1990s Web frenzy, generic descriptive domains became the rage. Investors scooped up *Pets.com, Furniture.com, Shoes.com,* and *Webvan* in a gold rush of IPOs, but all ultimately failed.

The Gold Standard for Company Names

Descriptive Names Continued:

- Descriptive names offer clarity in explaining your product or service, but can limit your potential. Imagine if Jeff Bezos had branded his online book business *Bookstore.com.* He would have never built the retail/entertainment/tech juggernaut that *Amazon.com* has become. Consider *Burlington Coat Factory,* which did not have Bezos' foresight. When *Burlington* expanded its product line, the company had to add the clunky tagline, *"We're more than just coats."* Finally, in 2013 they dropped *"Coat Factory"* altogether.

3. **Lyrical** — Unlike descriptive names, lyrical names communicate brand qualities. *Apple Computer* has nothing to do with fruit, but suggests friendly technology. Many great brands have lyrical names:

   - *Starbucks* was named after a character in *Moby-Dick,*

   - *Google* came from an accidental misspelling of the number "googol,"

   - *Nike* is the Greek goddess of victory,

   - *Zappos* is derived from the Spanish word *zapatos,* meaning shoes, and

   - *Twitter* is derived from the dictionary definition: 'a short burst of inconsequential information' and 'chirps from birds.'

The ideal name works three ways: It's descriptive, lyrical, and it communicates your brand position.

- **The best names speak to your brand position –**
  Your name should punctuate your position without sounding generic. Snappy lyrical names with clear positions include:

  - *SmartWater:* Just like spring water, but *smarter* and better.

  - *Dropbox* suggests a no-brainer way to store your files. They could have chosen, "Cloud-Based Data Storage Inc.," but instead, they coined a product name that sounds tech-easy to use.

  - *Netflix* is self-descriptive (rent flix over the net). Originally a way to rent DVDs through the mail, today, the company streams and produces original films.

  - *OneBlade* is a non-cartridge, high-end razor company with the brand position: *Award-winning, single-blade razors.*

  - *Farm Burger* is an Atlanta-based burger chain that serves farm-to-table grass-fed beef.

  - *Kids Fly Safe* sells FAA-approved seat harnesses for children on airplanes. It's not the slickest brand, but the name directly addresses a parent's concern.

  - *UNTUCKit* sells shirts designed to be worn untucked. I wonder if my school principal would have approved.

Granola bars deserve special mention for weaving brand positions into their names:

  - *Luna* is a nutrition bar aimed at women.

  - *Clif Bar* targets wannabe rock-climbing men.

  - *Kind* suggests "Doing kind things for your body."

Go for SHORT!

- One to two words is the ideal length. The gold medals go to companies that boil their brands down to two letters: (GE, GM, and HP). Platinum goes to Oprah, who nails it with a single letter for her brand: (O).

- Long names create challenges for logo designers. Ultimately, successful brands shorten their names:

  - *PricewaterhouseCoopers* became *PwC*,

  - *Federal Express* became *FedEx*,

  - *Dunkin' Donuts* dropped the donuts,

  - *Home Box Office* became *HBO*,

  - *Kentucky Fried Chicken* became *KFC*, and

  - *Weight Watchers* is now *WW*.

kæn ˈpip(ə)l prəˈnaʊns ði neɪm?

Can people pronounce the name?

Foreign words add *panache*, but can also hobble your efforts. I helped a French couple launch *Au Pan Crêpe* ("the crepe pan" restaurant), but their Georgia customers stumbled with the French expression. Eventually, the restaurant became *French Gourmet Bistro*.

- **Avoid creative spellings** — *Lyft*, *Tumblr*, and *Grindr* get away with odd spellings because they invested millions building brand recognition. Funky spellings create trouble when you'e forced to spell out the name over the phone or before the elevator stops at your floor. You may even discover (too late) that Siri is misdirecting your customers to someone's correctly-spelled site. For example:

  - **Flickr** – One of the most famous high-cost screw-ups from cutesy spelling is *Flickr*. When Caterina Fake launched her company, the *Flicker.com* domain belonged to *Flicker Beer*, so Caterina dropped the "e." As *Flickr* grew, so did the mistyped Web traffic going to *flicker* instead of *flickr* – an estimated loss of 3.6 million visitors per year. At one point, *Yahoo!* (the new owner of *Flickr*) offered to pay $600,000 for *flicker.com* — a very expensive 301 redirect.[3]

  - **Kabbage.com** – If you choose a creative spelling and become wildly successful, you may need to fork over big bucks for the correct spelling – but that would be a wonderful problem to have. Witness *Kabbage.com* (small business loans online), which ultimately bought *cabbage.com* (for an undisclosed sum) to avoid Web spelling confusion.

Small Business Funding Options ✕ +

← → C G cabbage.com > > kabbage.com

---

3 "Yahoo Finally Takes Control of Flicker.com Domain Name," PetaPixel, June 15, 2010.

Great brands often break the rules by using fake words that are neither descriptive, fanciful, spellable, nor even pronounceable.

Iggli.com died a quick death as a travel startup. *Geniqe* is one of 1500 ready-to-go fake names you can buy ($3612) with matching domains from *Novanym*.

Fake words achieve the goal of being short and available as dot-coms, but shoestring startups should try to avoid them. They require bigger bucks to build awareness and cement the spelling.

Here are some notable fake-word brands:

- *Blinkist* – lets you read key ideas from nonfiction books in 15 minutes or less. Okay, "blink" is a word.

- *Fiverr* – online freelance services

- *Qdoba* – Mexican food chain

- *Kiip* – Mobile advertising.

- *Zumper* – Apartments for rent

- *Zillow* — Yes, a fake word can become a huge multinational brand, but it took serious investments to propel it to its $4 billion market valuation.

- *Trulia* – Tons of TV advertising made *Trulia* a national brand. *Zillow* acquired it in 2015 for $3.5 billion.

- *BHLDN* – Vowels are so passé for hipster weddings from *Anthropologie*.

- *Xobni* – "*Inbox*" spelled backward. This utterly unpronounceable software company ceased operations – and maybe for that reason.

- And what about *Spotify?* This great name for a laundry spot-remover proves that a global music brand can emerge from a made-up word.

zumper

Zillow

trulia

BHLDN

xobni

Spotify

Blinkist

fiverr

QDOBA
MEXICAN EATS

kiip

The Domain Name Gold Standard

Choosing a well-positioned brand name is the easy part. With over 220 million domains currently registered, finding a domain to match your company name requires creativity and perseverance. If you visit *dotweekly.com*, you will find a pricey market for lucrative domains. For this reason, fake names and spellings have become workarounds for the scarcity of single-word, unique URLs that end in dot-com.

Since we're following the progress of Donnie's *Lilliputian Lawn Care*, I can report that Donnie is excited to build his Web site. He checked *GoDaddy.com* and discovered that *lilliputian.com* is available — for $9,880. If it's any consolation, the URL was reduced from $27,300 the week before. Fortunately, Donnie can register *LilliputianLawns.com* for $11.99, so he buys it. Donnie plans to paint the Web domain on his truck and market to the neighborhood.

After spending his $11.99, Donnie has second thoughts. *LilliputianLawns.com* is a mouthful. "And, who can spell "Lilliputian?" he wonders. "How about *LilliputLawns.com* — named after the island of the little people?"

When Donnie shares the idea with his friends, he learns that none have read *Gulliver's Travels*, nor watched the 1939 movie or the 1977 and 2010 remakes. "Maybe, I'm a literary outlier," he laments.

Donnie remembers that his brand position focused on "sustainable lawn care," so he rethinks his name. He searches a long list of URLs with *"Sustainable," "Earth Friendly," "GreenPlanet,"* and so on. None captures his quirky idea.

Finally, Donnie settles on *"Carbon Free Lawns."* It's hardly poetic, but it offers differentiation and clarity. Importantly, *CarbonFreeLawns.com* was available for $11.99. The brand also allows Donnie to advertise manure-based lawn-feeding as an alternative to petroleum-based synthetic fertilizers.

? Premium Domain

lilliputian.com is available
$9,880.00 ❓

Domain Available

lilliputianlawns.com is available
$11.99 $17.99 ❓
for the first year

LilliputianLawns.com?
LilliputLawns.com?
Carbonfreelawns.com

The domain name check-list

Before you freak out, "Everything's taken!" Realize that a tight, catchy domain name that is identical to your company name (example: *Bombas.com)* is only necessary if you are *building a brand.*

So, isn't that the premise of this book? Yes! But, if you're starting *Allentown Orthopaedic Medical* or *South Kingsboro Pest Control*, finding a dot-com should be easy. Your customers will be able to find you on Google just fine. But, if you want a memorable brand that conveys substance and authority (for example, *Pest1.com* – available for $300, a steal! – instead of *SouthKingsboroPestControl.com)* you will need to go through the domain drill below. Ready? Let's start:

a faux brand

☑ **The Gold standard = Alignment** — When your company name and domain match exactly, your domain becomes "aligned" or unified with your brand. Alignment is a must with "pure-play" online brands, like *Bombas*, and pretty much every major national brand meets this standard. Examples:

- **Aligned National brands** – *Facebook.com, McDonalds.com, Wholefoods.com, Amazon.com, Walgreens.com*, and pretty much every big compay paid what it took to get a matching dot-com, or they got in early.

- **Shortened names** – Domains that shorten the company name especially meet the gold standard. Examples: *Experian Information Systems = experian.com. Hyatt Hotels = hyatt.com. Sunkist Growers = sunkist.com.* In each case, the brand became known by its shortened name.

☑ **Add a descriptor** — The single-word domain you want probably won't be available unless you create a fake or made-up spelling. A better approach is to add a second word as a descriptor. Examples:

hyatt.com
experian.com
sunkist.com

- *OneBlade*, the single blade razor company, uses *OneBladeShave.com*

- *Bounty* paper towels uses *BountyTowels.com* (Bounty.com is a UK maternity site.)

- *GoGo,* the wifi service for air travel, uses *GoGoAir.com.*

- *Snyders*, the leader in pretzels, uses *SnydersofHanover*.com.

- *Mute*, the anti-snoring device company, uses *MuteSnoring.com*

- Restaurants and bricks-and-mortar retailers often add the city as a descriptor — *companynameNY.com.* In my neighborhood, *Revival*, a Southern-style restaurant, uses *RevivalDecatur.com.*

OneBladeShave.com

RevivalDecatur.com

☑ **Add a prefix** — Adding a small word in front can also help you buy a domain:

- The famous British newspaper, *The Manchester Guardian*, could not get *Guardian.com*, so its digital news portal became *TheGuardian.com*.

- *Facebook* started as *TheFacebook.com*.

- *MARTA*, Atlanta's public transit system, uses *ItsMarta.com*.

- Adding "get" and "join" also work. (*JoinDrift.com, JoinPapa.com*). *Quip*, a new electric toothbrush uses *GetQuip.com*. *Dropbox* started with the clunky *GetDropbox.com*.

- Adding "go" can work. *PatientCo*, a healthcare payment site, uses *GoPatientCo.com*, and there's the most famous Go domain, *GoFundMe*. Or, turn "go" into a suffix, or two of them for indie funding: *IndieGoGo.com*.

www.getdropbox.com

.COM

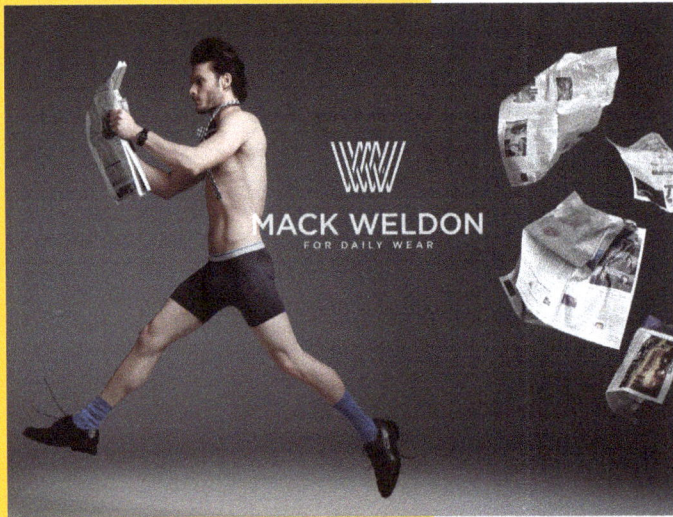

☑ **Add a suffix** — Adding *ify* can turn your noun into a verb.

- Example: *Shop* becomes *Shopify.com*. Adding "vine," spawned *Bridgevine.com*. But, to avoid an awkward spelling moment in the elevator, I don't recommend using a domain extension to spell out the word. *Bit.ly* and *Mother.ly* require some help from Libya (.ly) to spell out the domain.

☑ **Sneak in initials** — If *JoesPlumbingandHeating.com* is too clunky, consider *JoesPH.com*.

- Initials can add clout (*Bryn Mawr Trust* is *BMT.com*), but dot-coms with all initials can be hard to find.

☑ **Invent a proper name** — An entirely fictitious proper name is not out of the question.

- When the CEO founder of the "digitally-native vertical" underwear brand, *Mack Weldon*, introduces himself at meetings, you must first process the fact that his name isn't Mack. CEO Brian Berger sought to reinvent the way men's underwear was designed, marketed, and sold, so he created *"Mack Weldon,"* a fictitious name that connotes masculinity and practicality. It was also an easy dot-com to acquire. Mack, rather, Brian, riffed off *"Weldon,"* a sleepwear brand from the 1940s to create his brand, but without the forties masculinity. The New York Times described Mike Sharits, the iconic *Max Weldon* underwear model, as "fatless, but… just goofy enough, rubbing his belly or tripping out of a pair of trousers, to be relatable."[4]

---

4 Wilson, Eric, "Less Ab, More Flab," New York Times, 2013/05/23

"Python hyphen Publishing dot com"

- ☑ **Don't add a hyphen** — If PythonPublishing.com isn't available, don't succumb to a hyphen between the two words, even if it seems an easy fix.

  - Warning. You will endure the rest of your days in business reciting, *"Python hyphen Publishing dot com."* No hyphens, ever.

- ☑ **Avoid extreme misalignment** — Customers expect the domain name to match, yet even large companies can go off the deep end with non-matching domains such as these:

  - *Google's* parent company, *Alphabet,* uses the extremely-misaligned *abc.xyz* as its domain. Huh?

Alphabet
abc.xyz

  - Until 2012, the web address for software-maker, *37Signals*, was the misaligned *BasecampHQ. com* (their lead product is Basecamp). Later, they achieved perfect alignment when they paid big bucks for *Basecamp.com*, and renamed the company to *Basecamp.*

37signals
BasecampHQ.com

Basecamp
Basecamp.com

  - *Advanced Plan for Health* offers a proprietary healthcare analytics system, called *Poindexter* (named after the nerdy scientist character in the *Felix the Cat* cartoon). Their Web domain, *MyPoindexter. com,* takes misalignment to the extreme. I encouraged them to follow the example of *37Signals* and change the entire brand to the quirky, but memorable, *Poindexter.* Alas, perfect alignment was a bridge too far.

Advanced Plan
FOR HEALTH
MyPoindexter.com

  - Extreme mismatch is appropriate when the brand stands on its own apart from the company name. Example: *Stokely-Van Camp, Inc.* promotes its sports drink at the perfectly-aligned *gatorade.com.*

GATORADE

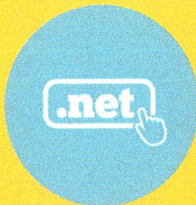

-

- According to statistics, 47.1% of all websites use a domain that ends with ".com." A new round of alternative URL extensions came out in 2014 to solve the scarcity of dot-coms. Domain purchasers could register *legal.guru, brucemiller.agency,* and *fridaynightpoker.club.* Ultimately, the market spoke, and the new extensions tanked. Dot-coms still rule.

- **Cute country extensions** — Don't even consider using country extensions like *eat.me* (Montenegro) or *Smart.ly* (Libya). But, the extension .io (British Indian Ocean Territory) is hugely popular with multiplayer games and online applications. And what about *Notion*, the all-in-one productivity app? Business users log in at *notion.so* (Somalia) — huh?

- **When to use other top-level domains** — .Net is a legitimate option if *dot-com* isn't available. Example: *Stitch.net* (Services for seniors). *Dot-Org* works well for non-profits, but *edu* is reserved for legitimate schools. Of the new domain extensions, *dot-co* (company) seems to have the most credibility.

- ☑ **When to pay a premium** — Registering a dot-com typically costs around $10 - $12. Domain registration often comes free with a web hosting plan. When registrars like GoDaddy ask a premium price (example: $9,800 for *lilliputian.com*), they are acting as a broker for a privately-owned domain. Should you pay a premium price?

- **Example** – My client, Sara Anderson, was starting a shoestring brand for her original fashion designs. Through a brand story workshop, we positioned the brand for *women who embody feminine sophistication but identify with a free-spirited ethos.* In the spirit of *Martha Stewart, Donna Karan,* and *Laura Ashely,* Sara wanted *Sara Anderson* for her brand. We searched for domains: She could choose *SaraAndersonDesign.com* for $11.99 or *SaraAnderson. com* for $2400. Sara was a stay-at-home mom looking to reinvent herself, but wasn't ready to make a big investment. She thought long and hard, "Do I have what it takes to become a fashion brand or is this a hobby?" Once Sara visualized the label, spending $2400 was a no-brainer.

☑ **What if the domain is not for sale?** — Suppose you want PythonPublishing.com. You search and get: *"This domain is not available."* All is not lost.

- **First, check usage** – In this example, I typed *pythonpublishing.com* into my browser, and a shell of a Web site appeared. As of this writing, Python Publishing does not appear to be fully in business.

- **Check the ownership** – *Whois* (whois.icann.org) lets you search ownership of the domain. Sometimes the administrative contact (owner) is listed and you can contact them directly. You may also find that the registrar is a reseller. In the above example, *NameSilo. com* (a reseller) is offering *pythonpublishing.com* via auction for a premium price.

- **Contact the registrar**– In most cases, you will need to go to the registrar's website and contact support. Tell them you wish to purchase a domain they host and ask them to forward your message to the domain owner. Include your name, company, email, phone, and Web site if you have one. Your credibility and willingness to offer a price will help you get through to the owner.

pythonpublishing.com	
Domain Information	
Domain:	pythonpublishing.com
Registrar:	NameSilo, LLC
Registered On:	2019-01-21
Expires On:	2020-01-20
Updated On:	2019-01-21

"I am interested in buying your domain to publish my book of poetry. Is it is available?"

Accept or reject the domain name transfer

- The domain name transfer is complete.
- Select either the Accept or Reject button to accept or reject the domain name transfer. The domain name inspection period ends.
- If you Accept, Escrow.com will release your payment to the seller.
- If you Reject, you will have to submit a domain name transfer to the seller. Once the seller accepts the d refunded to you, less the escrow fee. The escrow fee is non-refundable.

| Accept | Reject |

Merchandise				
No.	Item Description	Quantity	Unit Price	Total Price
1	▮▮▮▮▮	1	$200.00	$200.00
			Subtotal	$200.00
			Escrow Fee	$5.00
			Express Deposit Fee	$2.60
			Total Transaction ID: 4095867 Escrow ID: 1160674	$207.60

Terms

MyBrand.com

SOFTWARE PACKAGE

Name Game™

name-o-matic

- **Make an offer** — If the owner is interested and you are serious, offer an amount that is more than $500 and under $1000 for a low-value name, and between $1500 and $2500 for a high-value name. They may come back with a $5000 price. At that point, you need to know what the domain is worth to you. If you are like Sara, $2400 may be a good deal.

- **Use escrow or a broker** — If you negotiate directly with the owner, you will need to use an escrow service (example: *escrow.com*) to handle the transaction. If you purchase through a service like *GoDaddy*, they will manage the sale. You can also use the broker *afternic.com* to negotiate on your behalf.

Go for the Gold! Or maybe Silver or Bronze? — Yes, you want a cool, two-word, two-syllable dot-com that uses real words to express your brand position and is identical to your company name (for $11.99 please). I hope I've given you every tool to get there, but don't lose sleep over this because you will never start your business.

In the end, your customers are hiring *you*. Whatever Uniform Resource Locator (URL) you choose, your domain is pointing, not to an IP address in the cloud, but to *you* — the *Unique Real Living expression* of the universe that you are!

Before you go: Product Names

The Name Game™ goes beyond your Web domain and company name. You can also brand (and trademark) products, services, processes, methods, and formulations.

For example: Adding a TM symbol to *Name Game*™ suggests a proprietary naming service. The next chapter discusses trademarks.

"The Name Game" was also a 1964 novelty hit that – like a perfectly-positioned brand – snuck its way to the top of the pop charts.

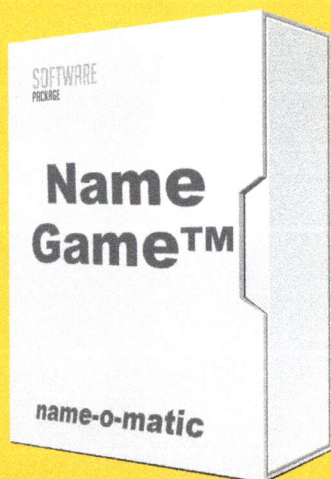

CONGRESS

CG-230

Produced by Charles Calello

THE NAME GAME
(Ellis/del. Calello)
SHIRLEY ELLIS
Arranged by Charles Calello
K-8643

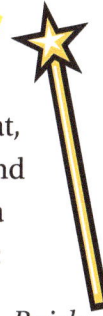

TM = Too Many Names – Like an apprentice donning the wizard's hat, once you start anointing products and processes with TMs, your brand universe can quickly run amok. You will confront the thorny dilemna between a *House of Brands* and a *House Brand*. Here's the difference:

A House of Brands – GM famously tried to juggle *Chevrolet, Cadillac, Buick, Oldsmobile, Pontiac, Saturn,* and *Geo* in an unmanageable House of Brands.

Microsoft, with its suite of distinct products is also a House of Brands. The downside: Every Microsoft brand must be managed and marketed.

A House Brand – With a House Brand, you have only one brand to build, manage, and promote. *Google* is a case in point. Compare *Google* versus *Microsoft*. A House Brand suggests an integrated product ecosystem (examples: Google, Apple, Ryobi Tools, Prime, Salesforce, etc.).

Google: *House Brand*	Microsoft: *House of Brands*
Google.com	Bing.com
Chrome	Microsoft Edge, Internet Explorer
Google+	Yammer
Google Hangouts	Skype for Business
Gmail	Outlook
G Suite for Business	Office 365, Exchange
Google Docs	Word
Google Calendar	Outlook

Google: *House Brand*	Microsoft: *House of Brands*
Google Slides	PowerPoint
Google Sheets	Excel
Google Currents	Microsoft Teams
Google Drive	OneDrive
Google Cloud	Azure
Google App Maker	PowerApps
Google Hangouts	Skype for Business
Chromebook	Surface

Brand Nirvana – If your company name, key product, brand position, and secret sauce merge into oneness, you attain brand nirvana.

Gusto!, a hip and healthy bowl restaurant in Atlanta, offers a choice of seven "gustos" – seven secret sauces to top your meal. The tag line proudly asks, *"What's your gusto?"*

ON YOUR MARKS, TRADEMARK!

Whether you prefer *Coke®* or *Frappucino®* or *Lavender Love™ Kombucha™ Enlightened™*, these superscript marks tell you the brand is legit — well, sort of.

The ® symbol signifies a federally registered trademark, while the TM symbol has no legal significance. Marketing folks will slap a TM on any name their company uses to 1) suggest they own the name, and/or 2) signal their intent to register the name.

For that reason, Michael and I sprinkled TM's on our client projects like M&Ms (examples: *Fuel IQ™* and *PriceQuery™*) because the marks suggest proprietary, innovative solutions. I have since learned that if you're not planning to register the mark, don't use TMs indiscriminately. You may invite objections from other trademark owners. This chapter encourages you to make the effort to register the real deal and obtain the ® symbol.

Most small businesses don't register their trademark, and if you're operating in a small geographic area (contractors, stores, and local servces), it's not always critical. But if you sell products on the Web, or plan to expand to other states, regions, or countries, a Federal trademark lets you move into new markets while protecting your brand.

If your business activity is only in-state, you can apply for state trademark registration. It's easier, cheaper, and it records the date you first used the mark if you are accused of infringement.

Green Planet Lawn Care
THE SUSTAINABLE CHOICE

Green Planet
LAWN CARE®

If you conduct business overseas, you can also apply for an international trademark. You may remember how Ivanka Trump was granted sixteen trademarks from the Chinese government after her dad lifted the ban on the Chinese company ZTE for violating US sanctions. This little bit of political intrigue underscores the strategic and financial value of holding trademarks in other countries.

Even for our young lawn guy, Donnie, trademark registration protects his future options — and future unknowns. Here's how:

Scenario – Suppose Donnie named his business *Green Planet Lawn Care*. In this *Green Planet* scenario, Donnie continues to cut lawns during college, and over time, his business grows. After taking courses in horticulture and landscape design, Donnie decides to scale up his business after graduation — two crews, then three, and so on.

Meanwhile, Joe Jones, the owner of *Green Planet Lawn Care* in Allentown, PA, is getting ready to retire. Joe has a hot-shot son with an MBA who is looking for an investment niche. The son is intrigued by *CertaPro Painters®* — the largest residential and commercial painting company in North America. *CertaPro* sells franchises for $57,500, so Joe's son decides to apply the *CertaPro* franchise model to lawn care. Joe and son apply for a trademark for the *Green Planet* name, assemble a franchise package, and start selling. They sell one of the first franchises in Donnie's town. When the franchise owner sees one of Donnie's *Green Planet* trucks at a job site, he gets pissed.

Boom. Donnie receives a strongly-worded letter to cease and desist using the *Green Planet* name — a name Donnie has used since high school.

Donnie may have a common law right to use the name in his geographic area, but rights don't matter if you can't afford the fight. If you don't trademark your name, an infringement claim can become an expensive legal liability.

That's what happened in my neighborhood when some locals opened an authentic Irish pub, *The Grange Public House*. After a few years of business, the *National Grange of the Order of Patrons of Husbandry (aka The Grange)* took notice and demanded that our sweet little pub change its name. A sensible person would ask, "Who would confuse a fraternal farming organization with our hip Irish pub?" It doesn't matter. If you don't have the resources for a legal fight, you might be forced to buy new signage, print new menus, and restart your business. Our little pub is now *The Marley*.

My mom's Los Angeles public relations agency, *Nann Miller Enterprises,* also got into a trademark fight when an upstart PR person named Nan Miller (with a trademark) challenged my mom's use of her un-trademarked business name. My mom added a second "n."

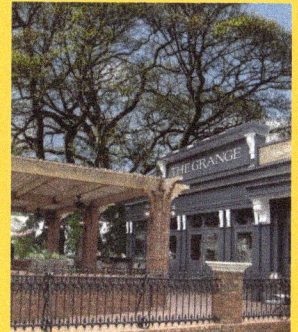
The Grange Irish pub was...

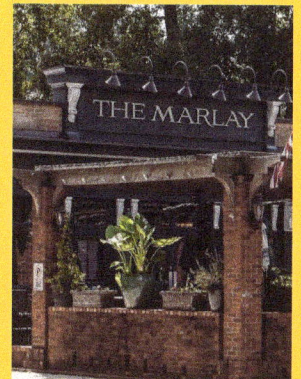
...forced to become the Marlay.

Overview of Initial Application Options	
Questions	TEAS Plus
What is the filing fee per class of goods/services?	$225

Most people don't trademark their business name because they think it's expensive, not necessary, or too complicated. The shoestring approach below helps protect against future damages — and only costs $225.

Full disclaimer – I am not a lawyer. I am an advocate for shoestring startups getting trademark protection at a price they can afford. I offer no guarantee that the USPTO will grant your trademark or that you will avoid legal wrangling with your name. I recommend a lawyer if you can afford one, but I've always applied for trademarks on my own.

What is a trademark? – A trademark is a type of intellectual property (usually a brand name, tagline, or design) that the Federal government will register to provide nationwide rights to its use. The government will not register marks that are similar to other, active trademarks to prevent confusion in the marketplace. If you create a new kombucha drink and brand it *CocaBucha, Coca-Cola*® may cry foul because consumers might think it's a Coke-branded product. The government may also reject it. Trademarks prevent this confusion.

The Federal examiner – The examiner serves as a referee in reviewing your application. As with football, most plays are easy calls; others require the rule book. The examiner follows the *Trademark Manual of Examining Procedure* (Google it).

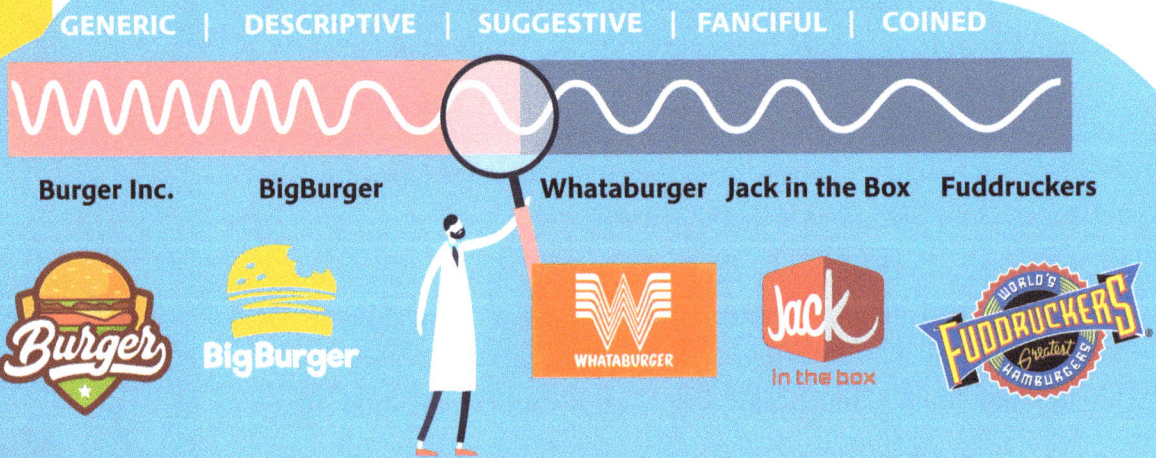

Trademarkability

GENERIC | DESCRIPTIVE | SUGGESTIVE | FANCIFUL | COINED

Burger Inc. BigBurger Whataburger Jack in the Box Fuddruckers

The Spectrum of Trademarkability – The diagram above wil help you understand how the examiner determines the *Likelihood of Confusion* surrounding your mark. Potential trademarks live on a spectrum from *generic* (an everyday word) to *coined* (a made-up word). You can't claim ownership of *burger*, whereas *Fuddruckers* is unique. The examiner will make a judgment call if your trademark lives in the middle.

Thirteen factors guide the examiner's decision on possible consumer confusion (Search: "*Trademark Dupont Factors.*")

To determine the Trademarkability of your mark, place your name on the spectrum to see if you're in the red:

- **Generic** – You generally can't register a commonly-used term for a product or service as a trademark. *Steak 'n Shake*® (1934) would have a tough time getting a trademark today.

- **Descriptive** – Words that describe the generic product name can also be hard to trademark. Example: *Hot Pockets*®.

- **Suggestive** – Marks that suggest feelings and qualities associated with the product can be trademarked, but live in the gray zone. Example: *PizzaFire*®.

- **Fanciful** – Common words used in novel ways become inventive trademarks for the product, i.e. *Apple Inc.*®

- **Coined** – The strongest type of mark is an invented word or phrase that's not in the dictionary, i.e. *Häagen-Dazs*®.

Trademark Step-by Step

Trademark Procedure — Much of what's written about trademarks can be confusing. A brief overview exists at NOLO. com: *"How Do I Register a Trademark?"* which I invite you to read, then follow this step-by-step:

1. **Determine your International Class** – Search: *USPTO Trademark Classes* to locate the appropriate category for your trademark. The list shows 34 classes for goods (001 - 034) and 11 classes for services (035 - 044).

   - I find it quicker to search at *Nolo.com Trademark Classes.* Click on a class, then scroll down to *Complete Listing of All Goods in Class XX Based on Taxonomy.*

   - Donnie's lawn service lives in 044 (Medical, beauty, and agricultural).

2. **Name Lookup** — Visit the US Patent and Trademark site's Trademark Electronic Search System (Search *USPTO TESS*) to see if other businesses use your chosen name.

   - Click: *Search our Trademark Database*

   - Click: *Basic Word Search* and enter the key words in your business name. Instead of *"Green Planet Lawn Care,"* search on *Green Planet.* 51 records are returned.

   - Click on each record. Review the *Goods and Services* description, and see if they are in the same IC Class.

   - Instead of *Basic Word Search,* you can focus your search to a single class. Select *Structured Word Search.* Enter the following into the fields using your terms:

     » Row 1: Search term = *Green Planet,* Field = *Full Mark.* Operator = *AND*

     » Row 2: Search term = *044,* Field = *International Class*

   - Review each record. If no records are returned when searching on your International Class, your mark likely can be trademarked.

   - Instead of "Field = *Full Mark,*" try "Field = *BasicIndex.*" This returns names that use parts of your chosen name (example: *Envirogreen*).

Goods

001 Chemicals	018 Leather goods
002 Paints	019 Non-metallic building materia
003 Cosmetics and cleaning products	020 Furniture and articles not othe
004 Lubricants and fuels	021 Housewares and glass
005 Pharmaceuticals	022 Cordage and fibers
006 Metal goods	023 Yarns and threads
007 Machinery	024 Fabrics
008 Hand tools	025 Clothing
009 Electrical and scientific apparatus	026 Fancy goods
010 Medical apparatus	027 Floor coverings
011 Environmental control apparatus	028 Toys and sporting goods
012 Vehicles	029 Meats and processed foods
013 Firearms	030 Staple foods
014 Jewelry	031 Natural agricultural products
015 Musical instruments	032 Light beverages
016 Paper goods and printed matter	033 Wines and spirits
017 Rubber goods	034 Smokers articles

Services

035 Advertising and business	041 Education and entertainment
036 Insurance and financial	042 Computer, scientific and legal
037 Construction and repair	043 Hotels and restaurants
038 Communication	044 Medical, beauty and agricultur
039 Transportation and storage	045 Personal
040 Material treatment	

Trademark Electronic Search System (T

d on Fri Oct 4 05:36:29 EDT 2019

FREE FORM BROWSE DICT **SEARCH OG** BOTTOM HELP

ARCHING THE USPTO DATABASE. EVEN IF **YOU** THIN
E REGISTERED AT THE USPTO. AFTER YOU FILE AN AP
V, AND MIGHT **REFUSE TO REGISTER** YOUR MARK.

ar ⚪ Singular
⚪ Live   ⚪ Dead

Green Planet Lawn Care

Combined Word Mark (BI,TI,MP,TL) ▾

All Search Terms (AND) ▾

Start   List At: OR Jump to record: 51

Refine Search (live)[LD] AND (Green Planet)[COMB]   Su

Current Search: S1: (live)[LD] AND (Green Planet)[COMB] docs 51 occ

	Serial Number	Reg. Number	
1	88611700		GREEN PLANET
2	88472806		ECOGREENFEET WALK GENTLY ON OUR PL
3	88586891		G GREEN PLANET STRAWS
4	88580680		KEEP OUR OCEANS CLEAN AND OUR PLAN
5	88366188		VERDE PLANET
6	88364801		GREEN POWER PLANET
7	88289522		GREEN PLANET HERBAL MOUTHWASH
8	88156752		GREENPLANET PHARMA.
9	88034032		PLANET GREEN SLEEVES
10	87403478	5323204	GREEN PLANET PRODUCTS
11	87570076	5386732	PLANET + ALL GREEN, ALL THE TIME
12	87506640	5495647	SUSTAINABLE SOURCING S HIMALASALT T GARLIC HIMALAYAN SEA SALT NET WT. 6 02
13	87459316	5431468	GREEN PLANET

Search Term: Green Planet*   Field: Full Mark   Operator AND ▾

Search Term: 044   Field: International Class

Submit Query   Clear Query

T. Markey

BRAND STORY®

Marketing and consulting services in the field of promoting and tracking the goods, services, and brands of others through all public communication means

Term ID		Advertising services, public relations and marketing services, namely, promoting and marketing the goods and services of others through all public communication means
035-2126	035	

Gray areas to consider:

- **Same name, same class** – You will likely discover existing marks with the same name, same class, but with *Goods and Services* descriptions in a different industry (example: *Green Planet Tattoos,* also in Class 44). The examiner will determine if confusion in the marketplace could result.

- **Similar class** – If you discover a trademark for *Green Planet Landscape Architecture* – in IC 042 (a different, but similar class) – you should be okay. But, the examiner could conceivably reject your request if *Green Planet Lawn Care* (044) and *Green Planet Landscape Architecture* (042) might create consumer confusion (even though archtects use computers and landscapers use mowers).

- **Similar sound** – Search sound-alike words. If your t-shirt business is *Marquee Tees,* and a fashion line owns *T.Markey,* the USPTO might reject your request. The examiner follows "The Dupont Factors" to make these decisions. Same class, similar class, or similar sound – it's a $225 roll of the dice.

- **Using an attorney** – If you are in a "same name/same class" situation, hiring an attorney is recomended. They will search the existing marks and advise you to the level of risk you would encounter in (a) attempting to register your mark and (b) living with your mark in the real world even if it gets through the Trademark Office. A search report might cost $300 to $600 based on how extensive a search you desire.

- **Accuracy is everything** – I have screwed up several times. Recently, I tried to help my friend Sara trademark *Après Wear* for her after-yoga line of kimonos. During our initial search on TESS, I queried *Apres* without inserting the accent (*Après*). "You seem good to go," I told Sara. And yes, I blew through $225 of Sara's shoestring funds.

Après Wear

- Remember: You are applying for federal protection for the entire United States.

3. **Understand how International Classes protect you.** Your $225 trademark protects one business class.

- **Stay in your lane –** Trademark classes explain how *Dove* (*Class 3 - Cosmetics and Cleaning Products*) doesn't conflict with *Dove* (*Class 30 - Staple Food Products*). Each brand stays in its lane, so customers don't get confused. If the chocolate *Dove* tried to jump classes and introduce a chocolate-scented shampoo, the soap *Dove* could sue chocolate *Dove* for trademark infringement.

Class 3   **Class 30**

- **Extending brands –** Some brands, like *Arm & Hammer*, jump lanes to expand into new markets. *Arm & Hammer* extended its brand into many classes (baking soda, toothpaste, laundry detergent, cat litter). The *GE* brand pops up in countless industries (light bulbs, appliances, financial services, jet engines, medical imaging, etc.).

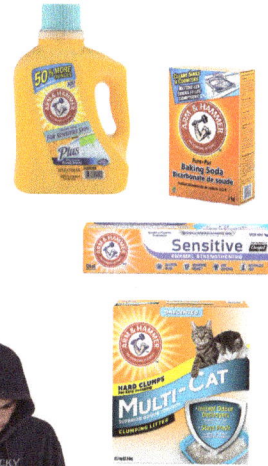

- **Multiple classes** – Like *Arm & Hammer*, you can apply for a trademark in multiple classes, but they will cost $225 for each class. For example, if you want to trademark *Kentucky Lucky Whiskey* in Class 33, but also want to trademark a fashion line to go with your whiskey – example: *Kentucky Lucky* hoodies in Class 25 – you must file and pay fees for two classes.

 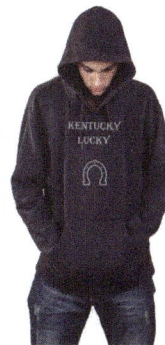

Class 33   **Class 25**

- **Multiple products** – An application for "pants, shirts, shoes, jackets, hats," although five separate products, requires a fee for only one class since all of these products fall within Class 25 for clothing, footwear, or headgear.

Class 25

Find *Goods and Services* descriptions that match your business.

Term ID	Class	Description	Status	Effective Date	Type	Notes	TM5	NCL \
012-672	012	Cars	A	04/02/1991	GOODS		T	07-19
028-1278	028	Toy cars	A	11/22/2007	GOODS		T	09-20

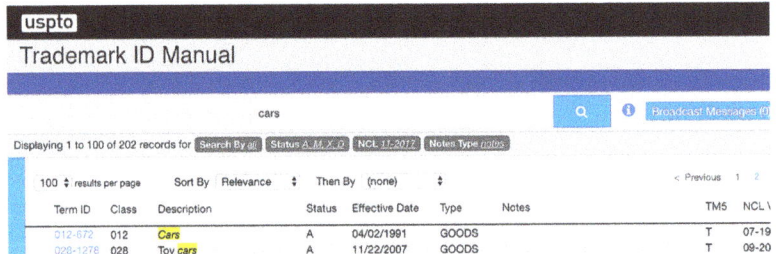

- **Search the manual** – To expedite the $225 process, you will be choosing *Goods and Services* descriptions that have been approved in the past. You will search the Master ID List and copy the description into your application.

  To get started, search for *"USPTO Trademark ID Manual"* and open the manual.

  Submit several search terms into the Master List until you find a description that fits your business. For Donnie's *Carbon Free Lawns* business, he first searched on *Landscaping* and reviewed all 28 results. He also searched on *Gardening*. The closest description for Donnie is *044-119 Landscape gardening*.

- **Choose a description**– Donnie searched on *lawn* and got 61 results, including *044-2571 Lawn care* and *044-2572 Lawn mowing services*. Donnie decided to use both *044-119 Gardening* and *044-2571 Lawn care* for his trademark. Both are in class 44.

- **Copy the description(s)** – Donnie clicked on the ID Link (example 044-2571) and copied each description he wanted to use.

Term ID	Class	Description
044-2440	043	Beer garden services
044-182	044	Garden tree planting
044-181	044	Garden or flower bed care
044-120	044	Landscape gardening design for others
044-119	044	Landscape gardening
044-247	044	Garden care services
044-659	044	Garden design, installation and maintenance of interior botanical displays, streetscape container plantings and rooftop gardens for others
044-2331	044	Rental of gardening implements
044-2268	044	Providing information about gardening
044-183	044	Gardener and gardening services
044-2747	044	Rental of animals for gardening purposes
044-2601	044	Gardening

044-2572	044	Lawn mowing services
044-2571	044	Lawn care

- **Custom description** – If you can't find an appropriate listing (for example, *Marijuana Edibles)*, you must use the TEAS RF application ($275) and create a customized description of your goods and services. A custom description is needed when you have a unique product or service that isn't listed in the manual. Side note: Since marijuana is still illegal under federal law, good luck with your trademark.

5. **The specimen** — The Trademark agency (USPTO) will ask for a specimen of your mark used in *actual* commerce. The rules state:

- **The rule** – *"Use in commerce" must be a bona fide use of the mark in the ordinary course of trade, and not made merely to reserve a right in a mark."*

- **The Catch-22** – You want to trademark your name *before* you invest dollars into the brand, because you don't want to discover later that it can't be trademarked. The USPTO insists on the opposite — start your business, then trademark the name.

- **The Solution: Intent to use** – The USPTO recognizes this dilemma, so they offer an *"Intent to Use"* form. The form entails additional fees to hold the trademark for six months (extensions available) while you get ready to launch. If you sell products, the *Intent to Use* form is often necessary (explanation next page).

- **Service businesses** – If you are a service business and ready to accept your first sale *today*, you are technically *in commerce*. Go ahead and apply. The USPTO will ask for the date you were first in business.

- **Website specimen** – If you are a service business, you can show your Website as a specimen. Print your Web page to a PDF file from your browser to capture the *application date and URL* in the header/footer.

1/30/2020

uspto

Latest News

https://www.uspto.gov

- **Press release** – A press release announcing your launch can serve as an un-arguable specimen that your service business trademark is actively in use ($49 at *NewswireNEXT, PR Underground,* and others). You can also scan your marketing brochures.

- **Business cards** – Business cards make for a quick and easy specimen for service businesses. If a Fedex store is in your neighborhood: Go to *Fedex.com* and select Printing Services. Choose a relevant design and include your business name/address. Add descriptive bullets for your services that match your *Goods and Services* description, pay $25, and submit. A few hours later, *voila* — 250 business cards. Take a photo of the cards that shows that these are actual cards and not a design file.

- **Selling a product?** – If you are producing *Goods*, for example, ceramics, T-shirts, software, or cookies, it's more complicated. You will need a photo showing the trademark on the bottom of a mug, a garment label on a shirt, the packaging, a software start-up screen, etc. All of these will require an actual salable product – not a prototype. If you trademark t-shirts, you must show a t-shirt. If ceramics, photograph a mug. And yes, I made this mistake with Sara's kimonos.

- **Take it step-by-step** – Your trademark specimen is one of three places in the process where it's easy to make a mistake. The three places are:

  1. Searching the TESS database adequately to ensure there aren't Existing Registrants in a similar type of business,

  2. Selecting the correct ID Class/Description from the ID Manual, and

  3. Submitting an Acceptable Specimen (of an actual product, if applicable).

6. **Fill out the form** — The trademark application asks for simple information, but be warned: the confusing layout keeps lawyers in business.

- Because you have selected your *Goods and Services* listing from the ID Manual, use the TEAS Plus application.

- Search on *"USPTO TEAS Plus Application"* to locate the form. Then click *"Fill out TEAS Plus online."*

- Go slow and focus on the information requested. Double-check each page; it's a merciless, poorly written form. Your trademark submission is likely for the "words only" (not a design or stylized font).

- Because you already have a photo of your specimen and your *Goods and Services* description, filling out the form should be straightforward.

Once you're done, celebrate your deep dive into bureaucracy. Importantly, your baby has a name, and with trademark protection, your name is in a class of its own.

One final bit of business — If your trademark is accepted, open your calendar app, count five years ahead of your registration date, and write, *"File Declaration of Use of Mark in Commerce Under Section 8."* The USPTO will remind you to file, but your email must be current. Plan on getting rip-off notices from scammers posing as trademark agencies.

Again: *Between years five and six after the initial trademark registration, you must fill out a Section 8 form, which currently costs $100.*

While you're at it, count nine years ahead. You'll have to pay a bigger fee between years 9 and 10, as well as every 10th year onward, for the rest of your trademark's life — a small price compared to receiving a cease and desist letter someday in the future.

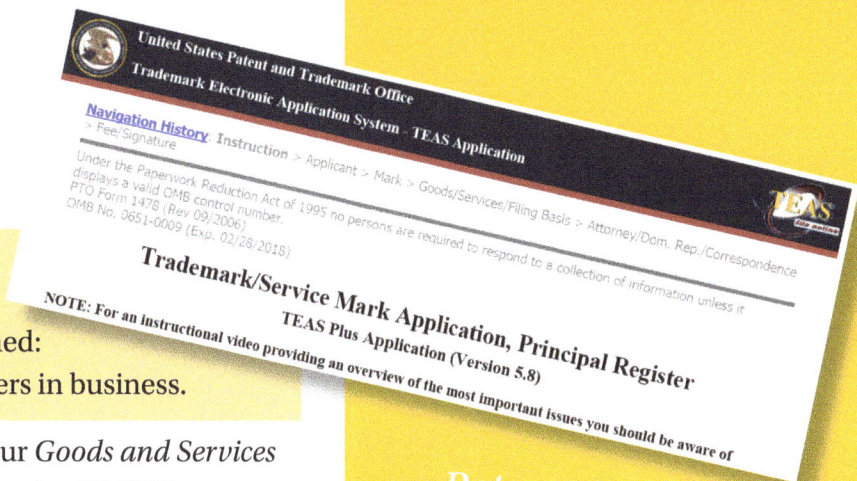

Between years five and six after the initial trademark registration, you must fill out a Section 8 form.

Carbon Free Lawns ®
THE SUSTAINABLE CHOICE
CarbonFreeLawns.com

CREATE A LOVE RELATIONSHIP with CUSTOMERS.

There is a hip new food truck roaming Los Angeles run by a multiracial, twenty-something trio called the *WOKE! Truck.*

More than dishing up food, the *WOKE!* crew wants to change the way people interact with their food — and with each other. *WOKE!* grew out of a community service restaurant that donated food to low-income families, and employed and trained employees with criminal, addiction, and teen pregnancy backgrounds. Newly sober and needing purpose, the founder, Max Daniel, turned the operation into a roaming foodie hotspot for cheap but eclectic fusion food.

When asked to give their brand pitch, the trio of Max Daniel, Kashmir Bianca Hughes, and Michael Douglas Powers replied:

"We are Irish, Black, and Asian. We sell fusion food and teach history at the same time. And we use our business to give back to the community. We hire employees fresh out of rehab, train teen mothers for the job, and we do stuff for the community, as well."[1]

Their tag line: *Feeding Your Body and Your Mind.*™

Whether you call their elevator pitch a brand story or a way of spreading a political message, the *WOKE!* crew has created is a way to connect with their

---

1 Esther Tseng, "This Los Angeles Food Truck Isn't Afraid to Call Itself 'Woke'," VICE.com, 2-27-19.

customers – a love relationship. Connecting with customers is the whole point of your Brand Story.

Jen Rubio, co-founder of *Away*, the travel luggage brand, also got her start connecting customers to L.A. food trucks by using social media to create brand stories. As she tells it:

"Before launching *Away*, I had built my career as a storyteller... In order to truly be successful, you have to understand who you're trying to reach, and what they want to hear. I think more and more brands are starting to recognize and appreciate the importance of people-first marketing. It can't just be about the consumer, but about the human who's making the choice to interact and consume.

"We created a brand, *Away*, that was so synonymous with better travel that customers were calling us... asking for tips and recommendations ahead of their upcoming trips!"[2]

This love relationship between the *WOKE! Truck* and its food fans, and *Away* and its travel fans is called *brand affinity*. *Brand affinity* describes a felt relationship from shared values. It's different than *brand loyalty* (for example, loyalty to *Tide* detergent because your t-shirts come out whiter).

The people who love Jen Rubio's brand have never been to her factory nor met her in person — but they have strong emotional hooks to her brand story. *Away* promises more than a suitcase; the brand promises *adventure*. In their words: "Getting Away means getting more out of every trip to come." *Away* is the only piece of luggage with a magazine, written "for travelers, by travelers." The magazine "tells compelling, thoughtful, and unique travel stories through the lens of local, creative, and influential people" — and in the process, creates fans for the brand.

If you're wondering how you're going to create a cult following for your gutter-cleaning business, consider this:

---

2 "How Away Brings Its Brand to Life through Content Marketing, https://insights.newscred.com/away-content-marketing/ April, 2018.

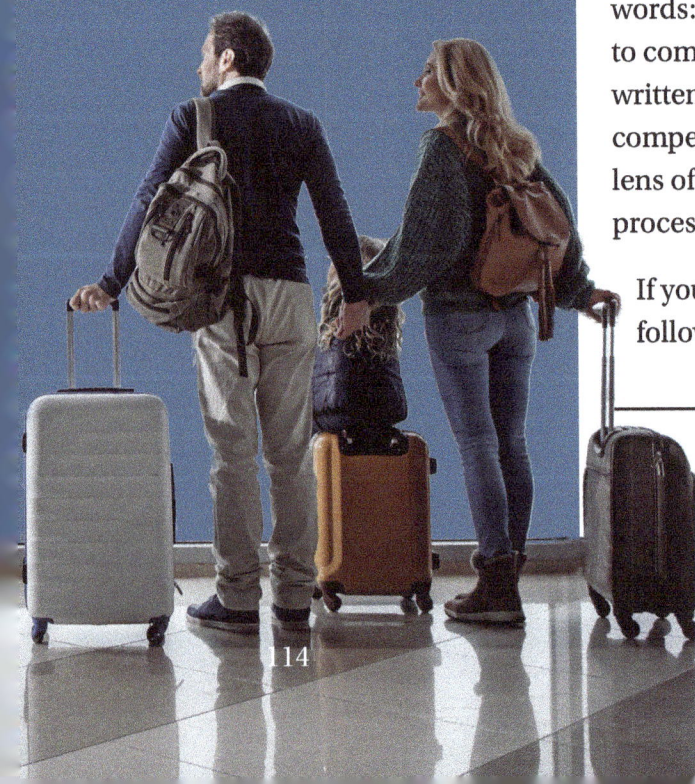

Cults identify with stories. Same with brands. Whether you plan to groom dogs or write wills, every business has a story. Even the driveway gypsies who knocked on my door falsely claiming they had leftover asphalt from a big job had a brand story. It was a great story – and I bought a truckload!

What I call a Brand Story is also called a "brand platform." Whether you prefer a platform or a story, it's all the pieces and parts that form a brand. In the same way that a movie has a storyline, setting, characters, costumes, and conflict, a Brand Story has its component parts.

A Brand Story starts with a positioning statement. It functions like a logline for a movie. Here's the logline for The Godfather: *The aging patriarch of an organized crime dynasty transfers control of his clandestine empire to his reluctant son.*

Here's my made-up positioning statement for *Away*:

- *For travel warriors tired of broken bags and dying phones, Away designed the perfect suitcase to accompany a lifetime's worth of travel adventures.*

Away is building a brand story that goes: "Since you love to travel, you should love your luggage. Away makes luggage lovable."

Building Your Brand Story — I know what you're thinking: Please, no more homework; I just want to sell my widgets!

I feel your pain, but building your brand story upfront avoids a streak of fumbles later on. When it comes time to build your website, write an ad, send out social media, create a brochure, exhibit at a trade show, speak at a lunch-and-learn, create a YouTube video, or pitch a big client — you won't have to sweat it.

Your Brand Story platform will make it plug-and-play easy to build brand consistency and grow customer loyalty in the months and years ahead.

Let's build your Brand Story!

Whether you plan to groom dogs or write wills, every business has a story.

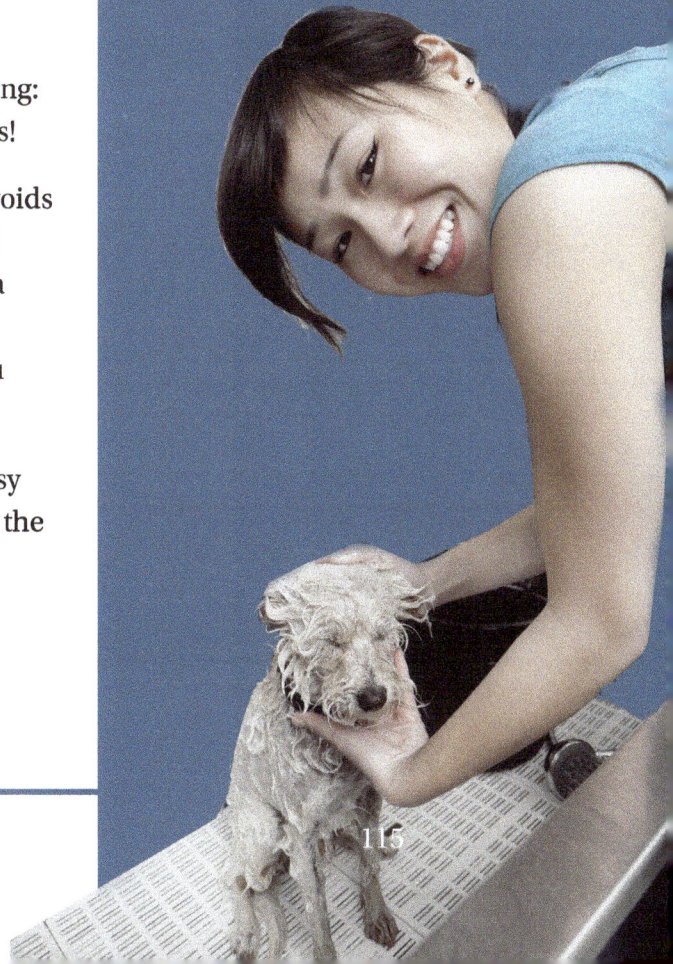

Ten Elements that form your BRAND STORY

Learn how each one helps build a love relationship with your customer.

Scene 1	Frame:	Duration:
Brand Positioning Statement		
How you uniquely meet your customers' needs in a competitive market.		
Audio:	Shot size:	

Scene 2	Frame:	Duration:
Target Customer		
The most-likely person to purchase your product or service.		
Audio:	Shot size:	

Scene 6	Frame:	Duration:
Brand Drivers		
The emotional benefits that connect your brand to customers.		
Audio:	Shot size:	

Scene 7	Frame:	Duration:
Brand Character		
The brand's personality in look, feel, voice, and tone.		
Audio:	Shot size:	

For hipsters seeking a gourment treat

Volvo = safety

Download the Brand Story Platform at MillereMedia.com. Fill out each of these Ten Elements the best you can. It will be a work in progress through the life of your business.

1. Brand Positioning Statement — A brand owns a position in the mind of the consumer. The brand positioning statement identifies your target customer's need, and how you solve it trough your unique approach or expertise.

Good news, you crafted your brand position in Chapter 4.

2. Target Customer — You've also identified your target customer (the purchasers at the top of the bell curve). That's two down.

You can build out this section further by describing the full range of customers or discuss expansion into future markets. For example, *King of Pops* started selling popsicles from pushcarts for its target customer — *hip pedestrians seeking a gourment treat* — but ultimately expanded into retail stores and catering.

3. Brand Concept — When your customers think of your business, what word or concept should instantly come to mind? Examples: Volvo = *safety* (or it did in the past). Southwest Airlines = *No-Frills* (at least when they started). Zappos = *Great Customer Service.* Chick-fil-A = *No Beef* (those cows on the billboards).

Scene 3	Frame:	Duration:
Brand Concept		
The Big Idea that captures what makes your business unique.		
Audio:	Shot size:	

Scene 4	Frame:	Duration:
Brand Promise		
How you build customer loyalty by meeting expectations.		
Audio:	Shot size:	

Scene 5	Frame:	Duration:
Brand Vision		
The goal or ideals you hope to achieve.		
Audio:	Shot size:	

Scene 8	Frame:	Duration:
Brand Look		
The visual consistency that confers credibility and quality.		
Audio:	Shot size:	

Scene 9	Frame:	Duration:
Brand Rituals		
The gestures, customs, and tokens of appreciation that bond with customers.		
Audio:	Shot size:	

Scene 10	Frame:	Duration:
Brand Messaging		
The taglines, slogans, headlines, and descriptive copy that tell your story.		
Audio:	Shot size:	

And for Donnie, the big idea for his lawn business is *No Carbon.*

During the golden age of advertising, *Avis* car rental built their business around a big idea, *We Try Harder,* because they were number two after *Hertz.* Your brand concept is the core message that is always communicated by your brand. The brand concept should drive the headline in an ad, form the key statement on your website, get printed on a t-shirt or a button, or if you hire a skywriter, spell out the message in the sky.

4. Brand Promise — When you keep a promise to a child, you fulfill their expectations. Same with your customers. Your brand fulfills their expectations, meets their needs, and builds their trust so that they become customers for life. Your Brand Promise should be pretty straight-forward.

BRAND PROMISE –
Tell your customers what they can expect from your brand with these three C's:

Frame:
Duration:

Sick kids need attention
That's why we return all calls within 2 hours.
– Dr. Lois Martinez

Shot size:

Audio:

- **Compelling** — The Brand Promise must be something your customer values, like a pediatrician who promises to return all calls within 2 hours (Hah! Making this up).

- **Credible** — It can't be pie-in-the-sky jargon like *Ford's "Quality is job one."* A down-to-earth promise is better: *"Every BMW goes through optical 3D coordinate measuring technology for quality assurance."*

- **Consistent** — The promise must be kept every time, and include a mechanism to fix the wrong if you mess up. For example, with *Amazon's A-to-Z Guarantee,* Amazon will reimburse you even if it's a third-party seller who screws up.

of our food is 100% clean.

Here are other examples: *Panera* promises *"100% clean food."* *FedEx* built its business by promising "when it absolutely, positively has to get there overnight." And, *Geico* promises a simple metric: *"15 minutes or less can save you 15% or more on car insurance."*

Some promises are less overt. *McDonald's* makes an implicit promise to serve an inexpensive, familiar, and consistent meal delivered quickly in a clean environment. Nutritious isn't part of the promise.

Even Donnie promises to never to use a gas-powered blower on the job — only a rake. Firing up the blower would quickly undermine his brand promise.

Frame:

Duration:

"We're in business to save our home planet."
Patagonia

Audio:

Shot size:

Sharing your brand's vision is the way to measure success.

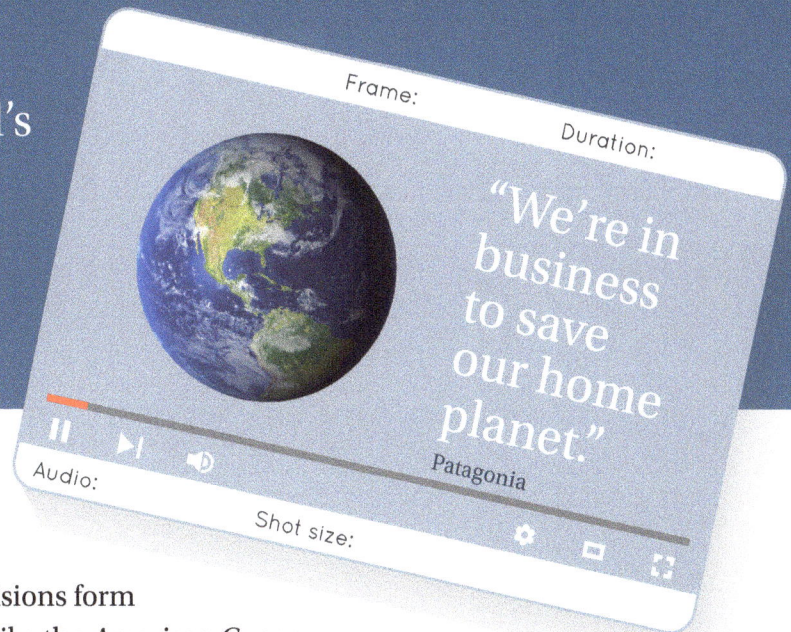

5. Brand Vision — If your brand embraces ideals, goals, or aspirations, promoting your vision is a way to measure success. Brand visions form the core of medical research brands like the *American Cancer Society* (dedicated to eliminating cancer) as well as new brands launching on *Kickstarter* that hope to build a better mousetrap. *Apple's* vision of making technology friendlier was a guiding force for the company. Each product (Mac, iPod, iPhone) marked a stepping stone toward that vision.

If your company exists for more than making money, by definition, you have a vision – a reason for being. For example, *Patagonia:* "We're in business to save our home planet."

My friend Cindi runs *Side By Side,* a day program for people with brain injuries, guided by the vision:

"To use community involvement, education, and research to guarantee the opportunity for all people with a brain injury to lead a quality life."

Your vision does not need to be grandiose. A local home renovator in Atlanta states as his vision: *"We believe old houses are worth saving..."*

Even a hot dog guy like my neighborhood *Doggy Dogg* offers a vision: *"Elevating hot dogs into a gourmet experience recognized by serious foodies."*

"Elevating hot dogs into a gourmet experience..."

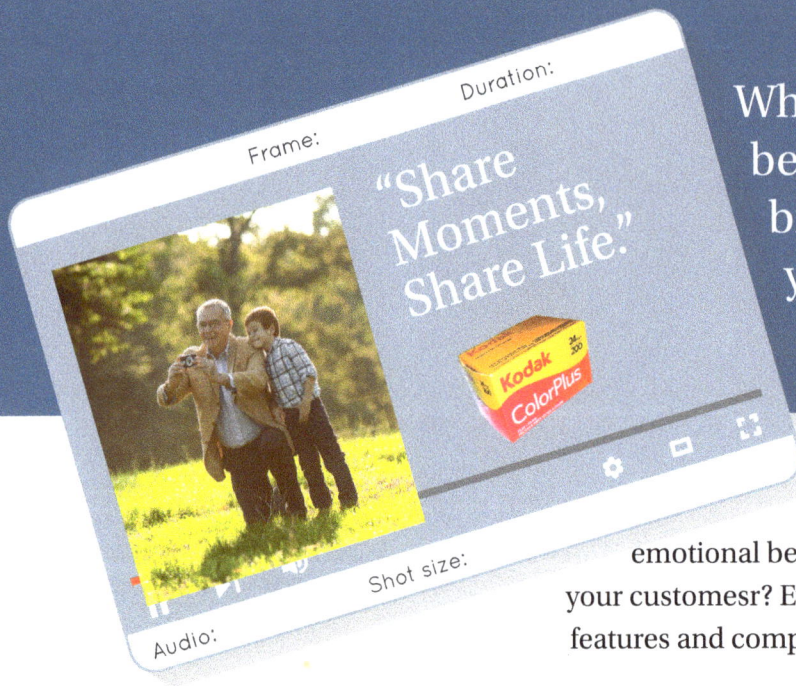
"Share Moments, Share Life."

Kodak ColorPlus

What emotional benefits make your brand relevant to your customer?

Kodak sold the nostalgiac warmth of capturing memories.

Cialis promises mid-life kinkiness.

6. Brand Drivers — Brand Driver is a fancy word for *feelings*. What are the emotional benefits that make your brand relevant to your customesr? Even though the benefits come from key features and competitive strengths, you sell with feelings.

For example, *Volvo* could cite their NTSB statistics of crash-worthiness, but instead, they sold soccer moms with the feeling of *safety*.

Coca Cola offers no nutritional reason to drink their product. Their iconic brand is built on feelings — of shared humanity, lifestyle moments, and the joy of living.

Back in the day, *Kodak* didn't tout their technical superiority over *Fuji Film* — they sold the nostalgic warmth of capturing memories.

Pharmaceutical companies love Brand Drivers. The *Cialis* bathtubs promise mid-life kinkiness, and *Humira* promises joint-flexible fun with your kids.

When you pull the trim off, car companies sell very similar products – so they use Brand Drivers for differentiation: *BMW* is a precision-driving machine, *Lexus* sells the ultimate customer experience, *Subaru* offers confidence in challenging terrains, and *Jeep* promises adventure. And, for your inner outlaw, there's always *Harley Davidson*.

Donnie quickly latched on to his Brand Driver — *Feel eco-good by reducing carbon emissions in your own backyard.*

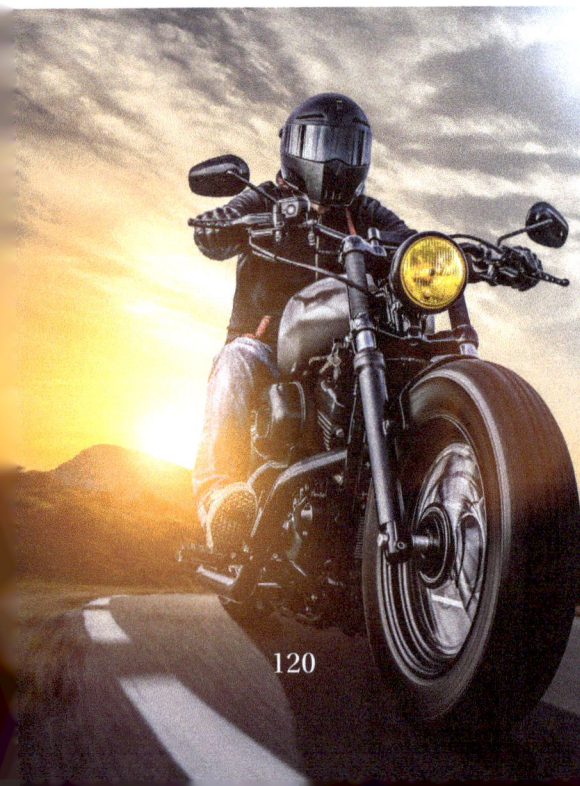

For your inner outlaw, there's always *Harley Davidson.*

> Character drives your story when it stretches your brand beyond the genre.

Frame:

Duration:

Should cold medicine be sold by a ball of green snot?

Audio:

Shot size:

7. Brand Character — Brands have personalities that shape their look, feel, voice, and tone. When the Brand Character is spot on, it seems obvious. Consider *Harley Davidson* versus *Vespa*, both selling two-wheeled transportation:

Harley   *Vespa*

The difference between the two is a no-brainer. But when it comes to your brand, it should be just as obvious: Are you **friendly** like a *Vespa*, **badass** like a *Harley*, **happy** like a *Coke*, **playful** like *Skittles*, **helpful** like *Allstate*, **trustworthy** like *Charles Schwab*, **futuristic** like *Tesla*, **authoritative** like *Forbes*, or **stuffy** like *Grey Poupon*?

For most start-ups, the Brand Character reflects the founders' personalities. Our fast-food chicken wing client, *Wing Zone*, was started by two college frat guys at the University of Florida, and they created a brand personality to match.

Character drives the brand when it stretches beyond the genre, for example, auto insurance sold by a goofy girl (Flo) or cold medicine sold by a ball of green snot (Mr. Mucus).

Study award-winning TV spots on YouTube to recognize the role of character. What personality would help your customer connect to your brand? Write a sentence that describes your brand's character. Even a couple of words — *warm and friendly, refined and elegant, knowledgeable and authoritative* — will help create a memorable brand that resonates with your customers.

"Free-spirited and fun."

121

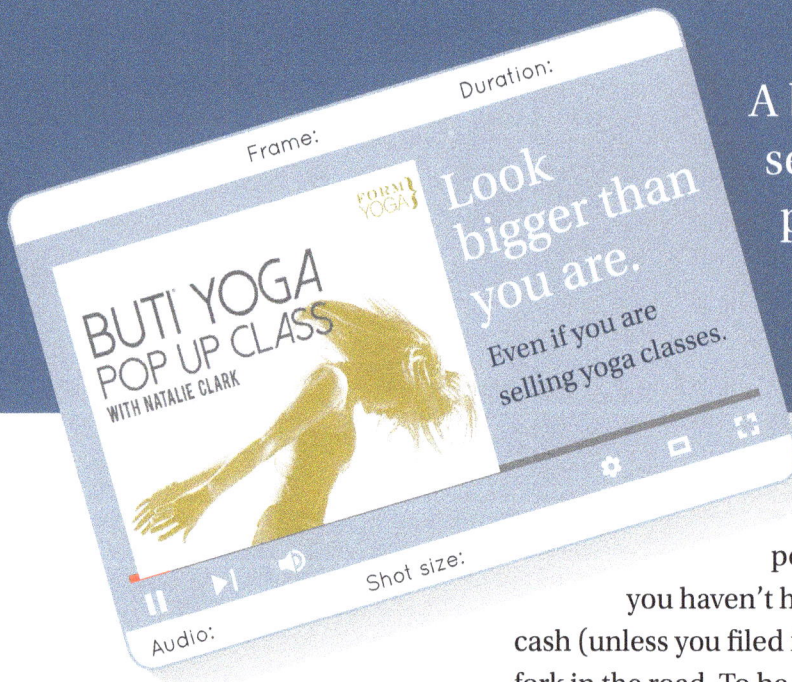

BUTI YOGA POP UP CLASS WITH NATALIE CLARK

Look bigger than you are. Even if you are selling yoga classes.

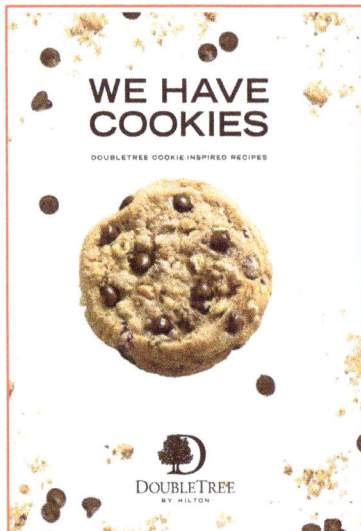

WE HAVE COOKIES

DOUBLETREE COOKIE INSPIRED RECIPES

DOUBLETREE BY HILTON

A brand's look and feel separates mom and pops from national brands.

8. Brand Look — The brand's visual look separates mom-and-pops from national brands. Until now, you haven't had to spend a dime of brand-building cash (unless you filed for a trademark). Brand Look is the fork in the road. To be credible, you need to look credible, and that means professional design for your logo, Web site, collateral, advertising, etc. My neighborhood yoga studio grew to become one of the city's largest on the strength of its brand. We will discuss Brand Look for shoe-stringers in chapter 8.

9. Brand Rituals

"Welcome to Moe's!" Whether you love or loathe it, the ubiquitous welcome injects the burrito chain with personality each time you walk in the door. If you've ever stayed in a *DoubleTree Hotel*, their warm gooey check-in cookie connects your tastebuds to the brand.

And, before the era of peanut allergies, *Southwest Airlines'* bag of peanuts underscored their core concept: No-frills *Southwest* lets you fly for peanuts.

Brand rituals connect customers viscerally to the brand. Remarkably, while so many brands try to build affinity with tiresome social media posts, a cookie or a donut can do so much more.

Years ago, when I worked at *CheckFree Corporation*, Denise, the owner of a local copy shop, would visit our department every morning and call out, "Hey guys, got anything for me today?"

Brand rituals connect customers viscerally to the brand.

Frame:

Duration:

"Hey Guys."

Got anything for me today?

Audio:

Shot size:

What made Denise's visit compelling was the ritual box of *Krispy Kreme* donuts she discretely placed on top of a cubicle. Denise owned a quick-print shop, so we started giving her little jobs — notepads, business cards, and forms. The donuts continued to appear every morning, and we leaned on the in-person convenience: "Denise, can you print a sales sheet? How about this color brochure?"

Denise always answered in the affirmative. We guessed she had a printer friend somewhere, so we didn't ask how she got the work done. One day, I was walking out to the parking lot and spotted the secret to her brand. A stack of *Krispy Kreme* boxes sat in the back of her car. Denise had mastered the Brand Ritual.

10. Brand Messaging — Writing tight, persuasive copy is hard work — that's why you only want to write it once. A Brand Messaging platform provides ready-to-go text that you can drop into proposals, web pages, collateral, digital ads, slide decks, and video scripts. A page or two will serve you well.

To create your Messaging Platform, write a phrase or short paragraph for each component of your business, including:

- **Tagline** — This is a punchier version of your positioning statement. The best tag lines are memorable, form a great slogan, differentiate the brand, and communicate the key benefit. The tagline can be short, like "Got Milk?" Or long, like MasterCard's: *"There are some things money can't buy. For everything else, there's MasterCard."* Taglines can become iconic: *"Melts in Your Mouth, Not in Your Hands."*

Writing tight, persuasive copy is hard work. That's why you only want to write it once.

"Melts in Your Mouth, Not in Your Hands."

©

> Your slogan announces your brand like a flag in the sky.

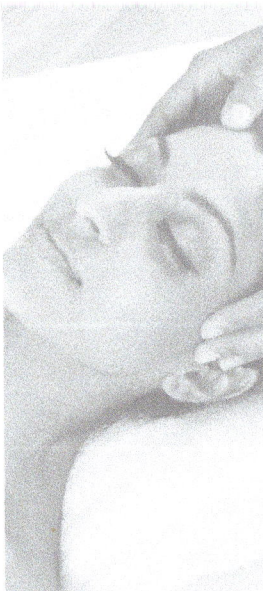

- **Slogans** — Slogans are similar to the tagline. Think of the slogan as the trademarked flag that waves atop your brand: *Intel Inside®*, *Just Do It®*, *Where's the Beef?®*, and *Bring Out the Best™*. Slogans often communicate your secret sauce or differentiator: Walmart – *Save money. Live better.*

- **Descriptor** —These generic words live under your logo and describe what you do, for example, *Meineke "care care center."* Or *CertaPro "Residential. Commercial. Interior. Exterior.* Major brands usually avoid descriptors because their customers don't need an explanation.

- **Product messaging** — Create an official description for each of your products or services. Here are some service descriptions I wrote for a friend's brand messaging platform. She can pull from these as needed:

Eleanor's Bodywork Service Descriptions

- *Biodynamic Craniosacral Therapy* is a healing art that works with the forces that create and maintain health in the human system…
[more]

- *Polarity Therapy* works to restore the natural flows which energize and support the major systems of the human body…
[more]

- *Reiki* transmits Universal Life Energy to the client to deepen relaxation, enhance healing, reduce pain, and decrease other symptoms…
[more]

Describe your methods the same way in all communications.

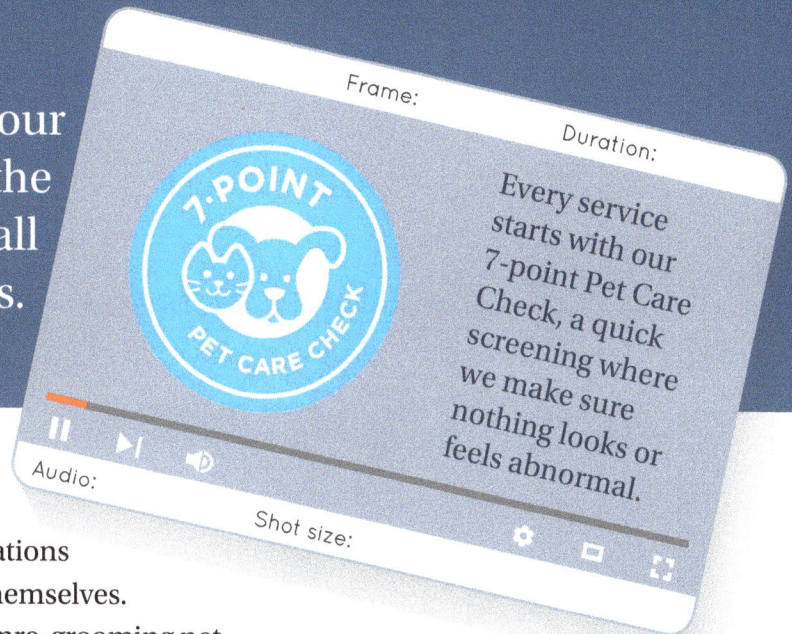

Frame:

Duration:

7·POINT PET CARE CHECK

Every service starts with our 7-point Pet Care Check, a quick screening where we make sure nothing looks or feels abnormal.

Audio:

Shot size:

- **Methods and processes** — Describe your processes the same way in all your communications so that they become brands in themselves. For example, *Petco* describes its pre-grooming pet screening as a *7-Point Pet Care Check*.

- **Boilerplate** — This is the About Us page of your website. It explains who you are and what you do without hype or spin. The About Us page is often read by the purchasing department or the banker who wants to know what you do before approving a purchase or loan request.

- **Bios** — The style of your staff bios is different for each industry. Does your target customer want to know that you studied biochemistry at Duke or that you do yoga with a goat? Rather than telling too much, each element in your bio should build confidence in your capabilities or approach.

- **Elevator Speech** — I left the most important for last. This three-minute pitch pulls it all together. The Elevator Speech is so essential, it gets a whole chapter coming right up.

Marvel at how your brand is taking shape as a living being, just like a toddler forming a personality. The roots you plant today will continue to grow in the years ahead into love relationships with your customers.

Your brand is taking shape as a living being.

125

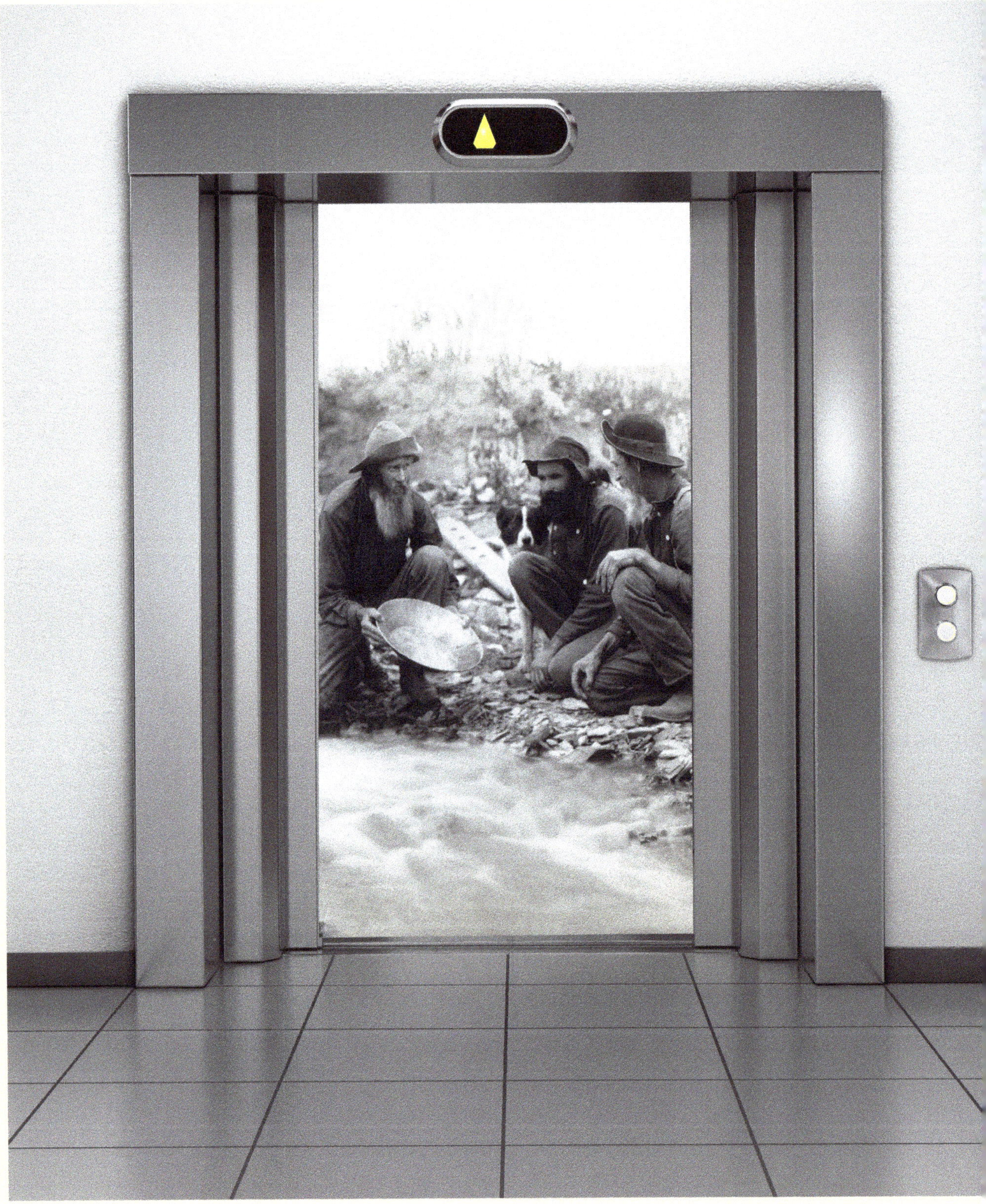

The ELEVATOR PITCH.

During the Gold Rush fever of Silicon Valley, everyone thought they could make vast sums of money on the Web.

It was the dawn of the Internet, circa 1999. All you needed were backers for your big idea. My buddy, Bill Green, caught the fever, sold his house in Atlanta, and moved to the Bay Area to "get into tech."

When Bill arrived in California, Silicon Valley legend and former Chief Evangelist of Apple, Guy Kawasaki, was staging "boot camps" to help wannabe tech entrepreneurs get into the game. Bill paid $1100 for the two-day *Garage.com* seminar and learned how to connect with venture capitalists – and hopefully pitch an idea.

At the "Boot Camp for Startups," Kawasaki taught participants how to condense their business idea into a 10-slide deck and then distill the deck into a short elevator pitch. The purpose of the exercise was to prepare for the day when you bumped into a mover-shaker while riding to the top floor. The unspoken joke, of course, was that in real life, the elevator moment never ever happens.

During the breaks, the boot campers practiced their pitches, swapped business cards, and prepared to strike gold. In real life, gold pans from wannabes pitching each other only come up empty. During a break, Bill broke ranks and headed to the men's room. Expecting an uneventful pit stop, Bill leaned over his shoulder. There was the guy leading the training, Guy Kawasaki's Vice President of Entrepreneur Development, Mike Scanlin.

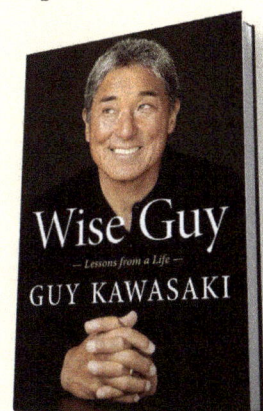

127

> ## "I pitched their idea right there in the men's room, and he was highly receptive."

"I realized that I had come all this way and spent my money to get my foot in the door," Bill recalled. "And now I had ten seconds at the urinal with someone who could change my life. He could give me access to one of the most storied angel investors of the era. My big problem was that I didn't have a deal. My mind raced. Earlier that week, I had met with some people starting *TeamFuel*, a high-tech supply chain start-up that hoped to reduce fuel costs for utilities. So, I pitched *their idea* to Scanlin, right there in the men's room, and he was highly receptive.

"The next day, I phoned *TeamFuel* and told them that I had a solid lead for Silicon Valley venture money. As it happened, *TeamFuel* needed a credible CEO. Boom. I became a player in the clean technology sector."

Only Bill would have the chutzpah to pitch *someone else's project*, unsolicited, off-the-cuff, to one of the most storied investors in Silicon Valley. And, unlike Bill, you probably won't make the deal of your life in an elevator, let alone at the urinal. For this reason, I teach people not to prepare for a 30-second elevator speech, but to craft a longer pitch – three minutes – that distills your company's reason for being.

In writing your 3-minute pitch, think of yourself as a trial lawyer preparing an opening argument. Does your case hold water? Will your customers follow a simple logic to understand what you are offering and why they need it? In this way, the Elevator Pitch is the long-form version of your positioning statement. It will form the backbone of your Web site, slide decks, collateral, advertising, and more.

Best of all, if you do meet Mr. Big in an elevator (or Ms. Big in the ladies' room), you'll be ready to go.

Think of yourself as a trial lawyer preparing an opening argument.

Prepare your pitch: Step-by-step

Step 1: Develop a voicemail pitch — Approaching Guy Kawasaki in the men's room might be too confrontational, so pretend you just swapped cards and now want to leave a follow-up voice message.

What three or four points would you leave in a plain-spoken message, free from jargon, over the phone, and without PowerPoint to support you?

These five concise points communicate the value proposition to an investor:

"Leverage *scalable technology that earns ongoing fees on a huge commodity without taking physical delivery.'*

*Ka-chin*g!

Create sales sheets, headlines, digital ads, and Web banners – all using your 5-point pitch as the template:

VOICEMAIL SCRIPT

1. **Overview**: [beep] Hi Guy, this is Bill Green from TeamFuel – the start-up that uses supply-chain technology to manage fuel for big users.

2. **Problem**: A little background: Fuel prices change every day, but unlike filling the tank of your car, big fuel users have hundreds of tanks to fill on a precise schedule. They can't choose to fill their tanks when prices are low.

3. **Solution**: That's what we do. We analyze the fuel market, streamline procurement, and purchase fuel for our customers when prices go down.

4. **Results**: We guarantee millions of dollars in savings through scalable technology, market optimization, and volume purchasing. We manage the enormous volume of fuel that moves through the market everyday – and we earn a fee on that volume by optimizing procurement.

5. **Call to Action:** I'd like to discuss opportunities to invest in TeamFuel.

Still filling your tanks when prices are high?

TeamFuel optimizes your fuel procurement

If you're like most companies, you have found ways to cut costs in every area - except where it hurts the most: Fuel.

Today, the world's largest fleet organizations employ full-time professionals to cut costs and streamline operations. But for most fuel users, old fuel technology, non-expert buyers, and rising administrative costs hinder efficient procurement.

What's more, rising prices in a volatile market make it difficult for your fuel buyers to make effective refill decisions — especially with rising fuel prices, complex forecasting, delivery logistics, and more.

Our Solution:

TeamFuel has developed the industry's first end-to-end solution that manages fuel needs throughout the supply chain. Our value proposition is simple:

- We study your fuel operations to optimize your supply chain.
- We implement intelligent fuel technology to streamline procurement and operations.

You enjoy guaranteed savings when you let TeamFuel serve as your outsourced "fuel department."

teamfuel

Positioning Statement – *For fleets and other volume fuel users that don't have full-time fuel professionals to make effective purocurement decisions in a volatile market, <u>only</u> TeamFuel employs supply-chain technology, forecasting tools, and procurement expertise to reduce fuel costs. As your outsourced fuel department, TeamFuel leverages our volume purchasing and scale of operations to deliver guaranteed fuel savings.*

1. **Attention Grabber** — Ask a provocative question that dramatizes how what you do matters to the prospect.

2. **The Customer's Problem** — Detail the pain points your customer faces.

3. **Our Solution** — Explain your unique approach or secret sauce and how it fits the customer's needs.

4. **How it Works** — Describe features, methods, and processes.

5. **Results** — Offer proof that it works; show documented metrics or savings. Share customer satisfaction.

TeamFuel 3-minute example

Attention Grabber:

If you invest $100,000 in stocks, do you time your investment when prices are low? Of course!

How about $100,000 worth of fuel? Do you fill your tanks when prices go down? If you think that's impossible, you're wrong.

TeamFuel has developed technology to help you take command of your entire fuel picture. We act as your outsourced "fuel department" to get the best prices from the marketplace.

The Customer's Problem:

You've probably found ways to streamline costs throughout your organization — in HR, IT, employee benefits – everywhere except the one area it hurts the most: fuel management.

Large fleets and airlines employ full-time fuel professionals to manage procurement. Smaller users, like you, must deal with old fuel technology, non-expert buyers, and rising administrative costs.

More importantly, price volatility makes it difficult for you to make effective refill decisions — especially with rising prices, complex forecasting, delivery logistics, and smaller volumes.

Our Solution:

TeamFuel has developed the industry's first end-to-end solution that manages fuel needs throughout the supply chain. Our value proposition is simple:

TeamFuel 3-Minute Example
(continued)

1. *We study your fuel operations to optimize your supply chain,*

2. *We implement intelligent fuel technology to streamline procurement and operations, and*

3. *You enjoy guaranteed savings when you let TeamFuel serve as your outsourced "fuel department."*

How it Works:

1. **Fuel IQ™**: *First, TeamFuel studies your enterprise-wide fuel operations to develop a 14-point fuel profile to guide fuel procurement throughout your organization.*

2. **ThinkTank™** – *Next, we network every tank in your system and integrate them into our national storage picture. We optimize procurement decisions at a tremendous scale, system-wide.*

3. **PriceQuery™** – *Finally, our system searches for market trends and spot opportunities and delivers the best fuel price every day through demand aggregation, market timing, freight cost consolidation, and contract leveraging.*

Results:

Starting with a baseline assessment of your current costs, we build a cost-reduction model that tracks your actual savings in ten key areas.

Total cost savings are guaranteed. Save up to 65% in operations and 35% in fuel costs when you outsource your fuel operations to TeamFuel.

Step 3: Practice Your Pitch

Read through your pitch a few times, then fit your entire speech onto a 5x8-inch card using high-level bullets. Memorize the bullets (not the speech), then just wing it without concern for mistakes.

TeamFuel 3-Minute Pitch

Grabber:

- Invest $100k in stocks and real estate. Time the purchase?
- Proprietary technology
- Outsourced fuel department
- Get best prices

Problem:

- Large users have full-time professionals
- Streamline operations, but not fuel
- Old tech, non-expert, admin costs
- Rising costs, effective decisions

Solution:

- Study operations
- Intelligent technology
- Guaranteed savings - outsourced fuel dept.

How it Works:

- Fuel IQ
- ThinkTank
- Price Query

Results:

- Baseline, cost-reduction model
- Tracked savings areas
- 65% operations, 35% costs

With high-level bullets, you can adapt to the people, the setting, and the time available.

With the outline set, your elevator pitch always comes off fresh and alive!

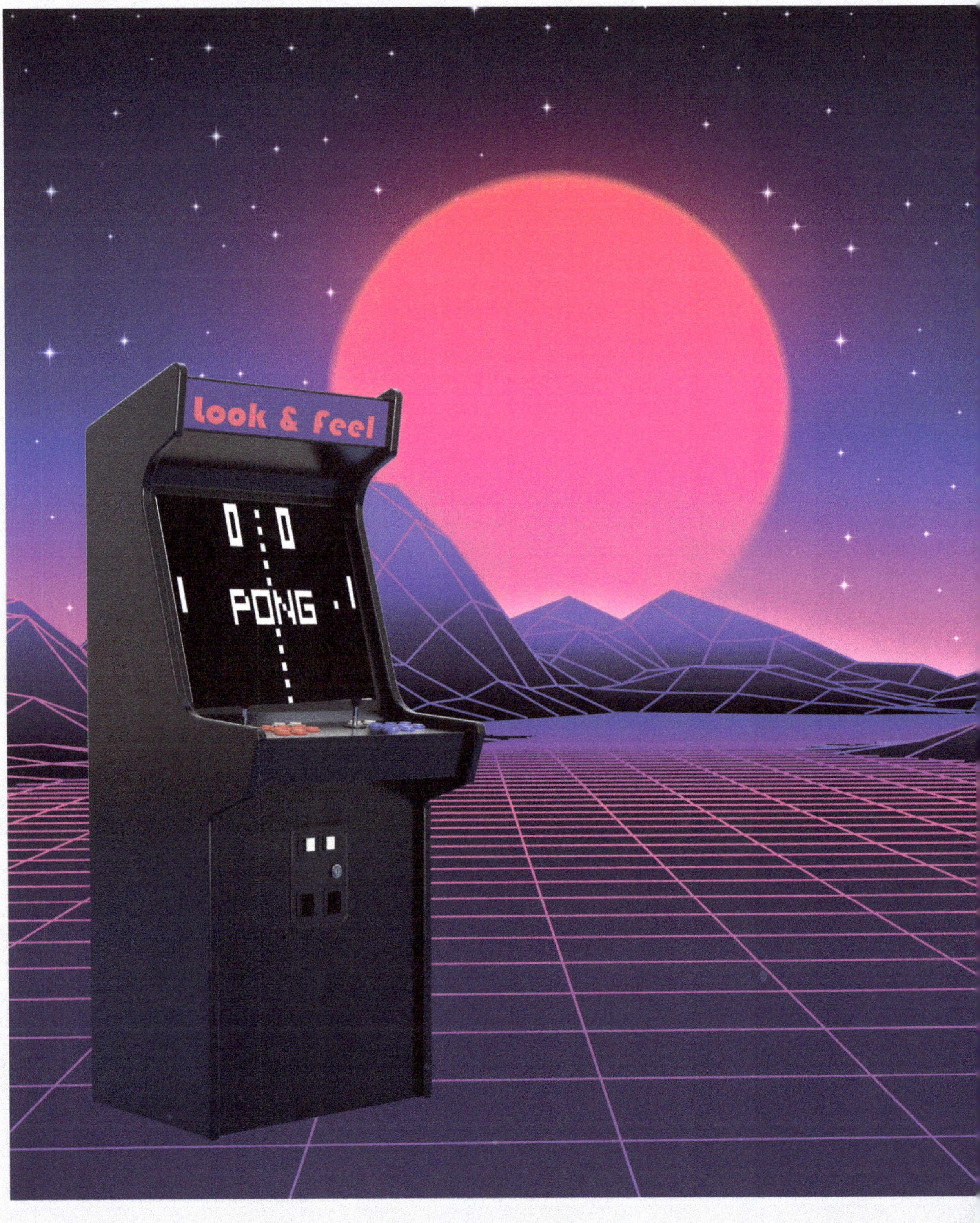

look & feel
0 : 0
PONG

LOOK and FEEL.

In 1976, Steven Lisberger became intrigued by *Pong*, the world's first commercial video game, so he spent the next five years creating *Tron* – the first film built from computer animation.

Variety wrote at the time, *"Tron is loaded with visual delights but falls way short of the mark in story and viewer involvement… Lisberger has adequately marshaled a huge force of technicians to deliver the dazzle, but even kids…will have a difficult time getting hooked."*

As a brand builder, getting people hooked is your mission — but like with *Tron*, it's easy to make the same mistake and cast the *visual delights* in the leading role. *Nike's* swoosh, *Coca Cola's* iconic typeface, and *Apple's* bitten fruit form memorable logos but they are not the brand.

I've postponed talking about brand design, aka look-and-feel, for a reason. The design supports the story, but it's the story that hooks the customer. Films as varied as *The Lady and the Tramp, Harry Potter,* and *Game of Thrones* "delivered the dazzle," but it's their *stories* that built affinity with their fans. When you build your brand, customer affinity with the Brand Story is your measure of success.

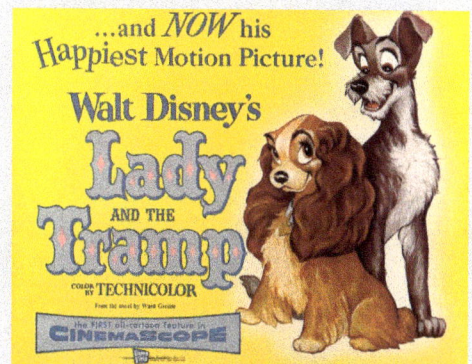

Think of your unadorned brand as Cinderella getting ready for the ball. The work of the designer is to find the right gown.

Should she slip into a slinky black dress — like this logo from Chanel?

Or make a playful statement with Crayola colors?

Or beckon with something feminine and suggestive?

Or lift a pint with a lusty illustration?

Design supports the story — not the other way around. Here are two near-identical products with markedly different stories (and scents). One suggests an evening of elegance, the other a night of decadence:

Givenchy Dahlia Noir

Dior Hypnotic Poison

Whether you plan to hire a design firm, engage overseas talent, or do it yourself, you will be steering the design ship because only you know your brand story. The higher the fees, the less steering you will do, but even the fanciest design firm will seek your direction. So, let's get to work on your logo.

Logo design for the shoestring start-up

Large creative agencies charge up to $600 per hour in New York, and $200 to $300 per hour in other major markets. That's not going to work, so let's move straight to plan B.

If you're on a shoestring budget, plan to spend $300 at the low end and $1500 at the high end for your logo project. (If you're not a shoestringer and reading this book anyway, consider spending 10 percent of your start-up costs to build your brand. An early-career freelance designer might charge $2500 for the full creative process. A small agency might charge up to $10,000 to build your identity. Yes, this is an investment, but you don't want to revisit it down the road. Like everything else, your budget should reflect your expected revenue, competitive market, and capital on-hand.

For shoestringers with $300 to spend, step one is to find an overseas designer who works via the Web. Freelance platforms like *Fiverr* and *Upwork* will stretch your dollars with their enormous body of overseas talent.

Here's the caveat: Hiring remote talent requires extra preparation, communication, and homework. The purpose of the step-by-step below is just that. If you put in the effort, you can develop an effective logo within your budget.

Step 1: Collect logos

Pinterest offers a handy way to collect logo ideas. If you've been collecting recipes on Pinterest, you know it works like a cork board. You will be collecting logos and pinning them to your board. So, go ahead and create an account.

- **Collect logos** — Start looking for logos that inspire your thinking. Using Google Images, collect logos from businesses that are similar to yours. For example, suppose you are opening a pizza restaurant:
  - If you search on "*pizza logos*," you will get a screen full of stock logos.
  - If you search on "*pizza brands*," images of frozen pizza boxes appear.

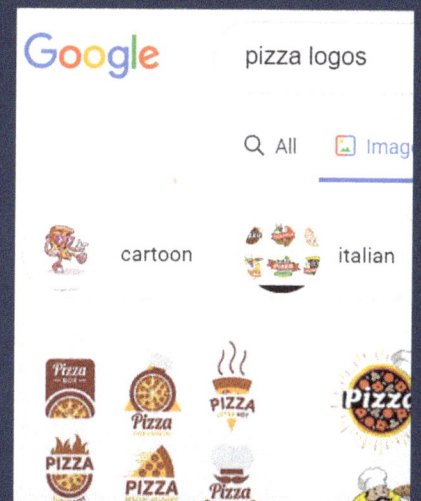

"Pizza logos"

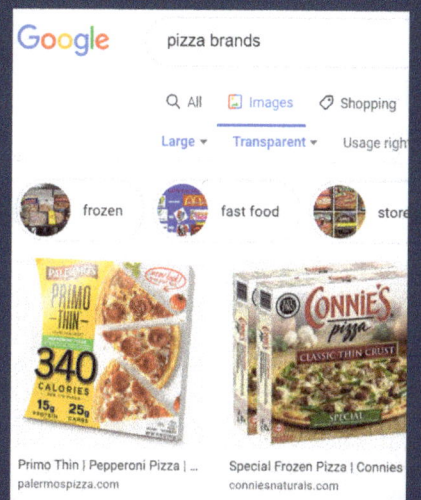

"Pizza brands"

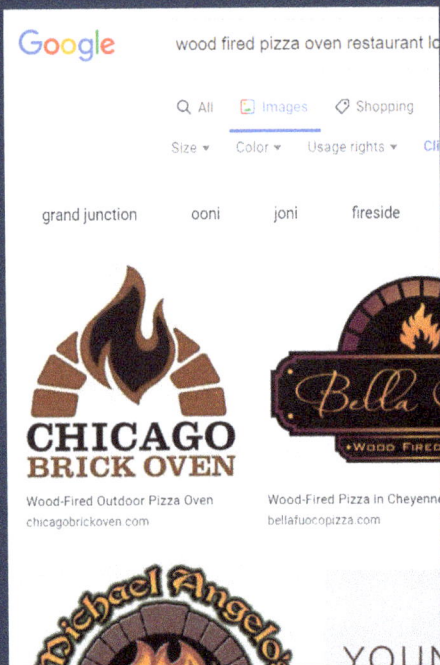

Add logos to your Pinterest board:

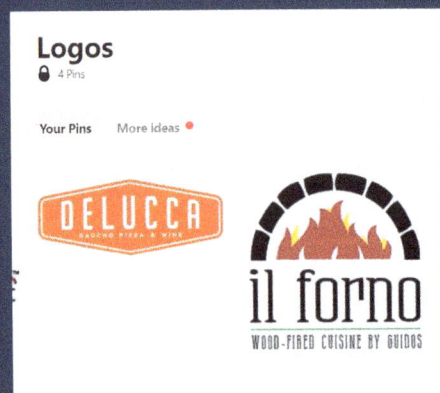

- The correct search term is *"pizza restaurant logos"* or *"pizza restaurant brands."* Logos for Pizza Hut, Papa John's, Domino's, etc. appear. Limit your search to graphics by selecting: *Tools | Type | Clip art.*

- Keep narrowing your search until you find logos that match your type of business. For example, you might search on *"wood fired pizza oven restaurant logo,"* then restrict to Clip Art.

- **Copy the image URLs of your favorites** — You're just starting your search, so don't be too picky. If a logo catches your eye in Google Images, copy the URL:

  - In Chrome or Firefox, click on the logo (it enlarges), then right-click on the larger image and select: *"Copy Image Address/Location"* from the menu.

  - In Safari, hold the Ctrl button, then click on the image. MS Edge does not have this function.

- **Pin the logos** — Build a Pinterest board of logos you like. You can also include logos you dislike for discussion.

  - In Pinterest, click your Account Name, then the "+" and "Create board." Name it *Logos*.

  - Create a Pin by clicking the "+" and selecting "Create Pin."

  - Select "Save from site" and paste the image address from Google (Ctrl V or Cmd V) and Enter.

  - Upload from the Web: Click the logo image and select "Add to Pin." Then "Save."

  - If prompted, select *Logos* as the Board to save the Pin.

- **Expand your search** — Continue searching for logos with Google Images and save them as Pins to your board.

- **Fine Tune:** As you get the hang of it, fine-tune your search. For example, search on *"Italian restaurants San Francisco"* or *"Trattoria New York City."* Trendier logos appear. In Google Images, select *Tools | Type | Clip art* to view just logos. Pin the ones you like.

- **Stock Logos:** You can also visit Shutterstock.com and search for stock logos to further spark ideas. For example, in Shutterstock, search on *"landscaping logo,"* *"medical logo,"* *"letter M logo mark,"* and so on. Click on any logos you like and pin them to your Pinterest board. Because of copyright and lack of exclusivity, don't plan on using stock images for your logo.

- **Competitors:** Now visit the web sites of your direct competitors and pin their logos to a Competitors board to help you position your brand against your competition.

- **Keep your Brand Story in mind** — A trattoria on Lake Como in Italy and an Italian restaurant in the mall have different brand stories to tell. Your logo design should suggest the brand experience in terms of price and quality for the customer.

  - As you search, select logos with your Brand Story in mind. Again, don't obsess trying to find the perfect logo; you will fine-tune your selections later.

  - Collect 20 to 30 logos. You will narrow them down after you study the Rules for Logos.

Fine tune your search:

Create a board of direct competitor logos:

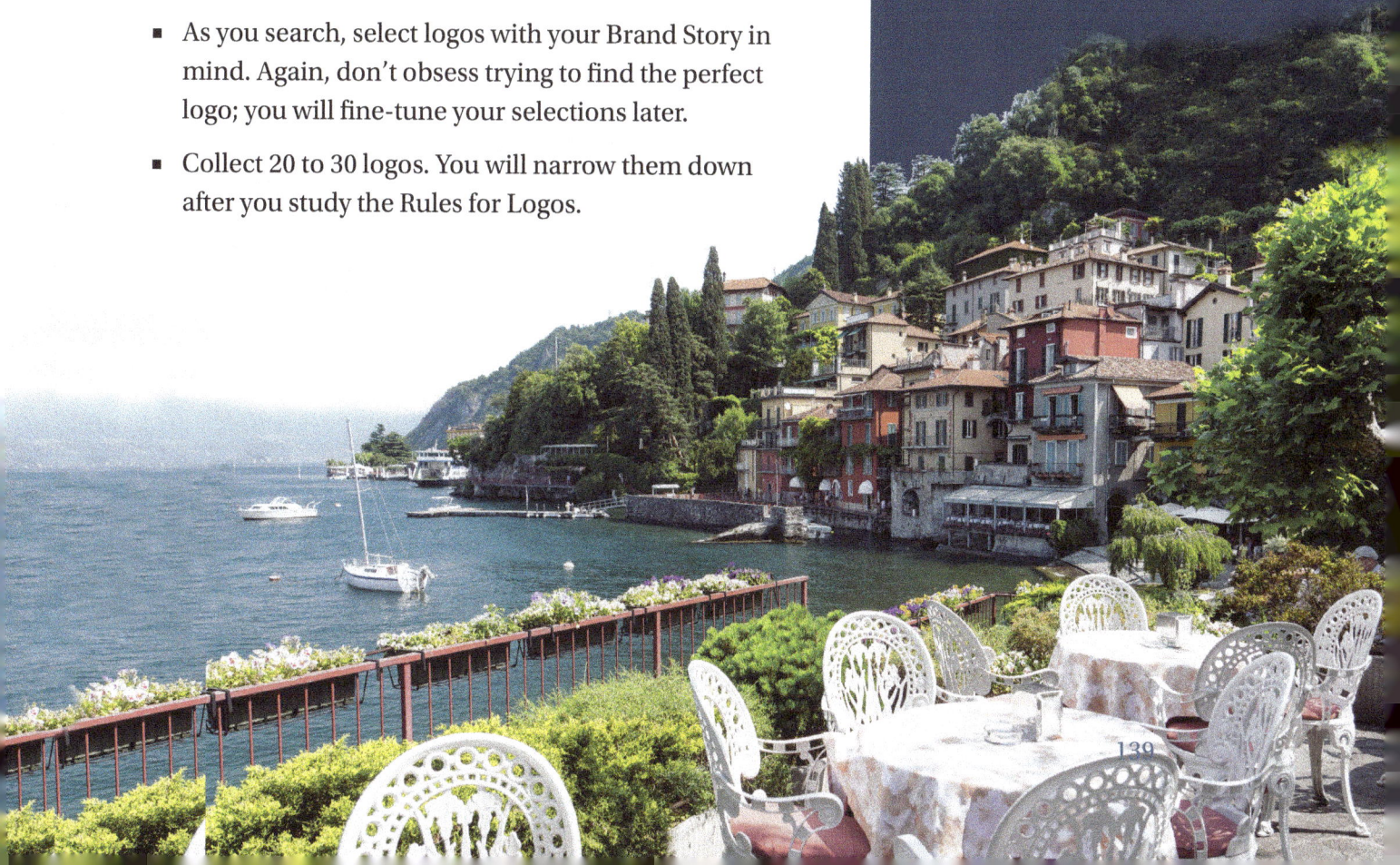

Learn the Rules for Logos

Iconic logos are simple:

Logos fall into three broad categories:

Successful logos communicate a feeling: *"This business knows what it's doing; it's the right brand for me."*

Shoestring brands make the mistake of using their logo to explain their concept, grab attention, or generate excitement – a laudable impulse early on, but you're in it for the long haul. Don't' confuse your logo with an ad.

- **Logo Rule One: Logos that go the distance are bold and simple:**

    - Perform a Google search on the *"most famous logos of all time"* and let each one sink in. The basic logo test is whether you could spot it at 60 mph. The most iconic logos work without a company name. Bold-and-simple logos win the day.

    - Consider *Delta Airlines* and the defunct *ValuJet*. Simple block letters form the *Delta* logo, whereas *ValuJet's* happy plane wants to make flying fun. If *ValuJet* had done its brand homework, they would have realized that travelers prefer a professionally run airline over one that is fun. Regardless, each logo supports the airline's brand position.

- **Logo Rule Two: Logos fall into three broad categories:**

    1. **Type Treatment + Mark**: Most logos start with a font, tweak the font, and add a distinctive mark. Type treatment logos are easier to create and get the job done — especially for business services.

    2. **Stylized logos**: Styling the font creates a more distinctive, recognizable logo. Consumer brands like *Frito Lay* use stylized font designs.

    3. **Illustration**: Illustrations paint a rich Brand Story when they are part of the brand. Grass-fed butter, baking soda, and badass IPAs use imagery to promote their brand.

Food products, restaurants, and consumer attractions are always a good fit for illustrative logos, (but they won't fit on a pen. See Rule Three below). Unknown to trivia fans, *Apple Computer* used an illustration for its first logo. Hand-drawn by co-founder, Ronald Wayne, *Apple's* first logo showed Sir Isaac Newton getting bonked by a piece of fruit.

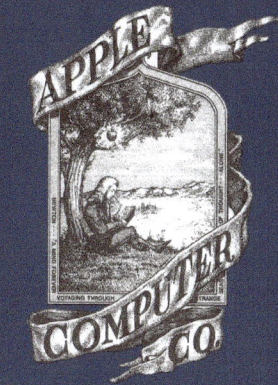

- **Logo Rule Three: Simple is more versatile.**

  - Logos live in lots of places — on websites (where it's good to be wide), on ball caps where tight logos fit the hat, and on pens and shirts where bold works best. As you sort through your logo ideas, ask: Can I print it on a pen? Embroider it on a shirt? Send it through a fuzzy fax? Stack it and spread it? Simple designs fit in all the places logos like to live.

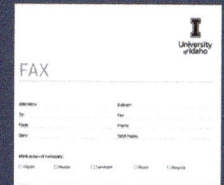

- **Logo Rule Four: Select a font that fits.**

  - Choosing fonts can be a dizzying process, but fonts ultimately fall into three categories: Sans Serif, Serif, and Decorative.

  - **Sans serif fonts** are pragmatic, effective, and direct. Most modern companies use sans serif fonts (no decorative strokes).

  - **Serif fonts** suggest elegance, intellect, and refinement. Serif fonts are great for fine wines, perfumes, serious journals, and haute couture.

  - **Decorative fonts** make strong visual statements, but also tend to be trendy and don't always age well.

Sans Serif	Serif	Decorative

Sans Serif

Serif

Decorative

Logo design is like fitting puzzle pieces:

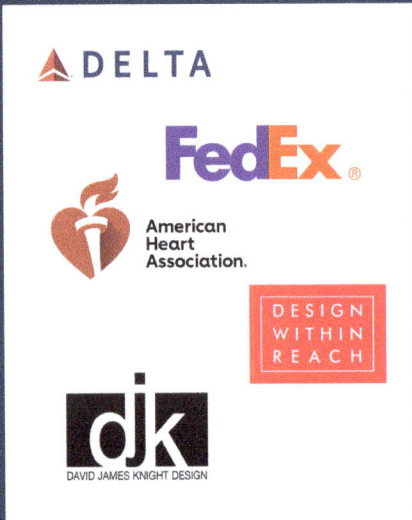

Design your logo in gray:

Study your industry for color ideas:

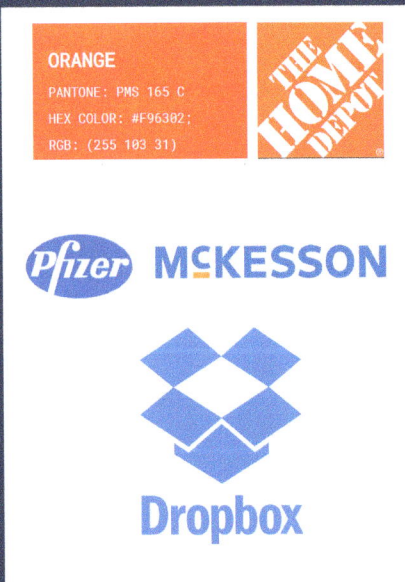

- **Logo Rule Five: Structure drives logo design.**

  - Creating a logo is less about art and more about getting the parts to fit. You start with a name, a description, and maybe some initials, then fit the pieces into a workable shape like a puzzle. For example:

  - *Delta* is short, so stretch it out (adding kerning spaces between the letters).

  - *FedEx* is two short syllables, so contrast the colors.

  - *American Heart Association* is too long, so stack the words.

  - *Design Within Reach* stacks nicely in a rectangle.

  - If the lower-case initials have ascenders, try snuggling them back-to-back. (David James Knight Design)

- **Logo Rule Six: Logos don't need color (at least in the beginning).**

  - Ask your designer to use grays to keep color out of the process. Plus, if the logo is ever reversed out of black, embroidered on a polo shirt, or sent in a fax, you'll already know that it works as a monochrome.

  - While your designer is working with grays, study your industry for color ideas. You can search for the color palettes of major companies on the Web. Search for "*company name* brand standards."

  - Let your designer guide your use of color, but you should understand the basics:

  - Healthcare and tech logos are often blue. Blue has become the most popular logo color — possibly because blue is associated with positive experiences (blue sky, blue sea, and baby blue). It's a safe color if you plan to sell to other cultures.

- Environmental and landscaping are almost always green.
- Browns are the least used, except for earthy, organic brands, and brown foods (coffee, bread, chocolate).
- Orange is playful, full of sunshine, and emotional warmth. In the 1950s, *Tide Detergent* took command of the grocery shelf with its trademark orange circle. *Home Depot, Shell Gas*, and *Amazon* use orange to their advantage.
- Purple can express mystery, spirituality, and royalty. Kids love purple, hence Teletubbies.
- Pink rhymes with kink (*Cosmo* magazine). It's also used in police holding areas to reduce aggressive behavior. Whatever you think of the *Lyft* logo, it catches your eye at the airport.
- Red cuts through clutter with a passion. Like a "power necktie," red asserts authority and thought leadership – examples: *CNN, Time,* and *CNET*. Red also prompts impulse buying. Red might tie with blue for most used in logos.

Step 3: Narrow your board. You've read the rules, now review your Pinterest board:

- Are you drawn to simple logos or logos with flair?
- Do your selected logos use serif, sans, or decorative fonts?
- What makes the most sense for your logo: Simple, Stylized, or Illustration?
- Do your selections support your brand story?
- Which competitor logo hits your sweet spot?

Support your Brand Story through color:

In Pinterest, select the logos that best reflect your Brand Story, and "Save" them to a new board. Call it, "Logo Selects." Use the description field to describe anything you like about the selected logo. Examples:

- *"Love the classic feel, openness, sense of balance."*

- *"Suggests high-tech without looking techie."*

- *"Soft and feminine, but strong enough to catch one's eye."*

- *"Cool-looking letter P."*

- *"I would leave my dog with these folks. They seem trustworthy and caring."*

==**Step 4: Search for a designer.** If you know a designer in your price range whose portfolio skill matches your Pinterest selections, you're set. Otherwise, visit *Fiverr* or *Upwork* to review the vast pool of domestic and overseas talent who can work within a shoestring budget.==

Here's how to choose and work with a remote designer and achieve agency results. I will use *Fiverr* for the example:

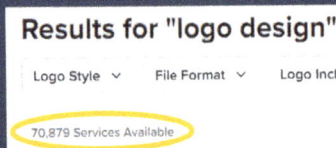

- Visit Fiverr.com and search on *Logo Design.* Good luck, over 70,000 results appear!

- Narrow your search, for example, *"Restaurant Logo Design"* This narrows the results to 2500

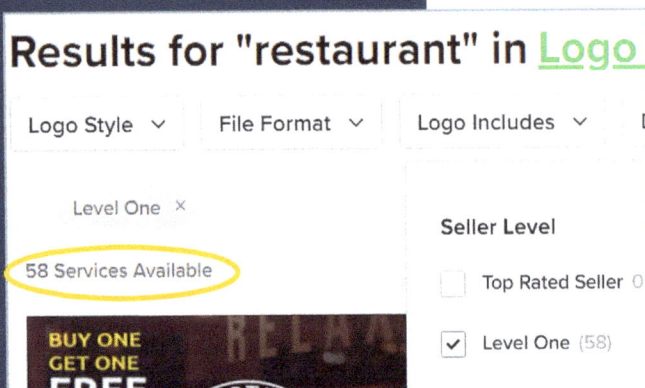

  - Search on *"Restaurant,"* Category = *Logo Design.* Click Seller Level: *"Level One."* Fifty-eight highly rated designers with restaurant samples appear.

  - Now that you have a sense of how the system works, spend an hour browsing for a designer with three parameters in mind:

1. **Search Terms:** Try searching with specifics that fit your brand, for example, *Logo Design Hand Drawn,* or *Elegant Feminine Logo, Logo Design Restaurant,* etc. Designers who list *Restaurant Logos* as a specialty (a "gig" in *Fiverr* talk) will appear in your results. Not all designers use *gigs* to specialize their services, so don't let this constrain your search. Select Top-Rated, Level 1, or Level 2 designers.

2. **Style:** Refer to your "Logo Selects" Pinterest Board to guide your browsing. Ask yourself, *"Which designers create logos that would fit on my board?"* Some are good at corporate, some have a flair for elegance, others are quirky, and still others can create pop art. Don't get swayed by cool-looking designs. Instead, hold the question: *"Does this designer have the experience to understand my brand?"* Click the "Save" button for each promising designer.

3. **Price:** Using your logo budget as a guide, save designers who fit your price range. Experience plus the local cost of living set the price (Romania is less expensive than Israel). At a minimum you will need as your deliverables:

   - 3 Concepts
   - 3 Revisions
   - Vector file
   - Jpg/png files

If your budget allows, choose high experience, plus a package with four concepts and unlimited revisions. Illustrations, mascots, 3D, and stylized/custom fonts cost more.

Studio – *Fiverr* also offers *Studio,* a mini agency approach where you work with a team of writers, designers, Web talent, etc. This may be a better solution if you need to build out more than a logo for your brand.

Stacey17'S Gigs

stacey17

I will create the perfect elegant feminine logo or...

★ **4.7** (129)

STARTING AT **$25**

♥ Save

Premium	Standard	Basic

PLATINUM PACKAGE $55

- 300 DPI - JPEG & PNG - 5000 x 3000 pixels - PDF & AI source file - vector file

⏱ 5 Days Delivery   ↻ Unlimited Revisions

✓ 2 Initial Concepts Included
✓ Logo Transparency
✓ High Resolution
✓ 3D Mockup
✓ Source File
✓ Social Media Kit
✓ Vector File

Continue ($55)

Studio

Get the job done by a team of specialists, with a single point of contact.

Step 5: Hire a designer. Now the un-fun part. Consummating the deal is a bit like online dating. But since you are following a deliberative process, the results will far exceed what you'd get from a freelance friend of a friend.

- **Narrow your designers:** Go into your *Fiverr* saved list. Note each designer's experience, price, communication skills, and talent. Choose 3-4 designers.

- **Contact the designers:** Using the "Contact Me" link, send the following message to each designer:

Dear [Name],

I am reviewing logo designers on Fiverr and like your work. I am interested in your [Platinum] package for our new business. Some background about my project:

- Type of business: [from your brand story]

- Target customer: [from your brand story]

- How we are unique: [Your secret sauce]

- Type of logo we seek: [Type treatment with mark, elegant, illustration, etc.]

While researching logos, I created a Pinterest Board with logos I like. Click each logo to read what I liked about the design: [Use the Pinterest Invite button to copy the link to your Selects Board and insert here.]

Three questions:

1. Do you have experience with similar types of logo projects?

2. What is your logo design process?

3. Do you have any samples from similar projects that you can share with me?

Sincerely,
[Your name]
[Your company name]

Send the email and wait for replies. You want to start a conversatopm with each prospect before you commit. You are hoping to discover:

- Does the designer respond to your questions with an eagerness to work?

- Does the designer understand brand strategy, or just make cool designs?

- Are you comfortable with the designer's process and timeline? Is it a well-structured process or somewhat vague?

- What is their stated experience? Do their samples match the quality you are seeking?

Your decision will stem more from comfort than analysis, so feel free to ask more questions. You can also follow this selection process if you hire a local designer.

Once you feel comfortable, *Fiverr* will guide the hiring process and manage the payment. The good news, your Brand Story plus *Pinterest* Board will perform like a formal creative brief — just like the big-bucks agency approach!

You're not hiring a designer (yet). You are starting a conversation.

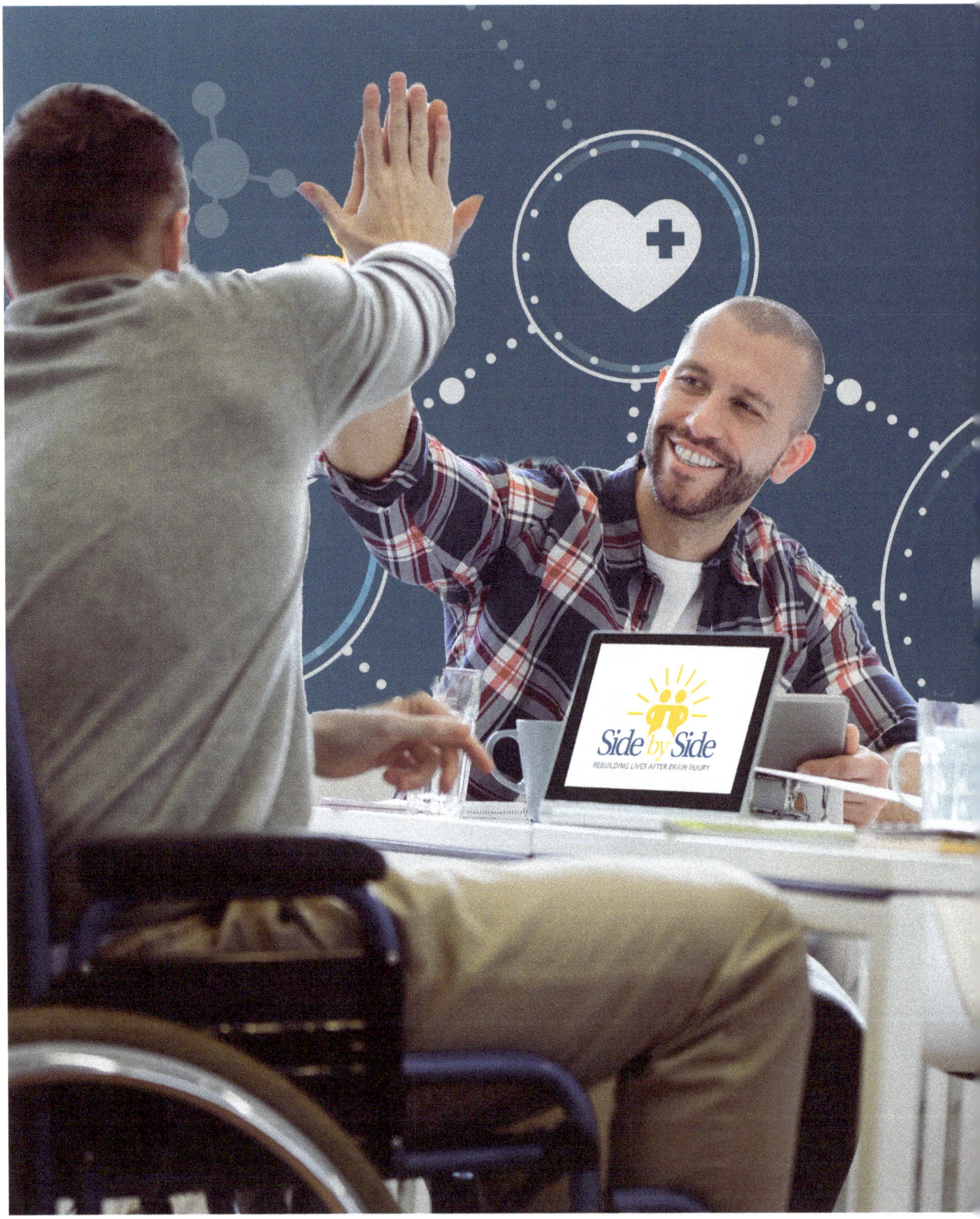
Side by Side
REBUILDING LIVES AFTER BRAIN INJURY

POSITIONING NON-PROFITS.

Whether you sell B-to-C, B-to-B, or Non-profit to Donor, ultimately everyone is a Consumer. Why? Because everyone responds to brands.

This fact was born out when I received an email from one of my non-profit clients:

"Bruce, guess what!" Cindi Johnson wrote. "We received a $100,000 check today for facility improvements. This was the meeting we created the case statement for!!! Thank you, thank you!"

Music to my ears and hooray — proof that brand positioning works in the non-profit world!

My client, *Side by Side Brain Injury Clubhouse, Inc.*, offers a day program for people with traumatic brain injuries. *Side by Side* was launching its first multi-million campaign — a $3 million effort to upgrade its facility, expand staff, add programs, increase visibility, and validate their clinical approach.

As a relatively small program run out of a converted house in Stone Mountain, Georgia, *Side by Side* needed to develop its Brand Story to help major donors understand the value of *Side by Side's* mission and feel confident funding the campaign. In a nutshell, *Side by Side* was preparing for its moonshot. There would be no second chance.

Side by Side planned to pitch to the prestigious Robert W. Woodruff Foundation, named after the philanthropist and long-time leader of *The Coca-Cola Company*. Here are the steps we took to position *Side by Side* to receive grants from major donors:

Side by Side Case Study:

Like with consumer brands, non-profit brands hold a place in the minds of their "customers" – their *donors*. And like a consumer brand, *Side by Side* had a branding problem. The organization was perceived as a warm and supportive "clubhouse" for brain-injured individuals, but the mission was bigger. We started the brand workshop with a question:

> *Will donors perceive Side by Side as a **Membership Community** or a **Clinical Program**?*

I researched *Side by Side's* collateral and found evidence for both. In our workshop, using a flip chart, we put "membership" messages on the left and "clinical" messages on the right:

Will donors perceive Side by Side as a Membership Community or a Clinical Program?

MEMBERSHIP MESSAGES	CLINICAL MESSAGES
• A **membership** organization in which members have responsibility and ownership of the Clubhouse.	• Work-focused programming
• Many return to resume **membership** as their needs change	• **Rehabilitation**
• Hope restored through a **community of peers**	• **Fostering** interdependence
• A place to belong, participate, develop meaningful **relationships**	• Employment **services**
• The path to recovery is through **relationships** and work	• Life skills **training**
• SBS must demonstrate its relevance as a high value **community** service provider.	• **Research collaboration** with Shepherd
• The Clubhouse is a safe, accessible and affordable **community** that families trust	• Examine and compare **outcomes**
	• Collaborative partnership with Clubhouse International and IBICA
	• Focus on measuring the positive **impact on health and well-being**
	• Establish credibility in accord with the **ACA, health cost reduction**, etc.
	• Hire four fulltime **clinical** staff

We studied the chart. The left column painted *Side by Side* as a:

> A **Membership Organization** *that offers a sense of community and purpose for people with brain injuries.*

It's a commendable mission, but will it play with major donors?

> The right column showed *Side by Side* in a **clinical role**, *teaching critical skills and measuring the clinical impact .*

Did Side by Side's messaging align with prospective major donors?

The Woodruff Foundation describes their Human Services mission as:

Supporting "**well-established** human services organizations that work to **improve the quality of life** for children and adults in need.

The goal of brand positioning is to align your brand to the needs of your target customer. In this case, the major donor was seeking *well-established* organizations that *improve the quality of life for children and adults in need.*

Houston, we have a messaging problem! *Side by Side* needed to strengthen its clinical message.

Determing the Secret Sauce: We addressed the messaging problem by crafting a new brand position for *Side by Side*. Following the Brand Story approach, we needed a Secret Sauce.

We took *Side by Side's* clinical approach (mentors working-side-by-side with clients), positioned it as the Secret Sauce, and branded it as the **Partnership Model**.

Here's the new Brand Positioning Statement. The bold words align with the major donor's needs:

Side by Side Brand Position

AUDIENCE: For donors, healthcare payers, and social service policymakers...

PROBLEM OR NEED: Who seek to make a cost-effective and **positive impact on the human cost of brain injuries to our society**, while **improving the quality of life** of the people impacted and their families...

UNIQUE SOLUTION (secret sauce): Only Side by Side, with its **unique Partnership Model, rebuilds shattered lives by engaging the whole person through a community of mutual support coupled with professional guidance.**

PROOF: The success of our Partnership Model is evidenced by our ability to: 1) Achieve incremental goals of self-sufficiency by 90 percent, increase the health and well-being of the family, 2) Reduce initial rehabilitation costs up to 85 percent, 3) Protect the payer's investment in rehabilitation gains, and 4) Lower the total cost of future care.

Following the Brand Story approach, we crafted a Secret Sauce!

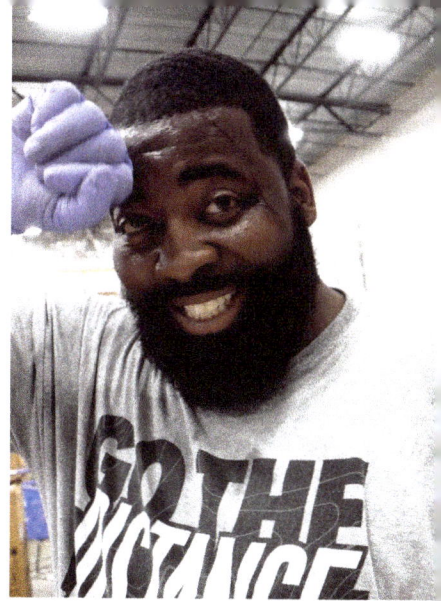

151

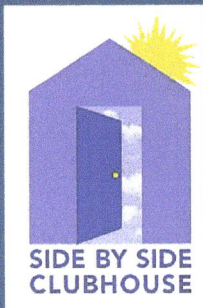

Old Logo

New Logo

The new positioning statement accomplished two things:

1. It pulled language, ***improving the quality of life***, directly from the Woodruff Foundation's grant guidelines.

2. It established a secret sauce — the ***Partnership Model*** — as a unique, branded clinical approach to working with brain-injured individuals.

Using the positioning statement as the starting point, we built out the remaining elements of a Brand Story:

Brand Concept: *Engaging the whole person through Side by Side's Partnership Model:* (this is the key idea expressed in all materials).

Brand Identity: In keeping with the new position, we changed the logo and shortening the brand name from Side by Side Brain Injury Clubhouse to *"Side by Side."* Executive Director, Cindi Johnson agreed to make the change despite sixteen years of equity built in the old clubhouse logo. We also branded the campaign as "Side by Side 2020" and branded their unique clinical approach (the secret sauce) as the *Side By Side Partnership Mode*l.

Elevator Pitch:

This two-minute pitch now guides *Side by Side's* messaging:

Problem: *With over 300,000 combat veterans back from Iraq and Afghanistan with traumatic brain injuries, public awareness of Traumatic Brain Injuries (TBI) has never been greater. Often overlooked are the millions of TBIs that occur in the United States at an annual cost of $76 billion. What's more, 2.5 million ER visits are diagnosed with TBI each year, usually from falls, sports, and accidents.*

152

Case Statement – If you're invited to pitch a major donor, the first thing out of your briefcase should be a case statement. It's a glossy document that illustrates your brand position and campaign mission.

Because we had done our brand homework, the elevator pitch guided the structure of the document.

One of the *Side by Side's* members had become a talented one-handed photographer after her injury, so we had access to a wealth of photos to tell the story.

Executive Director, Cindi Johnson was ecstatic with the campaign's success. As she explained, *"You want major donors to respond to what's in your heart, but you're ultimately judged by your professionalism and execution. And that's okay. Foundations have their own constituencies to be accountable to."*

BUDGET

LETTER FROM THE LEADERSHIP TEAM

Cindi Johnson, MA, CBIST
Executive Director

SIDE BY SIDE 2020
Building for the Future of Traumatic
Brain Injury Support in Georgia

While most people recover quickly from a mild concussion, a severe brain injury can disrupt family, career, and daily living – often for life. The big question facing providers, payers, and policymakers: After the person is released from medical care, what comes next? With 5.3 million Americans disabled by TBI, how do they rebuild their shattered lives?

Solution: *In the state of Georgia, only one organization offers a next step for persons with mild to severe TBI. Side by Side has pioneered a Partnership Model for rebuilding lives that have been broken by a traumatic brain injury.*
Our proven approach engages the whole person through a group setting of skills-based rehabilitation and mutual emotional support, coupled with professional guidance.

Proven Results: *The success of our approach is demonstrated by our program's ability to:*

- *Achieve incremental goals of self-sufficiency (by 90 percent of our members),*
- *Increase the health and well-being of the family,*
- *Reduce initial rehabilitation costs by up to 85 percent,*
- *Protect the payer's investment in rehabilitation gains,*
- *and Lower the total cost of future care.*

The Meher Archives

In 1884, Merwan Sheriar Irani was born in Pune, India, to Zoroastrian parents. From his teens and into his twenties — and after long periods of seclusion and contact with various teachers — Merwan underwent a spiritual transformation, eventually becoming Meher Baba.

Meher Baba maintained silence, underwent fasting, traveled widely, and performed works of charity with lepers and the poor. He also generated a remarkable number of books, talks, letters, and other materials in his vow of silence. His followers recognized him as a God-realized soul.

In the 1930s, Meher Baba began to attract Western followers until his death in 1969. Pete Townshend of The Who became a follower and dedicated his 1969 rock-opera *Tommy* to Meher Baba. Today, the mostly sixty- and seventy-year-olds who follow Meher Baba remain deeply dedicated to the path.

This backdrop also formed a set of challenges for a small group of Meher Baba's followers who hoped to raise $2 million to purchase and renovate a run-down former public school in the mountains near Asheville, NC to archive Meher Baba's papers and documents. The property included classrooms, an auditorium, and acreage, making it ideal for a spiritual center and the official archives for Meher Baba's life work.

Among the challenges:

- Meher Baba's documents were scattered in private collections around the world,
- There was no central organization to mobilize members to raise funds,

- Most members live simply, which meant the few wealthier donors were solicited frequently by competing Meher Baba trusts and organizations, and

- Like with any non-profit, politics and perceptions play an outsized role.

The target customer: Every branding project begins with the question: "Who is our target customer, and how do we solve their needs?"

We began our Brand Story workshop by sketching out fictional personas for two different target customers – or more accurately, donors:

1. **Major Donor Marjorie**: Marjorie, age 74, has benefited from a successful career, long marriage, and an inheritance. Unlike the spiritual nomads who characterize many Baba lovers, Marjorie maintains a financially secure, purposeful life. She feels a responsibility to see Baba's legacy preserved and made available for future generations. Marjorie needs to be solicited directly – preferably in person.

2. **Small Donor Sam**: Sam, age 68, is already retired, and lives on a fixed income. His commitment to Baba is intensely personal, devotional, and boundless. Major gifts are out of the question for Sam, because he saves his discretionary dollars to travel to Meher Baba centers in South Carolina and India. Sam can be solicited through an online campaign to give a few dollars per month via subscription.

Customer needs – We identified four core needs – the Big L's – the project could satisfy for our target donors:

1. **Legacy:** Building a digital archive with interactive access, preserved to archival standards using the latest technologies.

   "I want to make Meher Baba's legacy available to all – and preserved for future generations."

LEGACY- ARCHIVES

Digital FORMAT | URGENCY - RESCUE

Public Access to Materials

Online- Interactive Interface

Archival Spaces — climate, storage, security, staff / TECHNOLOGY Digital Transit

Preservation Future

LEARNING

- Study center — Audio/video Interviews
- Online Availability
- Study Groups
- Transition from Personal contact — Baba

- Poi LOVE - COMMUNITY

- Res Fellowship

Sahavas

Gatherings

Focal point for Asheville

Service opportunity

Worship

celeb_AND - Edifice

Meet MAJOR Building

Hub for Asheville + visitors

SIX ACRES

Space for large gatherings

Consecrated ground

Destination

Summer season Year-Round Welcome Climate

Family-friendly - All ages welcome

Garden potential- crops

Venue

I want there to be places dedicated to Baba."

I want to help build a center with land dedicated to Baba with a lasting future.

Anchoring the energy "planting the seed."

---

2. **Learning:** Offering a study center with research activities, classes, and online accessibility.

> "I want to learn and experience more about Meher Baba and his teachings."

3. **Love:** Establishing a community center focused on fellowship, gatherings, worship, and a meeting point for fellow Baba lovers.

> "I need opportunities for community and fellowship with other Meher Baba lovers."

4. **Land:** This major capital investment in a building with acreage offers a year-round destination for the Meher Baba community, a space for large gatherings, beautiful gardens, and family-friendly activities.

> "I want to help build a center with a lasting future on land dedicated to Meher Baba."

Where to focus – The project satisfied all four customer needs, but a brand position needs to focus on one. Since the immediate priority was to fund the purchase and renovation through major gifts, we focused our Brand Story on "Major Donor Marjorie" who wanted to preserve Baba's Legacy – Big L #1.

Later, we could focus on Love, Land, and Learning through subscription-based giving from smaller donors.

We also needed to demonstrate why a new non-profit entity was needed, given the existence of legacy organizations. Archival needs around climate, sea-level rise, humidity, and geologic stability would become part of our messaging.

"I want to make Meher Baba's legacy available to all – and preserved for future generations."

Meher Archives Positioning Statement:

- **Target Customer and Need:** *"For Baba lovers who want his legacy to be preserved and made available for future generations, and want to build a permanent center where Baba lovers can meet for fellowship, study, celebration, and community...*

- **Our Solution:** *Only the Meher Archives meets the needs of future generations – optimally suited for a changing climate and geology, and using open-access interactive technologies for a worldwide audience.*

- **Proof of Concept:** *With building and land in hand, this vision is already being realized and supported by significant contributions from major donors and committed volunteers.*

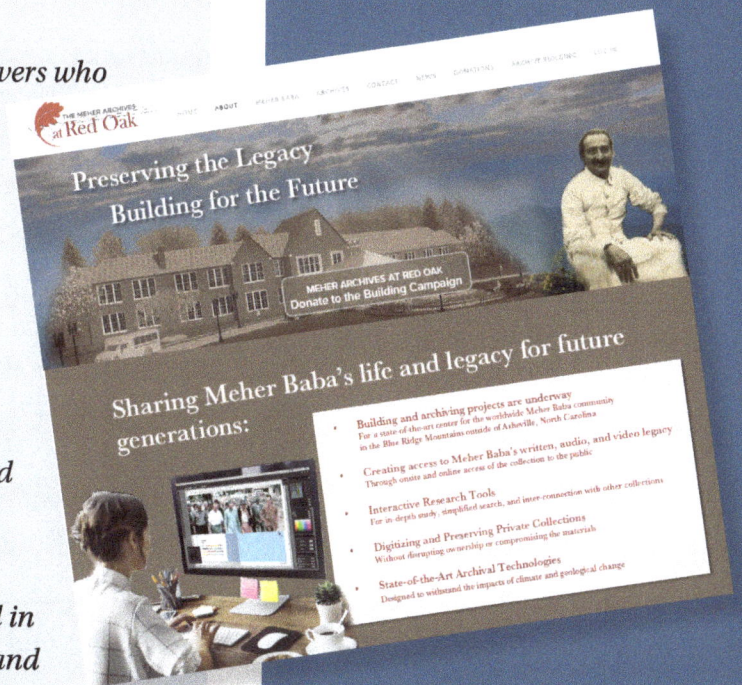

Implementing the Meher Archives Brand Story:
Each element in the positioning statement helped to structure the messaging for the Web site.

Know Your Donor

Non-profits are mission-driven to solve societal problems, but often forget the people who make it possible — the donors. Thinking of donors as target-customers informs your priorities and provokes deeper questions:

Why do people donate? Is it to solve societal problems and help the world – or for self-satisfaction?

According to research, altruistic desires are genuine, but they do not predict charitable giving. People give to a charity because giving makes them feel good.

Meher Archrives:
Rebuilding the roof

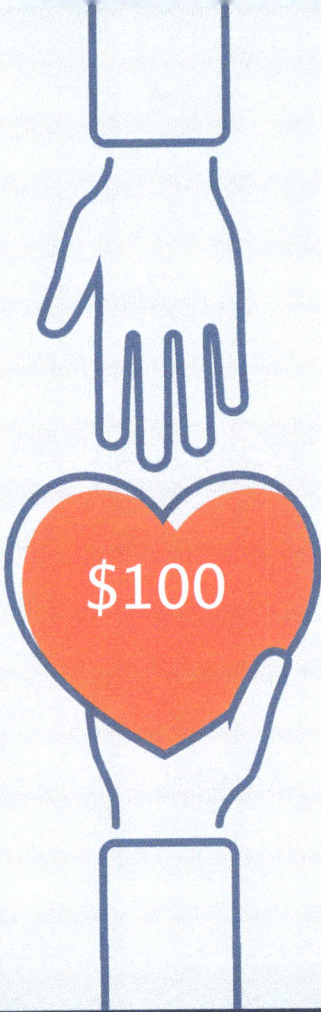

A successful Brand Story creates a "brand affinity" that engages the desire to give.

The Charities Aid Foundation asked 700 donors why they donate, and 42% agreed that the enjoyment they receive from giving was a key factor.[1]

The National Institute of Health took this question further by giving $100 to each participant in a controlled, experiment. When participants were allowed to donate a portion of their newly obtained $100, brain scans revealed activation of pleasure-related centers deep in the brain from those who made that choice.[2]

What does this mean for your non-profit?

Your donors give more from a *felt affinity* than a shared agenda. In other words, a successful Brand Story creates a "brand affinity" that engages the desire to give, activates the pleasure centers, and builds a donor relationship for the long haul.

Getting the non-profit Brand Story right means knowing your donor. *The Meher Archives* had four stories to tell — Legacy, Love, Land, and Learning. All were important, but only by aligning their story to the needs of their major donors, were they able to purchase and renovate the property for their project.

$100

Storytelling drives fundraising

Plain vanilla marketing to broad demographics (YMCA, United Way, Boys & Girls Club, etc.) no longer works with today's splintered audiences. Successful fundraising now requires intimate relationships with a close-knit circle of people who are invested in your story.

Instead of targeting the masses, cultivate the small circle of people who will respond to your Brand Story over the long haul.

Think tribal instead of societal. Story-based fundraising succeeds because it connects your audience with your cause – not by the facts of the case, but by a sense of shared community.

"Every successful charity is successful at fundraising because they have figured out how to be part of the culture – where people can proudly say, "Of course I support them, because people like us do things like this." – Seth Godin[3]

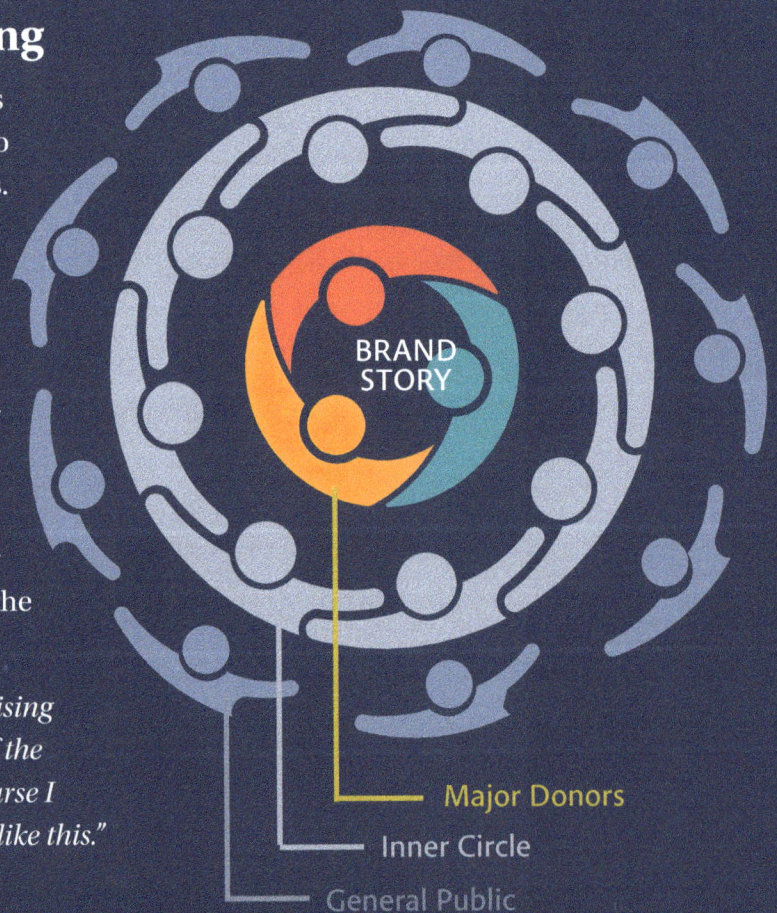

BRAND STORY

Major Donors
Inner Circle
General Public

The rules of brand affinity apply particularly to non-profits.

If you're providing hurricane relief work, your story is not: "Thanks to your donation, we filled ten dumpsters with debris and delivered 700 pounds of food."

Instead, your donors want to hear, "Friday afternoon, Pete, Judy, and Jennifer arrived on Grand Abaco Island and made a conch stew with the locals before getting to work."

Similarly, it's not, "Atlanta has five thousand homeless residents who need your support." Instead, "Every Sunday, David, Mary, and Jane set up lawn chairs in Woodruff Park and wash aching, blistering feet."

Instead of metrics and goals, share intimate stories – real stories. Your tribe will want to donate because it feels good to stay connected with your mission.

1. Charities Aid Foundation, Survey: "Why We Give," April 2013.
2. NIH, "Brain Imaging Reveals Joys of Giving," June 22, 2007
3. Seth Godwin on Successful Fundraising, YouTube, May 13, 2015

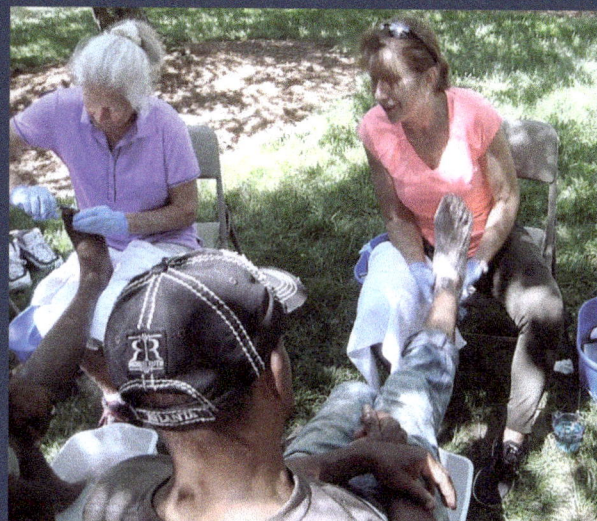

Church of the Common
Ground, Atlanta, GA

159

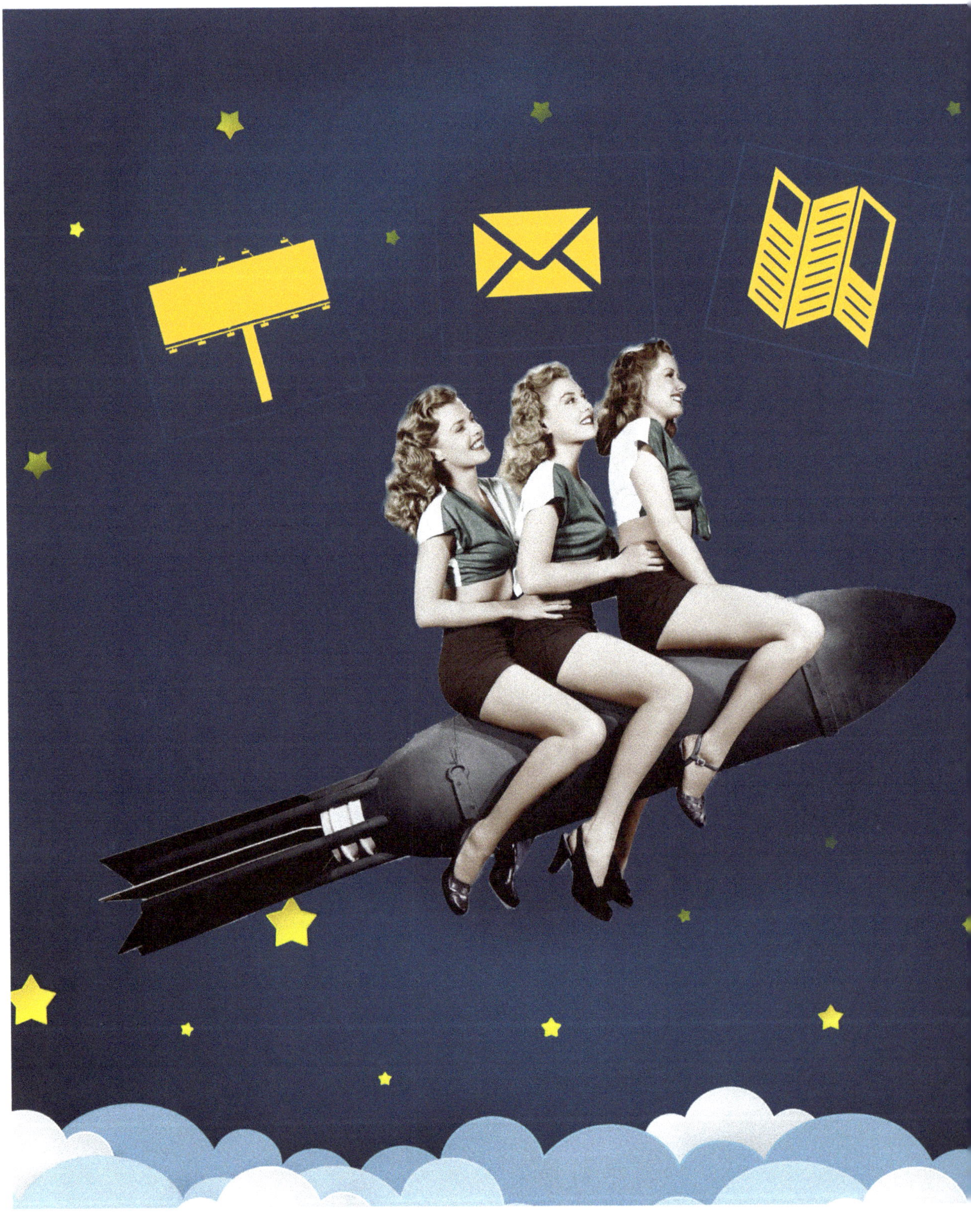

TOUCHPOINTS.

Marketing used to be simple. You had three basic choices: Advertising, direct mail, and collateral. You launched them into the market, and hoped for the best.

All this changed in the 1990s when marketers gave new meaning to the famous Monty Python sketch:

Man ordering breakfast: "Well, what've you got?"

Waitress: "Well, there's egg and bacon; egg sausage and bacon; egg and spam; egg bacon and spam; egg bacon sausage and spam; spam bacon sausage and spam; spam egg spam spam bacon and spam; spam sausage spam spam bacon spam tomato and spam."

Suddenly, bulk email bots overpowered our inboxes — that is until the CAN-SPAM Act hit the brakes a few years later (sorta).

Spam email was just the beginning. In 1994, *Wired Magazine* shocked the Web community by launching the industry's first web banner ad. Louis Rossetto, the co-founder of *Wired*, remembered the moment:

"People told us if you put ads online, the Internet would throw up on us. I thought the opposition was ridiculous. There is hardly an area of human activity that isn't commercial. Why should the Internet be the exception? So we said, 'Fuck it,' and just went ahead and did it"[1]

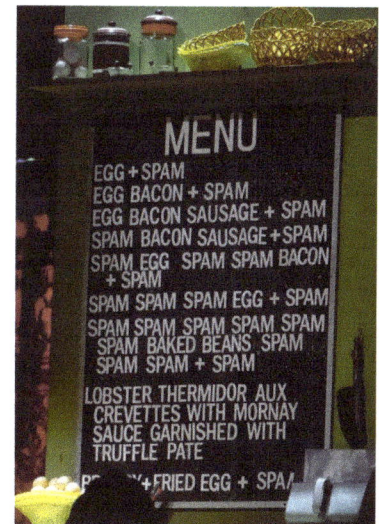

---

1 Ross Benes, "The beginning of a giant industry, An oral history of the first banner ad," Digiday, November 2017.

Have you ever clicked your mouse right HERE? → YOU WILL

The first banner ad: 1994

Try our fresh-brewed coffee for FREE before 10 am.

Wrapify

$390.00

Sally's
250 g
CBD
DEWBERRY
JAM
ORGANIC PRODUCT

Seven rules to simplify your marketing

The original clickbait spawned an explosion of digital messages that now seeps into every moment of our lives – and the momentum continues: Technology can beam proximity ads to your Apple watch via cell towers mapping your location. Fortunately, Apple is keeping that particular gate closed — for now.

And there's more: A company called *Wrapify* will wrap your car with advertising, connect you to their app, and pay you cents per mile. The next logical step is to bypass impression-based advertising altogether and implant messaging chips into our brains.

Lame joke aside, as a shoestring start-up, you rightly feel overwhelmed by the labyrinth of digital marketing, yer this complexity also offers enormous opportunity. Never before have everyday people been able to target millions of people without spending a penny — unless, of course, someone clicks. Today's digital platforms can target, place, measure, and analyze brand messages with remarkable precision. But mastering this technology is a fulltime career – and you just want to sell CBD-laced jam!

So, how do you get your message out without freaking out?

Take a breath. You're already ahead of the game because most marketing efforts are just spaghetti on the wall – *unless you have a brand position*. Since you've done the hard work building a Brand Story aligned to your target customer, your story will do the selling for you.

Seven rules to simplify your marketing

As a shoestringer, forget about marketing metrics, media buying, and balancing your marketing mix. Follow these seven simple rules to jumpstart your business:

Rule 1: Think in terms of touchpoints — Every place a prospective customer encounters your brand is a touchpoint. Handing a hotel guest a hot cookie is a touchpoint, as is greeting a burrito customer, *"Welcome to Moe's."* Sharing a business card or adding an email signature with your logo/

tagline are touchpoints. The "Carbon-Free Lawns" t-shirts Donnie's three-man crew wears on the job count for three touchpoints (at only $5 per shirt). In contrast, a Super Bowl touchpoint costs $5 million for 30 seconds.

Each Touchpoint is additive. If you start with three Touchpoints, your marketing footprint doubles when you have six.

Donnie's touchpoint marketing plan was simple and effective:

"I'll put a big logo sticker on the back of my clipboard," he mused. "Then I'll add my tagline to my estimates, wear a branded ball cap around town, post social updates to my Facebook page, sponsor a banner for my daughter's soccer team, and write a sustainable lawn care article for the The Intown Blog." Count the signage on Donnie's truck, and he's got seven no-brainer touchpoints.

Later, Donnie offered to give Saturday morning demonstrations in organic lawn care at his local Ace Hardware. Donnie handed out business cards while the store pushed bags of organic fertilizer. For Donnie's shoestring business, this coup was comparable to a CEO scoring a speaking slot at an industry conference.

Adding touchpoints — one at a time — makes marketing manageable.

Rule 2: Touchpoints must point — The purpose of Touchpoints is not to create brand impressions, but to *point* customers to your Brand Story.

You're building a touchpoint universe. Instead of the Dog Star and Betelgeuse, you've got bumper stickers, blimps, and business cards.

Adding touchpoints — one at a time — makes marketing manageable.

JUST DO IT.

Brand Story

These touchpoints point to your Brand Story via taglines, slogans, and campaigns. Simple touchpoints build into a small galaxy, and finally a touchpoint universe:

Yes, it's daunting to build a universe but remember – your touchpoints point. Since they connect to your Brand Story, they are viral by nature. Example:

"Can you believe it?" Joe tells his friend over coffee. "I saw this young guy pushing an old-fashioned lawnmower. *Carbon-Free Lawns*, he calls it. These kids are serious about climate."

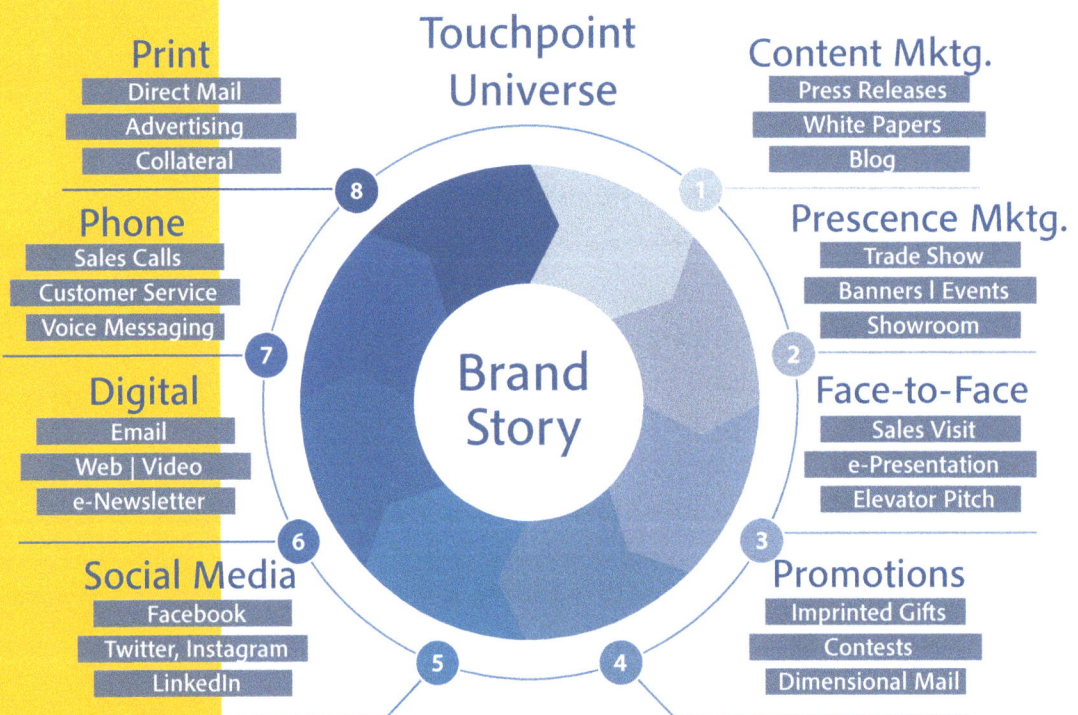

Touchpoint Universe

Brand Story

Print
- Direct Mail
- Advertising
- Collateral

8

Phone
- Sales Calls
- Customer Service
- Voice Messaging

7

Digital
- Email
- Web | Video
- e-Newsletter

6

Social Media
- Facebook
- Twitter, Instagram
- LinkedIn

5

Content Mktg.
- Press Releases
- White Papers
- Blog

1

Prescence Mktg.
- Trade Show
- Banners | Events
- Showroom

2

Face-to-Face
- Sales Visit
- e-Presentation
- Elevator Pitch

3

Promotions
- Imprinted Gifts
- Contests
- Dimensional Mail

4

Rule 3: The most effective touchpoint is free — And, that is your network. I never liked the word *network*, so I prefer the concept of *karass*, invented and explained by Kurt Vonnegut in his seminal book, *Cat's Cradle*. In the book, Bokonon, the leader of a fictionalized religion, explained how a *karass* works:

"Humanity is organized into teams that do God's will," Bokonon explained. *"These teams are called a karass... Karass ignores traditional boundaries like nation, occupation, and family. If you find your life tangled up with somebody else's life for no very logical reasons, that person may be a member of your karass. We find such people by accident, but we stick with them by choice. With any luck, we find a crew that we're happy to bond with."*[2]

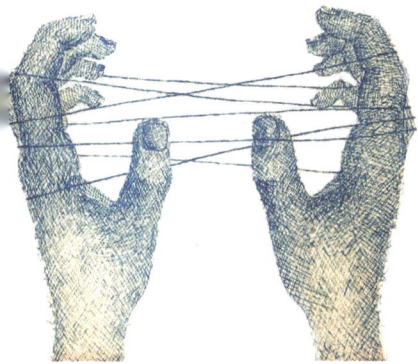

The problem with *network* is that it feels like work — something extraneous you create by handing out business cards at Chamber luncheons. With a *karass,* Vonnegut recognized that life gathers the crew. The people and connections you need to expand your world simply show up.

Working your *karass* has a *Hansel & Gretal* quality to it. You must remain awake to every breadcrumb along the path to see if it leads to a casual conversation - or better, a chance to share your elevator pitch.

Imagine being part of a boy band that nurtures its fan base through the decades. In this way, your *karass* of connections serves you for your entire working life — your friends from college, the corporation where you cut your teeth, old professors, parent's friends, your network of moms, golf buddies, and so on. For this reason, your *karass* should be nurtured and revered like tribal gold. You never know if one of the people on your "crew" will lead to an investor, a partnership, or your first big client.

Rule 4: Keep Social Media Social — The major social platforms offer great tools for pinging your people, but don't use them to directly solicit business. Social means *social.* Use your personal pages on *Facebook, LinkedIn, Instagram,* and *Twitter* to share what you are doing, but keep your marketing posts in a personal context. For example:

2   Kurt Vonnegut, *Cat's Cradle*, Dell 1998

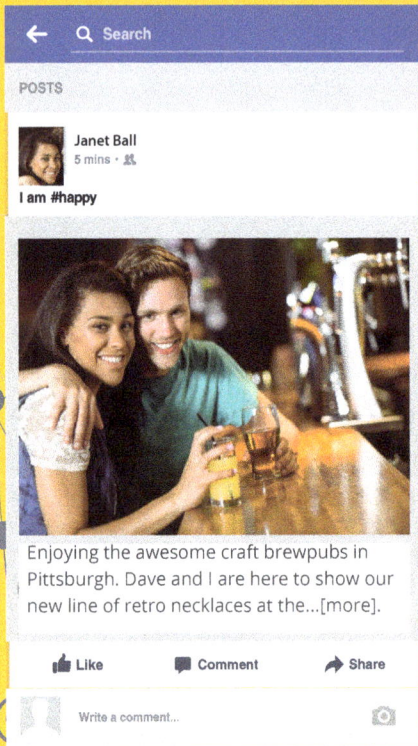

POSTS

Janet Ball
5 mins

I am #happy

Enjoying the awesome craft brewpubs in
Pittsburgh. Dave and I are here to show our
new line of retro necklaces at the...[more].

👍 Like   💬 Comment   ➡ Share

Write a comment...

"Enjoying the awesome craft brewpubs in Pittsburgh. Dave and I are here to show our new line of retro necklaces at the Independent Jeweler's Conference. Steel City's got more hip factor than we expected."

Your social network is interested in you and what you are up to — but your friends don't want to be prospects. You can buy some Adwords on *Google*, but your *karass* carries more weight. Someone in your yoga class might see your Pittsburgh post and mention your products to a friend who owns a jewelry shop. The ripple effect works virally.

Is multi-level marketing the same as working your *karass?* Your *karass* and MLM both leverage personal relationships — but differently. With multi-level marketing, distributors at the top of your "down-line" leverage *your* friends to feed *their* revenue stream. For this reason, MLMs are arguably unethical and not a *karass*. What's more, 73% of MLM distributors make no money (according to AARP), and 99% fail according to a report done for the Federal Trade Commission.[3]

People in your *karass* are on your team, and you are on their teams. They are generous by nature and want to help you out. Since you are leaning on bonds of trust, you have to deliver the goods and reciprocate by returning the favor. Social means *social.*

In my parent's generation, earning a customer's trust worked differently. If you needed life insurance, your nextdoor neighbor, Ned, might recommend Ted Macklevane. After mom fed the kids, Ted would show up in a suit and tie, shake hands, share how he and Ned go way back, then join you on the couch with his sales book. Ted built his whole book of business this way.

---

3 Jon M. Taylor, MBA, Ph.D., Consumer Awareness Institute, "The Case (for and) against Multi-level Marketing."

Rule 5: All roads lead to your Website

Websites are *useless*

if you expect people to find your site, get turned on by what you offer, and start placing orders. The premise of search engine optimization (SEO), referral networks, Google analytics, and referral networks assumes you can build a website that scoops prospects like a butterfly net. The truth is that 50% of all online retail sales come through Amazon. Yes, there are people looking for a chiropractor or dog walking service through a Web search, but more likely, they will encounter your brand in the real world or ask friends for a referral.

Websites are *indespensable*

because real-world touchpoints point to your website. Your friend's referral for a chiropractor or a dog-walker will typically lead to a Web look-up – often while you're on the phone with your friend!

Whether your web visitors come from personal referrals, business cards, bumper stickers, or other real-world touchpoints, your website must solve the visitors' problems, establish their trust, and close the sale. A strong Brand Story makes that happen.

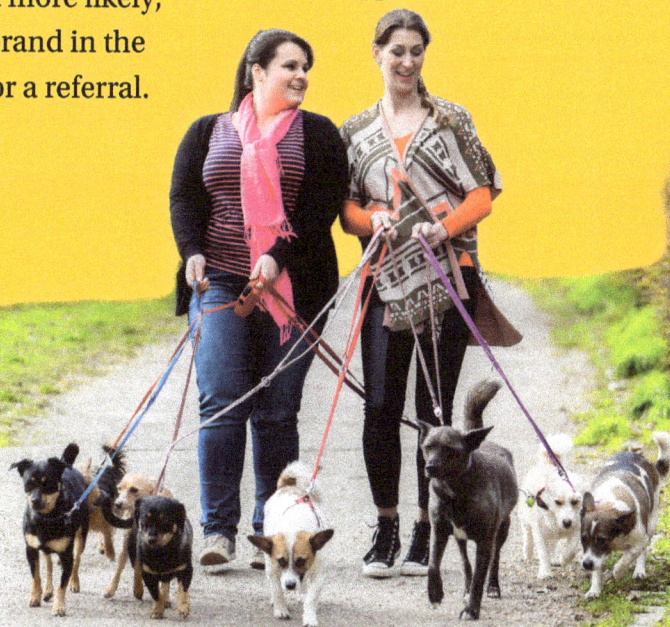

167

Today, the whole Ned-Ted line of trust has been augmented by the Web. Referrals are key, but people ultimately compare products by the *feeling* of the brand. They may not be able to articulate why they like a Web site, but subconsciously, they are responding to your Brand Story — do you feel legit? Is the position clear? Does your story align with *me*? The newest twist is that customers will go to *SelectQuote.com* where there is no Ted — *and no insurance company!* Just a bundler of brands with a click-easy, unassailable brand position: *We Shop Many, Highly-Rated Insurers for your Best Rates.*

Rule 6: Don't sell; build a sales engine — When all your touchpoints work together to drive sales, you have created a sales engine. Example:

Donnie discovered that his Saturday demos at *Ace Hardware* delivered some new customers, but talking about fertilizer was boring. He discovered that most people don't even bother to fertilize, but they all wanted a neat and trimmed lawn.

While Donnie gave demos, he learned more about his customers. They wore *Fitbits* and *Lululemon*, sipped *Keurig* coffees, and showed up pushing high-end jogging strollers.

Donnie asked the store manager to stock some manual reel mowers, and then took it a notch higher – asking him to stock high-end reel mowers from *Fiskars* (the scissors people). Donnie explained to the store manager, "Your customers are into double-wall stainless French presses for their morning coffee — they will want a *Fiskars* mower."

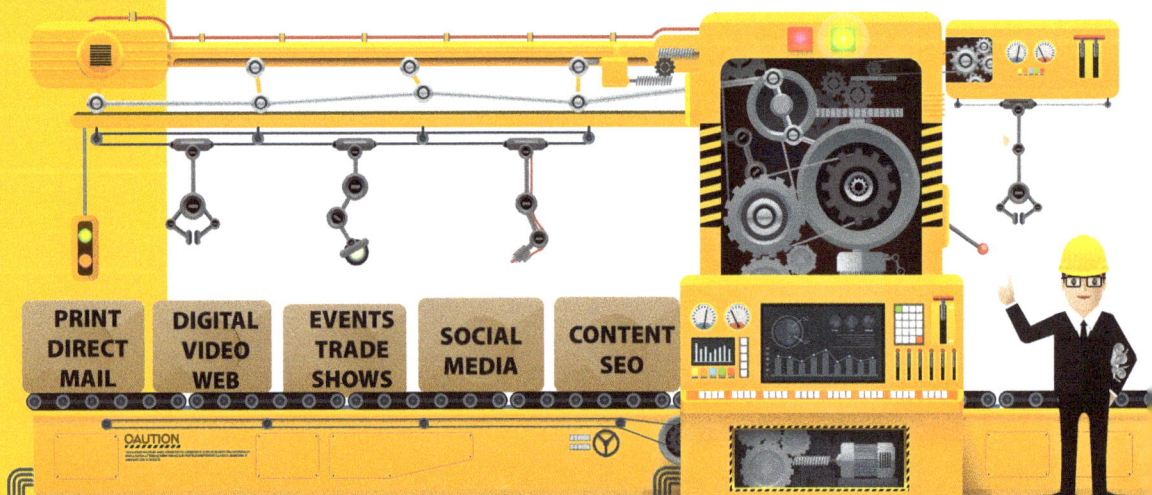

> When all your touchpoints work together, you have created a sales engine.

PRINT DIRECT MAIL

DIGITAL VIDEO WEB

EVENTS TRADE SHOWS

SOCIAL MEDIA

CONTENT SEO

In a stroke of genius, Donnie also purchased *Fiskars* mowers for his crews. Then he changed his brand color to *Fiskars* orange, created a big logo decal for his mowers, and used his decal mower for the store demos. "The hipsters will buy a *Fiskars* mower for the cool factor," Donnie reasoned, "but in the end, they will have me do the work."

The orange mowers became an important touchpoint — in the store and all around town. Importantly, via *Ace Hardware*, Donnie built a sales channel. To build his full marketing engine, Donnie went a step further. He launched a referral program — a free *Fiskars* scissors set for every sales referral from satisfied customers. Donnie could now hand out a branded promo item that reinforced his brand story: *Don't whack grass with gas; save the planet one clip at a time.*

Rule 7: Advertising costs; stories are free — Story-driven content marketing delivers the best bang for your buck for a simple reason: customers connect to stories. The first step in content marketing is to identify your Big Idea, i.e., your brand position. The goal of content marketing is to set the "tent pole" (your big idea) then anchor it with a broad footprint of "stakes."

Donnie built out his big idea — *the need for sustainable lawn care* — with social media stories, press releases for his local paper, topic landing pages to build SEO, a blog entry, and a *YouTube* video of his *Ace Hardware* demo. He reused this material for a series of *LinkedIn* posts and an email campaign.

CONTENT MARKETING

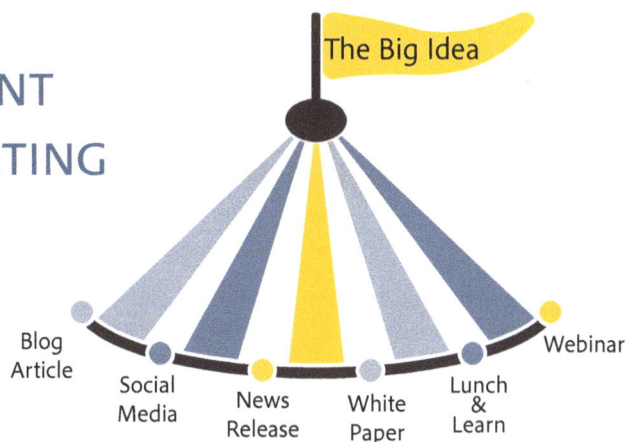

The Big Idea

Blog Article — Social Media — News Release — White Paper — Lunch & Learn — Webinar

Sustainable lawn care

Content Marketing

With *Sustainable Lawn Care* as Donnie's Big Idea, he created his content marketing plan: One new story per month released through multiple platforms. He came up with twelve short topics and tapped them into his phone calendar as a reminder each month: "March: *Petro products in your garden?*" "April: *Pollution-free lawn care,*" "May: *Ancient mower performs new tricks,*" June: *"Put Compost to Work..."* etc.

With this scalable approach, Donnie developed a suite of core stories to drive his brand message into a noisy marketplace — without any out-of-pocket costs.

Write your stories with your target customer in mind.

Let's create your Web site

Short of a Super Bowl ad, your Web site will form the biggest touchpoint in your marketing universe. This step-by-step approach leverages your Brand Story (via your elevator pitch) to create a site that actively engages prospective customers:

Step 1: Find your Brand Mentor — As a shoestring startup, you need help, but you don't have funds for a fancy agency. I suggest finding a successful web site to become your "Brand Mentor" to guide you through the process. Here's how:

Build a board: Follow the Pinterest steps in Chapter 9 to create a board of up to a dozen Web sites from your line of business that have strong brand positions.

- To capture screen grabs, install *FireShot* (or similar). This free extension for *Chrome* and Firefox captures entire Web pages as image files. (*Mac* users can also use cmd + shift + 4 to capture highlighted areas of the screen.)

- Click the *FireShot* icon to save the Web page as an image.

- Create a *Pinterest* Pin from the saved image. Add the pin to a board of "Sites I Like" and "Add a destination link." Comment to include what you like about each page.

Review the brands: Now, review your Pins and eliminate those that don't meet this criterion: "Does the Web site lead with a brand position?" It's easy to tell:

- Does the brand offer to solve a problem or fill a need?

- Does it differentiate itself from other brands? (The original, first, fastest, most convenient, experienced, better formula, new technology, better tasting, lower calories, faster-acting, cheapest, highest quality, and so on).

- Does it tell a Brand Story? Do all the pieces and parts add up, meaning, do the message, mission, design, back-story, people, and personality fit together to create a sense of brand or a cohesive story?

- Do you feel an affinity with this company?

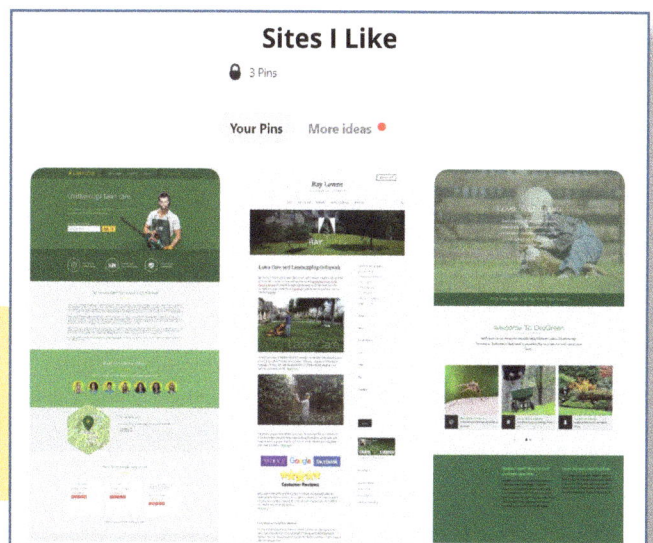

Create a board of sites you like.

Sara's "mentor:" Catalina Estrada

Let your mentor's thinking guide you across the blank pages.

Once you find your Mentor, you might ask:

- Is your Mentor's site sparse or verbose? Colorful or minimalist? Friendly or authoritative?

- Does your Mentor's site establish an unassailable position, lure you in with a story, or hit you hard with the offer?

- What Web components does your Mentor use: web forms, sign-ups, side-bars, widgets, testimonials, trial offers, videos, etc.?

Work with your Mentor: As you build your site, you will hit stumbling blocks. That's when you ask, "What would my Mentor do?" We used this approach to great effect when I helped my friend Sara Anderson navigate her path from stay-at-home mom to successful fabric designer.

Sara's Brand Story workshop identified her target customer as a successful mid-aged woman with wildness in her heart and a hidden artistic, bohemian flair. We found a kindred spirit with designer, Catalina Estrada (*catalinaestrada.com*).

"My heart needs rhythm, my mind needs harmony, and my soul needs color."

Catalina's brand position mirrored Sara's:

"My heart needs rhythm, my mind needs harmony, and my soul needs color." - Catalina Estrada

We built Sara's site, *SaraAnderson. com*, by asking when stumped, "What would Catalina do?"

Surprisingly, Sara's site and Catalina's site look completely different (as they should!), but their unconditional love of nature's colors, textures, and beauty are shared by both.

SARA anderson

Invites you to indulge your sensual nature

Sara's Web site:

Cachemira

Cachemira scarves celebrate nature with the luxury of cashmere.

Après Wear

Kimonos and caftans offer sensual sophistication after yoga or the beach.

>> View kimonos   >> View kaftans

Step 2: Build out your message

Good thing you crafted your Elevator Pitch. Now you're going to put it to work. We will pull language from the your Elevator Pitch and plug it straight into the Web site. Let's review the Teamfuel three-minute Elevator Pitch:

Attention Grabber:

If you invest $100,000 in stocks, do you time your investment when prices are low? Of course!

How about $100,000 worth of fuel? Do you fill your tanks when prices go down? If you think that's impossible, you're wrong.

TeamFuel has developed technology to help you take command of your entire fuel picture. We act as your outsourced "fuel department" to get the best prices from the marketplace.

The Customer's Problem:

You've probably found ways to streamline costs throughout your organization — in HR, IT, employee benefits – everywhere except the one area it hurts the most: fuel management.

Large fleets and airlines employ full-time fuel professionals to manage procurement. Smaller users, like you, must deal with old fuel technology, non-expert buyers, and rising administrative costs.

More importantly, price volatility makes it difficult for you to make effective refill decisions — especially with rising prices, complex forecasting, delivery logistics, and smaller volumes.

Our Solution:

TeamFuel has developed the industry's first end-to-end solution that manages fuel needs throughout the supply chain. Our value proposition is simple:

1. *We study your fuel operations to optimize your supply chain,*

2. *We implement intelligent fuel technology to streamline procurement and operations, and*

3. You enjoy guaranteed savings when you let TeamFuel serve as your outsourced "fuel department."

How it Works:

1. **Fuel IQ™**: *First, TeamFuel studies your enterprise-wide fuel operations to develop a 14-point fuel profile to guide fuel procurement throughout your organization.*

2. **ThinkTank™** – *Next, we network every tank in your system and integrate them into our national storage picture. We optimize procurement decisions at a tremendous scale, system-wide.*

3. **PriceQuery™** – *Finally, our system searches for market trends and spot opportunities and delivers the best fuel price every day through demand aggregation, market timing, freight cost consolidation, and contract leveraging.*

Results:

Starting with a baseline assessment of your current costs, we build a cost-reduction model that tracks your actual savings in ten key areas.

Total cost savings are guaranteed. Save up to 65% in perations and 35% in fuel costs when you outsource your fuel operations to TeamFuel.

Create Your Home Page

Think of your home page as your Brand Story with pictures. You will build out your Elevator Pitch as a scrollable page.

Since most Web visits are on the phone, scroll-down page layouts are easier for users. Each block of copy should include a link — again to avoid the menu.

For desktop visitors, the top-level menu should be logical and compact. In addition to the customary links, you may wish to include a top-level menu link for your secret sauce, big idea, or lead offering.

The home page uses a stack of horizontal rows (1-6). The sequence is logical:

LOGO HOME | ABOUT | SOLUTION | RESULTS | NEWS | CONTACT

1. Featured image or slider:
Big brand statement of the problem and solution
Learn more

2.  **SOLUTION**: Explain what you do and how your offering uniquely solves the customer's needs.

Image or video.

How it Works: One or two rows of product features that link to solution pages.

3.  Feature One    Feature Two    Feature Three

4. **Real world results:** Proof points that illustrate the effectiveness of the solution and the satisfaction of your customers.

Testimonial

5. **From the blog or news** Display the latest blog post, press release, or news story.

6. ## Call to Action Statement
Learn more

Let's look at each section:

1. Big Brand Statement: Grab the reader with a statement that explains why your brand matters. It needs to be short, direct, and scream differentiation. Tell the reader that you can solve their problem in a unique, new way. You can pose it as a question, a splashy introduction, or a pithy version of your positioning statement.

The full-width featured image can fill the entire screen or be narrower to reveal the content below the fold. An optional slider can run a sequence of images/statements – useful if you have several products or ideas to highlight. Still images are preferred over videos.

2. Solution: Your Web visitor might spend six seconds on your site to know what you're selling. Pull directly from your elevator pitch here to describe your product or service. If you have an overview video, put it here. Include a link that leads to your Solution page.

3. Features: If your visitor becomes curious to discover *How it Works,* you have won half the battle. Include 3 to 8 features (one or two rows). Include icons, images, and brand names.

4. Results/Testimonial: Offer real-world results, performance metrics, and benefit statements to show that you can deliver the goods. Testimonials add credibility with client names and logos.

5. News: Make sure your business looks alive. Update with fresh content from your news or blog pages. *Squarespace* uses Summary Blocks. The *Divi* theme for *Wordpress* uses the Blog Module.

6. Call to Action: What action do you want visitors to take? Restate your big idea by inviting them to solve their problem with your offer. Call now, get a free quote, take a survey, download a white paper, view a demo, and so on.

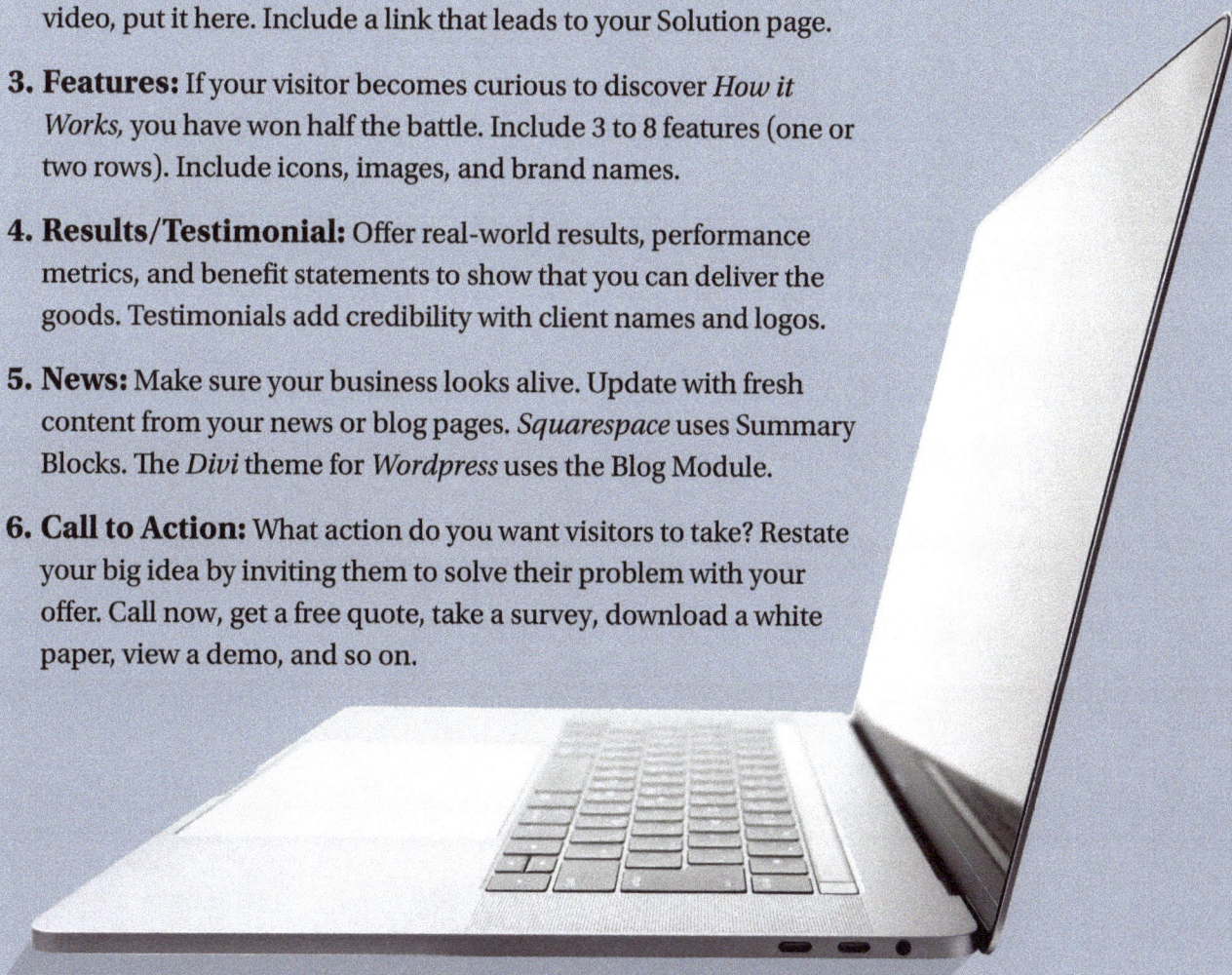

Step 3: Design Your Layout

Place your edited content from the Elevator Pitch into a rough layout. PowerPoint offers a quick and easy tool. This layout captures statements from the pitch and drops them directly into the Web template.

Your job is not be a Web designer – just a brand storyteller – so your PowerPoint layout does not need to be pretty. You can even use a pencil and a large pad. At some point, you will choose to hand the project to a Web pro, and this may be that point. Whether it's you or a pro, the designer will need structured Web copy and a basic layout as a starting point.

I created the Teamfuel web mockup using these easy-to-use tools:

- *PowerPoint*: Create a very tall layout: (In Office 365, use the Portrait setting from *Design | Slide Size | Custom Slide Size).*

- *Shutterstock*: For the images. You can *try* images without fees.

- *Coolors* (coolors.co): To create the color scheme.

- *TheNounProject.com*: For the icons.

- And the Elevator Pitch for the content.

teamfuel. HOME | ABOUT | SOLUTION | CLIENT SUCCESS | NEWS | CONTACT

REDUCE FUEL COSTS
When you take command of your entire fuel picture.

Learn how

TeamFuel has developed the industry's first end-to-end solution that reduces your fuel costs by managing procurement throughout the supply chain.
Watch the video

How it works: *Enjoy guaranteed savings when you let TeamFuel serve as your outsourced "fuel department."*

1. Fuel IQ™
We build a **14-point fuel profile** to guide procurement **throughout** your organization.

2. ThinkTank™
We **network your tanks** into our system to optimize fuel procurement at a nationwide scale.

3. PriceQuery™
We deliver the **best fuel price** through demand aggregation, market timing, consolidation, and more.

Save up to 35% in fuel costs:
We build a cost-reduction model that tracks your actual savings from day one. Save in fuel procurement, automation, productivity, overhead, management, service, maintenance, compliance and contingencies. more

Janet Roe
Pro-Fleet USA
"Teamfuel is always on duty, monitoring the markets. We saved 13 cents per gallon. Plus, their field monitoring reduced our maintenance overhead."

Teamfuel NEWS
See us at the *GLOBAL FLEET CONFERENCE*
June 4-6 | Hilton Miami

"Next generation fuel management is here..."
FLEET SOLUTIONS
Read more

Save up to 65% in operations and 35% in fuel costs when you outsource your fuel operations to TeamFuel.
Learn How

Capture content from your elevator pitch:

Attention Grabber:

TeamFuel has developed the tools and practices to help companies ==take command of their entire fuel picture==. In effect, we act as your outsourced "fuel department" to manage your operations and get the best fuel prices from the marketplace. Here's why effective fuel management is critical.

The Customer's Problem:

Today, the world's largest fleet organizations employ full-time professionals to cut costs and streamline operations. You've probably found ways to streamline costs throughout your organization — in HR, IT, employee benefits – everywhere except the one area it hurts the most: fuel management. Like most fuel users, you're likely handicapped by old fuel technology, non-expert buyers, and rising administrative costs.

What's more, rising prices in a volatile market make it nearly impossible for your fuel buyers to make effective refill decisions — especially with rising fuel prices, complex forecasting, delivery logistics, and more.

Our Solution:

==TeamFuel has developed the industry's first end-to-end solution that manages fuel needs throughout the supply chain.== Our value proposition is simple:

1. We study your fuel operations to optimize your supply chain,
2. We implement intelligent fuel technology to streamline procurement and operations, and
3. ==You enjoy guaranteed savings when you let TeamFuel serve as your outsourced "fuel department."==

How it Works:

1. ==Fuel IQ™: First, TeamFuel studies your enterprise-wide fuel operations to develop a 14-point fuel profile to guide fuel procurement throughout your organization.==
2. ==ThinkTank™ – Next, we network every tank in your system and integrate them into our national storage picture. This allows us to optimize procurement decisions at tremendous scale, system-wide.==
3. ==PriceQuery™ – Finally, our system searches for market trends and spot opportunities and delivers the best fuel price every day through demand aggregation, market timing, freight cost consolidation, and contract leveraging.==

Results:

Starting with a baseline assessment of your current costs, ==we build a cost-reduction model that tracks your actual savings from day one. Savings are tracked in ten key areas,== including fuel procurement, automation, productivity, overhead, management, service, maintenance, regulatory compliance and contingencies. Total cost savings are guaranteed.

Bottom line, your organization can realize significant savings: ==Up to 65% in operations and 35% in fuel costs when you outsource your fuel operations to TeamFuel.==

Step 4: Build Your Web Site

There are a million ways to skin this cat, but I will boil it down to two:

Squarespace: This all-in-one Web platform provides hosting and design templates in a self-contained environment. You select a design and customize it with your content, layout, and images. If you are competent with basic office applications, you can build a Website on *Squarespace*. Monthly fees are higher than *WordPress*, and the level of customization is lower, but most businesses should be able to tell their story within a stock template. *Wix* is another plug-and-play option.

WordPress: This open-source platform connects to a vast universe of 55,000 third-party plug-ins, plus design tools, templates, freelancers, and hosting companies. Whatever business niche you're in — non-profit, education, downloads, news, travel, music, food, sports, technology — you'll find themes and plugins to support your needs. You will also be able to integrate other business applications into your site through a vast range of API connections.

Choosing your platform: This decision should not hang on cost or technical abilities, but rather, functionality. *Squarespace* is well-suited for personal sites, small business, and the creative industry. The movie company, Pixar, reportedly uses *Squarespace*. *WordPress* does more — but requires regular maintenance.

Nearly every business application offers integration with *WordPress* — *Salesforce, Quickbooks, Meetup, Grubhub, Hubspot, Mailchimp, Zendesk, Slack*, etc. The downside with this flexibility is that greater technical skill is needed to build and maintain *WordPress* Web sites. Don't let this scare you. Plan on hiring a Web guy (or gal).

With your layout in hand and Brand Mentor for guidance, you can find a *WordPress* developer on *Fiverr.com* who can build a simple site for $500 that performs exactly to your needs. A U.S. designer might cost anywhere from $1500 to $10,000 depending on the complexity of the site. You can follow the same *Fiverr* hiring process as with the logo design.

If you build a *WordPress* site, consider working with a designer who uses *Divi* from *Elegant Themes*. *Divi* is a full-featured module-based platform that lets you build a *WordPress* Web site with some of the *Squarespace* ease.

The hosting savings from *WordPress* compared to *Squarespace* may help recoup your design costs. There are numerous low-cost hosting companies to choose from (*GoDaddy, Bluehost, Dreamhost*, and *Hostgator*). I often recommend *Siteground*.

SQUARESPACE

WORDPRE

You've cut costs in every area...
EXCEPT WHERE IT HURTS THE MOST.

TeamFuel optimizes your fuel procurement

Enjoy guaranteed savings when you let TeamFuel serve as your outsourced "fuel department."

The world's largest fleet organizations employ full-time professionals to cut costs and streamline operations. But for most fuel users, old fuel technology, non-expert buyers, and rising administrative costs hinder efficient procurement.

What's more, rising prices in a volatile market make it difficult for your fuel buyers to make effective refill decisions — especially with rising fuel prices, complex forecasting, delivery logistics, and more.

Our Solution:

TeamFuel has developed the industry's first end-to-end solution that manages fuel needs throughout the supply chain. Our value proposition is simple:

We study your fuel operations to optimize your supply chain,

We implement intelligent fuel technology to streamline procurement and operations, You enjoy guaranteed savings when you let TeamFuel serve as your outsourced "fuel department."

1. Fuel IQ™
We build a **14-point fuel profile** to guide procurement throughout your organization.

2. ThinkTank™
We **network your tanks** into our system to optimize fuel procurement at a nationwide scale.

3. PriceQuery™
We deliver the **best fuel price** through demand aggregation, market timing, consolidation, and more.

Save up to 65% in operations and 35% in fuel costs when you outsource your fuel operations to TeamFuel.
To learn how, call 800-000-0000 or visit teamfuel.com

Design a Sales Sheet

You can quickly make a sales sheet using the same elevator pitch content.

Whether you hire a *Fiverr* guy, have a friend versed in *Adobe InDesign* (the pro standard), or design it yourself with *MS Publisher* or even *PowerPoint* — I leave that to you. *MS Word* is not recommended. Make it a full bleed (images trimmed to the edge). Bottom line, don't hand out an amateurish design.

Use an online printer (*PSPrint, CatPrint, Imagers)* to print your sales sheets. Your *Fedex* print shop is an option if you need just a few copies.

Build out your Touchpoints

Let's finish where we began: Turning three touchpoints into six, and six into twelve. Consider all the places people might bump into your Brand Story:

WEB MARKETING

- Enhance your Website's SEO with targeted content.
- Offer quarterly Webinars.
- Submit your listing to online business directories.
- Sign up for *Google Local, Yelp*, and similar.
- Launch a *Google Ads* campaign

DIRECT MARKETING

- Distribute flyers into mailbox flags.
- Send direct mailers through *Every Door Direct Mail* from the *USPS*.
- Create an e-newsletter (and sign-up form), and send out quarterly, even if you are starting with a handful of contacts.

CONTENT MARKETING

- Create topical blog posts and articles to repurpose on *LinkedIn* and *Medium*.
- Write a short downloadable ebook to demonstrate thought leadership in your field.
- Create demonstration videos for *YouTube*.
- Create a Question/Answer UGC (User Generated Content) page to increase your *Google* footprint.

PRESENCE MARKETING

- Post a business card at your yoga studio or the hardware store. How about all the hardware stores?
- If you're a contractor, attach an outdoor acrylic brochure holder to your truck or place a yard sign on the job.
- Rent motorized searchlights.
- Build a float for your small-town parade.
- Order some pop-up banner stands.
- Attend trade shows and events as an exhibitor, or cheaper, don't buy a booth. Walk around the show to make connections and hand out cards.

SOCIAL MEDIA

- Purchase targeted advertising on social media.

- Use *LinkedIn* to start conversations with potential leads.

- Post regular updates on *Facebook* with a mostly personal (slightly business) angle.

PROMOTIONAL GOODS

- Order embroidered logo caps or polo shirts and wear them.

- Keep soft doggy Frisbees on hand (with logo/tagline) to hand out when you're out and about.

- Integrate a promo item with a direct mail campaign: For example, a free *Starbucks* card if a prospect takes a survey.

ADVERTISING

- Create a radio spot for *Spotify* or *Pandora*.

- Run a TV spot on your local cable network.

- Sponsor a kids soccer team.

- Create a low-budget Times Square-like postcard: Book a cheap digital billboard for a short run. Shoot a beauty shot of the sign at sunset, and turn it into a postcard promoting your launch.

AT THE TOP OF YOUR LIST, WORK YOUR KARASS

- Invite your friends to a launch party.

- Contact old business connections from years ago.

- Go to your inbox and send a personal email to every viable contact.

- Ask five business acquaintances if they know someone who might use your service.

- Call your mom. She's a shameless promoter.

Or give your services away free!

My massage therapist friend, Gail Cole, started this way – as does every major app with a free starter plan. Today, Gail is so booked she's not accepting new clients.

Cat's Cradle sums up what it means to be a DIY brand strategist:

> *"Self-taught, are you?" Julian asked Newt.*
> *"Isn't everybody?" Newt inquired.*
> *"Very good answer," Julian replied.*

Michael Jones (left), President of Thrive Farmers with two growers

BRAND STORIES.

The Story of Thrive Farmers Coffee

Great brands don't emerge *ex nihilo* – out of nothing. They begin with a story — often when life sends the founder a wake-up call.

What was working, suddenly does not. After an illness, break-up, financial failure, or career shift, the founder's creative engines rev up to reinvent oneself. In every instance, the disruptive force becomes the creative force — a message from the universe: "Time to stop what you're doing and change course."

Thrive Farmers, the farmer-to-table coffee brand that supplies over 2300 *Chick-fil-A* stores, began when three life-disruption stories intersected. For each of the founders, the disruptive force became the creative force to birth a paradigm-shfting brand. The saga began when a young twenty-something Costa Rican coffee farmer, Alejandro Garcia, realized that the family's coffee farm was no longer sustainable.

"Growing up on a coffee farm, I watched my mom and dad struggle to earn a living," Alejandro (Alé) remembered. "A whole year's work and then the money would not last for more than a few months for food."

Alejandro's five-generation coffee farm was at substantial risk of failure, so he became determined to do something about it. "I always had this feeling that it didn't need to be this way," Alé said.

"I wanted to find a way for my family to live well doing what we love – and that is growing coffee. I had a dream that if we had our own equipment and did our own processing, my family could make it. We would get enough money out of our crop to live a better life.

Alé and his dad

"So, I went to the States and worked in a family-style buffet restaurant in Pennsylvania Amish country for two long years," Alé continued. "I saved my money in a shoebox, and when I returned, my dad and me, we built our own processing mill. No other farmer in Monteverde had ever done something like this."

Alé saved $40,000 over two years. When he came back, he invested his hard-earned money in coffee processing equipment, and by so doing, changed the trajectory of the coffee farming business. The key was a chance meeting with Ken Lander, an American trial lawyer who also faced a crossroads. Ken had retired from Atlanta to Costa Rica and bought a coffee farm — mostly as a hobby. Ken had hoped to live off his real estate investments back in the States, but suddenly that plan came to a crashing halt.

MarketWatch

The Community Bank closed, 20th failure of the year

By John Letzing
Published: Nov 21, 2008 6:17 p.m. ET

SHARE | COMMENTS 0

SAN FRANCISCO (MarketWatch) -- Loganville, Ga.-based The Community Bank has been closed by regulators, the Federal Deposit Insurance Corporation said late Friday, marking the 20th bank failure of the year amid the ongoing financial crisis. All of Community Bank's deposits have been transferred to Bank of Essex, the FDIC said. The Bank of Essex, the FDIC said. The assets of $681 million and total the FDIC said.

"I was reading an article in *La Nacion*, Costa Rica's newspaper, on November 24, 2008," Ken remembered. "The title was '*20th Bank Para Romper en los Estados Unidos.*' It was a story about my little bank in Loganville, Georgia, where all of my exit strategy investments were centered. Reading the article, I discovered that my real estate and assets were going to disappear, and all I had was a coffee farm to survive."

Ken suddenly needed his gentleman's coffee farm to feed his family. He also learned that making a living as a coffee farmer didn't add up.

"I started a coffee shop, *The Common Cup*," Ken continued. "I gave coffee away by the cup to entice tourists to roast and buy coffee by the bag from my farm. I quickly ran out of coffee and went looking for other farmers in the area to see if they had any beans. Alejandro had a shop, and finally, I convinced him to join me and bring some of his beans to sell at my shop."

Over the next two years, Ken and Alé forged ahead. Without much thought to the implications, they achieved possibly the first vertical integration of the coffee supply chain by growing, harvesting, processing, roasting, serving, and shipping their coffee – albeit on a tourist shop scale.

Ken and Alé started the *San Rafael Sustainable Coffee Initiative* (SRSCI) to bring coffee farmers together. They began with three farmers who quickly grew to eight. More importantly, their humble initiative became the seed for a new approach to the business of coffee. Unlike "Fair Trade" and other marketing concepts, the SRSCI connected coffee from the farmer directly to the consumer.

The Common Cup
Monteverde. Costa Rica

At this point, a third entrepreneur, Michael Jones from Atlanta, entered the picture. Michael had built a medical device management company, *Implantable Provider Group (IPG)*, that revolutionized the supply chain for surgical implants. Michael could hardly imagine that his medical industry expertise as a "supply chain disrupter" would find new purpose in Ken and Alé's coffee business high in Costa Rica's cloud forest.

Michael had scored major contracts in the medical industry and built a successful company, but he would need venture financing to take his company to the next level. "Other people's money" would secure his dream to become an industry player, but also expose himself to risk.

Costa Rica, Cloud Forest

187

The investors forced Michael out as CEO. With this humbling turn of events, Michael chose to take a sabbatical.

"I was planning to take a year off, and I just couldn't do it," Michael recounted. "Within four weeks, I was bored to tears and needed something to give me focus. And that's how I landed in the world of coffee."

"By the time *Thrive* came around," Michael continued, "I had stopped drinking coffee altogether! I tried to find a coffee that didn't taste charred. My wife's dad, who was a *Blue Mountain Coffee* farmer in Jamaica, was also struggling. Japan was paying a lot for his coffee, yet he wasn't making much money. So, I helped him unravel the value chain for his coffee. As I studied his business, I began to see the social justice issues around coffee. This was at a time I was trying to redefine the purpose of my life."

An acquaintance introduced Michael to Ken Lander during Ken's foray into coffee farming. "I asked Ken about his journey and specifically, 'Hey, do you have any idea why my father-in-law isn't making any money selling premier coffee?'" Michael recounted.

"Ken opened the curtain to the business. He told me about the 'coyotes' — the middlemen — who have to buy as cheap as they can because they can't know for sure how the market will move. Suddenly, I felt a calling. Okay, this is what I'm supposed to do with my life."

Michael traveled to Costa Rica to meet with farmers. They explained how they didn't make enough to cover the cost of production and how they were being forced to quit. "I learned there was 70% farmer attrition in Costa Rica over a ten-year period," Michael continued. "So, I thought if somebody doesn't turn this around, we're not going to have coffee."

"I asked guidance from God, and at that point, I had already changed the course of my life. I asked, 'Lord, show me something that matters to You, and I will focus my efforts on that.' I recognized that these farmers were people who mattered to me – people who couldn't change their plight, and needed help."

I used my experience, and specifically my supply chain experience, to find a solution. This was during the start of the farm-to-table movement, so why not bring it to coffee?"

Michael Jones approached our firm, *Design Coup,* to build the new brand. We side-stepped the usual focus on flavor, aroma, mountain-grown, and the rest. Instead, we built the brand story around the farmer. Each bag had a farmer's story and picture. In those early days, each batch was sourced directly from a farmer to the consumer. We developed the brand name, *Thrive Farmers,* to push the key idea: *Helping farmers thrive.*

Michael (center) with two farmers

The *Thrive Farmers* business model removed the middlemen, brokers, and processors — all who took their cut. *Thrive* partners with farmers through a revenue-sharing model to bring the crop directly to market to give farmers higher, more predictable, and more transparent pricing. *Thrive* also invests in the farm communities to tackle their economic, social, and environmental challenges.

Original packaging

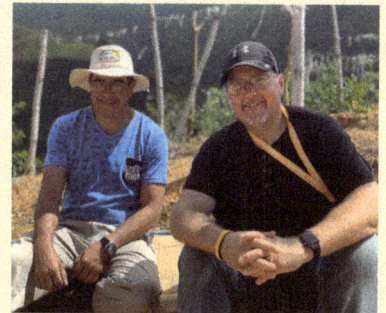

"One of our goals was to educate consumers," Ken Lander explained, "Once you understand how something is grown and who grows it, you begin to appreciate that products don't just show up in a store. You begin to see the humanity in your role as a consumer. You see how your desire to be appreciated for your work and to have a purpose in life is no different from what the people producing your food seek. With *Thrive,* we wanted to create a movement that would grow slowly and organically into the mainstream."

But that's not what happened. The idea of farmer-direct coffee caught on, and so *Thrive* had to scale quickly. Scaling a small-batch concept into mass distribution took vision — but also a big dose of destiny. The first door to open was *Earth Fare*, the North Carolina based healthy supermarket chain.

Ken Lander (right)

"A restaurant owner in Asheville, North Carolina, started serving our coffee," Michael Jones remembered. "He introduced us to an executive at *Earth Fare* who saw how our story would connect with their customer base. We took six *Earth Fare* executives to Costa Rica so they could pick coffee and meet our farmers."

Earth Fare, coffee demo

189

Unfortunately, *Earth Fare* was sold, and the new private equity owners dropped *Thrive*. One door closed, but a bigger one opened.

"One of our board members from Raleigh, North Carolina, ate breakfast two or three times a week at the local *Chick-fil-A* and began to make friends with the operator," Michael remembered. At Christmas, he gave a gift set of our coffee to the guy. The store operator was intrigued by the brand story on our package. As it turned out, he was the grandson to *Chick-fil-A's* founder — Truett Cathy!"

S. Truett Cathy had three kids – Dan (CEO), Bubba (Senior Vice President), and Trudy (Board member). When Trudy was still a teen, she moved from Atlanta to Birmingham to become the youngest operator of a *Chick-fil-A* — at age 19. Today, Trudy is a noted philanthropist. Following tradition, in 2008, Trudy's son, John White IV, left Atlanta to become an owner-operator of a *Chick-fil-A in* Durham, NC.

"So when the store operator read the blurb on our package, he got excited," Michael continued. "He said, 'Hey, I think our corporate guys need to know about this.'"

The brand concept – *supporting the farmer who brought this bag to your table* – created unique differentiation for a commodity product.

As fate would have it, *Chick-fil-A* was deep into a revamp of its coffee. David Farmer, the chain's VP of product strategy and development, explained (in something of an understatement), "Our customers might put up with our coffee… but it's not something we're proud of."[1]

---

1 "Chick-fil-A Replaces its Coffee for Specialty Brew," Business Week, 2014-08-12

Around this same time, *Chick-fil-A* was planning to relaunch its coffee with a national coffee brand as their supplier. Also, at this time, *Chick-fil-A* was embroiled in the same-sex marriage debate with proponents and opponents facing off in a cultural battle. Comments by Dan Cathy further inflamed the controversy.

"The national coffee chain suddenly pushed the pause button. They didn't want to associate their brand with a culture war," Michael continued. "So that was our opening. *Chick-fil-A* could rethink their strategy while we prepared to pitch *Thrive Farmers*. The national chain eventually came back, but it was too late. *Chick-fil-A* said, 'Yeah... we may not be a good fit.' *Chick-fil-A* went in another direction — and it was with us."

Chick-fil-A's David Farmer explained the company's decision to go with *Thrive*:

"The true magic of this relationship [with Thrive] is that not only does the coffee taste great, we also found a partner who shares our belief that business can be bigger than the bottom line. Now we can serve our customers an amazing cup of coffee that also will improve the lives of the farmers who grow it."

Like the proverbial dog that catches the car, *Thrive* now had a big problem — the nation's third-biggest fast-food chain consumed a lot of coffee. Michael Jones' faith was instrumental in meeting the challenge.

"The whole reason for pursuing coffee was to affect change, and I knew the only way to make meaningful change was through scale. From our earliest days, I would question, 'What does our company look like to scale?' We talked to bigger organizations and potential partners that had the capacity and knowledge to grow with us. When *Chick-fil-A* entered the picture, we had already identified partnerships that could help us meet those volumes. That was one of those providential things.

"Yes, we were selling a dream, but we would have never had the ability to make it come true if we hadn't sold that dream.

"I've always looked at talent through the same lens," Michael said. "The people I want to associate with, learn from, and ultimately hire are people who have more knowledge than me, especially in key areas. So whether it's supply chain or finance or operations or whatever, the key is to build a team of people and trust them to do their jobs."

It had been six years since I had helped *Thrive Farmers* launch its brand. I thought about the early days when we were hell-bent on challenging the status quo, launching a disruptive brand, and pitching it to *Chick-fil-A*. In this interview, I asked Michael, "Now that you've grown to a national scale, how do you keep your original brand values alive? As a much bigger company, how do you continue to connect to consumers and resonate in peoples' hearts?"

Michael thought for a moment and replied, "It comes down to the voice of the customer. You have to understand what's important to the customer. You can't fall asleep at the wheel. With every decision, we have to ensure it resonates with customers with what they want. The real question to ask, 'Is our brand promising something that matters to them?' If customers don't care, then why bother?"

NEW
FARMER-DIRECT
specialty-grade coffee

CoffeeWithAStory.com

"Ultimately, there has to be alignment between two things: Your core values and what's relevant to customers. I've heard it said many times: 'What people say about you when you're not there — that really is your brand.'"

I asked Ken if there was a visible change in the farming communities that produce the coffee for *Thrive Farmers*:

"Thrive is more than a brand," Ken answered. "In our farming communities, you now see kids going to college, houses being built, and more investment in the farms.

"Importantly, farmers have seen their perspective of the coffee business change. They now have hope. They have a new set of expectations when they sell their beans to other buyers. They are not just farmers; they are empowered to be business people and entrepreneurs."

If you're a coffee (or tea) connoisseur, visit *ThriveFarmers. com* and try a bag. You'll support farmers by sipping coffee.

"Is our brand promising something that matters to them? If customers don't care, then why bother?"

Mandy Roberts, Owner, *Form Yoga*

The Story of *FORM YOGA*

How Fortune, the mysterious fourth ingredient, intervened for a single mom.

A few years back, I fell in love with a fledgling yoga studio that opened around the corner from our agency. *Form Yoga* was started by a designer friend, Michele Emmons Dehaven, who launched the studio in the vacant half of her office space. Unfortunately, putting a yoga studio inside a design studio turned out to be one studio too many. This dubious idea for a business nearly failed, but eventually succeeded when Michele passed the torch to a new owner, Mandy Roberts.

Starting a business traditionally requires three ingredients: a product or service, some capital, and a market. I subscribe to a mysterious fourth ingredient that's critical, but wholly enigmatic. I call it Fortune.

Mandy Robert's journey with *Form Yoga* shines a light on Fortune – the mysterious force that opens doors, demands risk, and requires vigilance, self-confidence, and trust. Some people see a Divine hand in Fortune, others see the power of personal moxie, and still others call it luck. Regardless, we sense Fortune when it plays its cards. I asked Mandy to share her improbable journey from single mom to successful brand to see if she could shed light on the workings of Fortune.

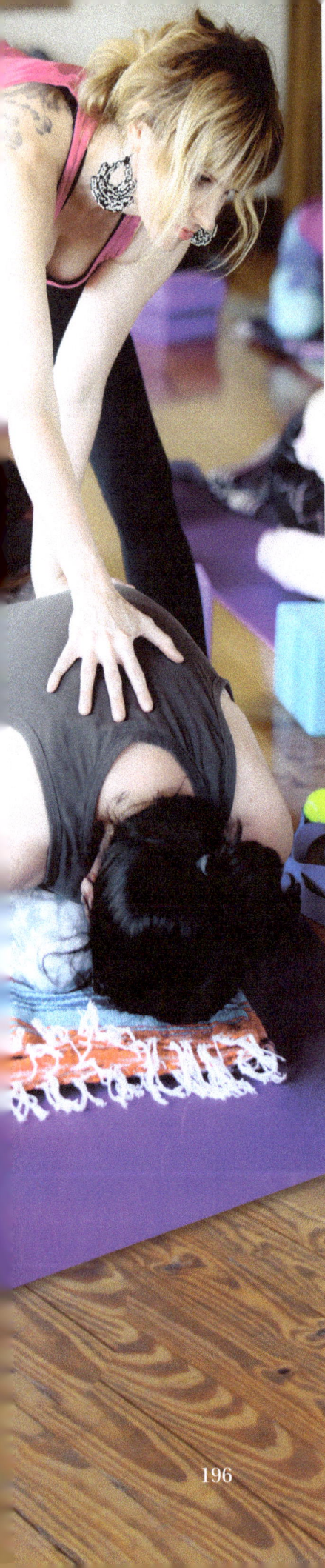

Bruce: Thank you for sharing your brand story. If I remember at the time, this was more than a business story. Yoga was instrumental in keeping you from falling apart — physically and emotionally.

Mandy: Very much so. I was married for fifteen years, and for much of it, yoga was my escape. I practiced seven days a week, sometimes twice a day. My marriage was crumbling, and the more it crumbled, the better I got at yoga. That was my release. When my husband and I decided to split, we had become two very different people, two different outlooks, and two different paths on how to get what we wanted in life. From the outside, it looked like we had a picture-perfect marriage, but we had our shit.

Bruce: So, what did you do?

Mandy: My friends would ask, "How are you going to support yourself as a single mom?" And my answer was always, "I don't know." And they would ask, "So what are you gonna do, be a yoga teacher?" And my answer was always, "No, yoga teachers don't make any money. I can't support my family on that." After being pressed and pressed, I conceded, "I guess I'll be a yoga teacher." I still thought I would be able to fix my marriage.

Bruce: What happened next?

Mandy: I realized I couldn't fix my marriage. It was my birthday when I decided, okay, I'm going to yoga teacher training. I got on the Internet and found a training that started the next weekend. I had never heard of the studio, never heard of the teacher, but wrote down the name. I asked around, "Ever hear of this guy?" My teacher's jaw dropped. "Oh my God, he's amazing."

Bruce: So, after that, you started teaching?

Mandy: Not exactly. The owner of the studio where I practiced wouldn't give me a class to teach because I wasn't a seasoned teacher. She only hired teachers who had a following. But she let me substitute.

Bruce: So now, you're a substitute.

Mandy: Yes. But interestingly, a very prominent teacher in town, Cheryl Crawford, happened to take my class — the very first class I subbed! As it turned out, Cheryl was helping a graphic designer friend, Michele Emmons Dehaven, start a new studio, *Form Yoga,* inside her design firm.

Sensing Fortune at work, I located Cheryl on Facebook to ask what she remembered of Mandy's first class. Cheryl wrote back immediately:

"Hi Bruce! I took Mandy's very first class and knew right away that she had what it takes to be an incredible teacher. I suppose you can call that instinct or an inner knowing. Most teachers are not in their authentic voice for many years. The big studio in town wouldn't hire Mandy, so I told Michele to hire her."

Cheryl Crawford

Back to the interview:

Bruce: So, Mandy, when did this breakthrough come?

Mandy: I had been subbing for just a couple of months, yet I was hired for the new studio without having to even teach for Michele. She just trusted Cheryl.

I contacted Michele for her memory, and she replied, *"Even though Mandy was a new teacher, she embraced the energy and flow of what Form Yoga was all about, plus, she had incredible music lists! Her playfulness and willingness to always try something new began to build a community."*

Michele Emmons Dehaven

Bruce: Mandy, what were your first classes like?

Mandy: I'm very shy, not that you'd know. I would get so nervous before every class that I would get butterflies in my stomach, and sweaty palms, dry mouth, the whole shebang. Oh God, I was so afraid of speaking in front of people. I'm very much an introvert, and teaching yoga was the hardest thing I've ever done, other than my divorce and giving birth.

Bruce: But you managed to pull it off.

Mandy: Mitchel, my teacher, told me, *"Just fake it. Pretend that you're on a stage, and this is your production. You're putting on a show."* As un-yogic as that sounds, that's how I was able to show up day after day and teach, because I looked at it as a production instead of me leading other people, which would be terrifying.

Bruce: But now, your new career was on a roll.

Mandy: Yes, but suddenly, there's bad news. The classes weren't growing. The new studio was losing money every month.

Michele explained: *"Our yoga business was becoming a distraction from our design business, and there weren't enough students for it to be self-sufficient. It was so hard for me to let people down, but I had put the energy into it that I could after-hours, but it needed more love."*

Mandy: I happened to be in Jamaica at the time. When I landed in Atlanta, I turned on my cell phone, and there was a voicemail from Michele:

> *"Mandy, I respect you and love you so much. I have decided to close the studio. I'm sorry, and I know you're on vacation. But know that I tried. I adore you, and I'm here to help you. However, you need to move on."*

Bruce: That must have been a terrible shock getting off the plane from paradise.

Mandy: I was a single mom. I was going through a divorce. My child came with me to teach because I was homeschooling him at the time. I felt stuck. My head was thinking, "Oh great, now how am I going to make this happen? What other yoga studio is going to let me drag my kid to work?"

198

The original *Form Yoga* space in Michele's design firm

Bruce: I remember the moment. All the teachers were heartbroken.

Mandy: Yes, but the other teachers had other gigs; I was one hundred percent invested in *Form Yoga*. I had no other options. So, I emailed Michele explaining, "I've given this some thought and figured out a way to restructure the studio where you guys will not lose money. We'll change the classes, change the teachers, change the pay structure, add a monthly membership. And I'll manage it for you. I'll make a dollar a head for people who walk into the space each month as a management fee."

Bruce: So, you offered to manage the business fulltime and make one dollar per student. That's not enough to live.

Mandy: I just wanted to keep the doors open. But what happened next is important. Michele read my email and replied, *"Okay, this sounds like a great idea. Why don't you take it and run with it."*

Bruce: Sounds reasonable.

Mandy: I thought the same thing; she's interested. She sent out an email to the community: *"We've got some good news. We might be able to keep the studio going after all. If you have questions, send them to Mandy."* So, I start working furiously — working the numbers, considering different scenarios, teachers, classes, researching other studios.

Bruce: I sense the hand of Fortune coming...

Mandy: I was gearing up and had a business question, so I emailed Michele. "Hey Michele, I need to know how to handle this issue." And she replied, *"What don't you get? It's yours. The studio is yours. I'm done."*

Bruce: Just like that.

Mandy: Yeah.

I was curious why Michele *gave* Mandy her business, so I contacted Michele again, and she replied: *"Mandy was at a time of change and evolution in her life, so I wanted her to take it and run with it. She had the energy and entrepreneurial approach to do it. Unlike the other teachers, Mandy always took charge of things when she saw an opportunity — even if it scared her a bit. So, I thought, what's there to lose?"*

Bruce: On one level, people were looking out for you – Cheryl, Michele, Mitchel – and on another level, Fortune, or your soul was watching out for you.

Mandy: When I realized that Michele was giving me the studio, it was magical. I knew that it was going to happen one day. Not *Form Yoga*, not Michele, but I knew I would own a studio. My teacher gifted me with an astrological reading at graduation. He knew why I went to teacher training. He knew what I was suffering from. We connected on a very deep level.

I sought to understand the workings of Fortune, so I asked Mandy's teacher, Mitchel Bleier, why he gifted her an astrology reading. He replied,

Mandy and I got close during training. I was aware of her life changes. I wanted to support that."

"But why, Mandy? I pressed further. "You probably have oodles of students."

"The moment of attraction is a mystery," Mitchel continued. *"And, it's in the force of being together that you understand why things are. But why something comes into being in a particular moment? That's the mystery."*

Mitchel Bleier

My conversation with Mandy continued:

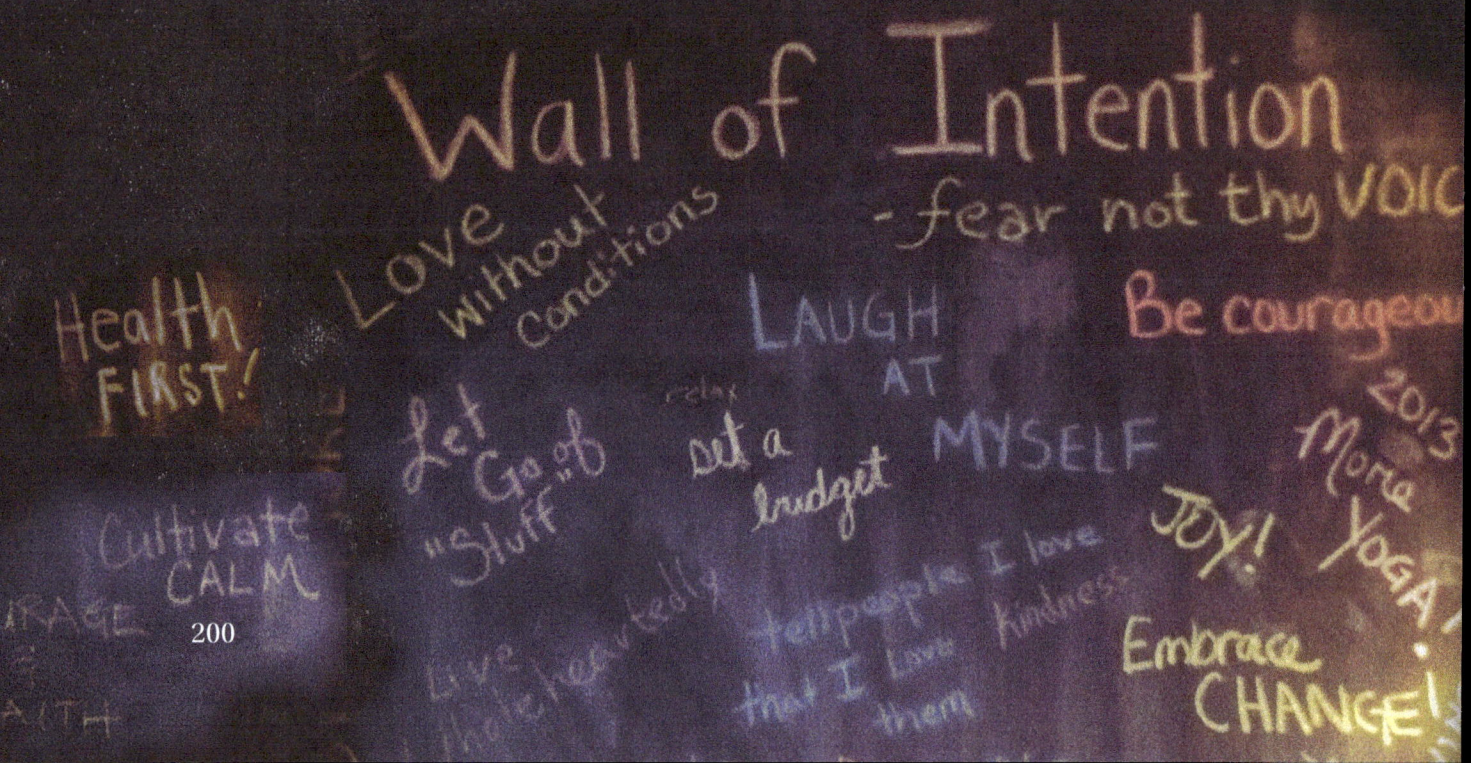

Wall of Intention

Love without conditions
-fear not thy VOIC
Be courageou
Health FIRST!
LAUGH AT MYSELF
2013 More Yoga!
Let Go of "Stuff"
relax
set a budget
JOY!
Cultivate CALM
Live wholeheartedly
tell people I love that I Love them
kindness
Embrace CHANGE!

Mandy: The astrologer predicted that I would own a studio. I was afraid of standing on my own two feet, and afraid of being the one in charge because I was afraid of screwing everything up. But I knew it was going to happen. She said it's my *dharma*. She said, *"The rose is always going to smell like a rose. It's never going to smell like a gardenia. This is already in the stars for you. It doesn't matter if you sit on your couch."* She said these words. I've got it recorded.

Bruce: Michele's offer was quite an affirmation.

Mandy: I was a divorced mom, thirty-four years old, who had never been out on my own. I had never even lived alone. And here I am, being catapulted into the role of business owner in a profession I just started doing. All these people now depended on me, all these teachers and students. It was affirming. I always believed in something – chance or will or divine intervention – but I never had proof. And now I had the proof.

Bruce: Did you have a sense of how you would do things differently?

Mandy: I never expected to be the business owner or building a brand. I started by asking myself, "What kind of environment would I want to practice in; who do I want to be surrounded by?"

Bruce: How did it feel to take the reins?

Mandy: I was terrified. My immediate reaction was, "No, no, I can't do this – especially becoming responsible for other people who depended on me. I didn't want to let anybody down. I didn't want to let myself down. It was very scary.

Bruce: Did *Form Yoga* start to emerge as a brand?

Mandy: I was dealing with a lot in my life, swinging like a pendulum, trying to figure out what was going to work. Building *Form Yoga* into a community began to take shape.

Bruce: Would you describe your brand concept as a *yoga community?*

The astrologer predicted that I would own a studio.

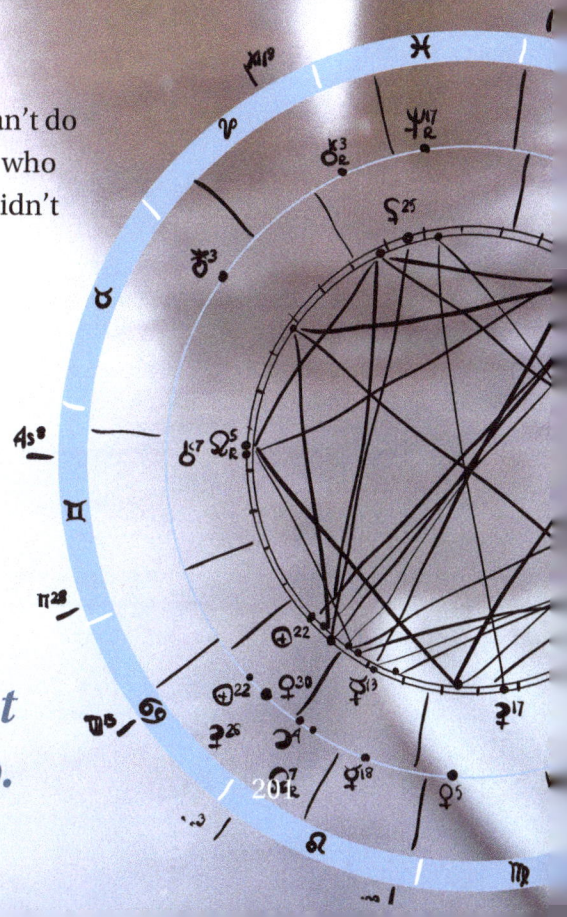

I had to decide, "Am I in this?

Mandy: Because I was single, I needed a community. It was all about me and what I needed. That's how it started, and then it became not about me at all. I think it was a byproduct of the life that I was struggling with.

Bruce: You're a fledgling yoga studio, operating in half of Michele's space, and paying her a per-student fee with no real risk from fixed overhead. Then came a dramatic shock – and a shock always enters from the outside in an enterprise. Michele lost her lease, and you had to find a space of your own.

Mandy: Dear Lord. That was a tough situation. It was kind of the piss or get off the pot moment. I had to decide, "Am in this? Can this be a business that survives on its own?" My deal with Michele was golden. There was no way I was going to lose money. The business was on a per-head basis, and I had set it up that way to avoid risk. But this was a whole new variable – uncertainty at its finest.

Bruce: Tell me about the calculation you made before rolling the dice on a space of your own.

Mandy: I sketched out how many students I would need, how many memberships, what to pay, and compared it with other studios.

Bruce: Was there doubt?

Mandy: Definitely, but still, I didn't have a choice. I was up against a wall, and the only way out was straight through – I just had to push through. I had to get through that wall. I still feel walls now. Maybe it was more fear than doubt – fear of failure.

Bruce: You found a space, moved in, and began to try out new ideas. We call it test marketing. I remember Wine Yoga.

Mandy: The business evolved organically. We had a student who loved wine, and one day he brought a bottle after class.

The author learns how to handstand.

Can this business survive on its own?"

The next week, somebody else brought a bottle. I thought, "Why not market it and sell it as Wine Yoga. It worked for a while until it didn't.

Bruce: And Ugly Sweater Yoga.

Mandy: Oh, my gosh, yeah. We also shot silly string during a core class, and I briefly offered a meditation class. I tried a Sunday free-form class where people could practice, and I would help them. Some things stuck to the wall and others not.

Bruce: You stayed in your new space for three years, then another big leap.

Mandy: I felt myself digging in too deeply – with no growth and no movement. Moving to a new space, three or four times bigger, raised the financial stakes considerably. But to move forward, I needed a better location. We were off the beaten path at the old location. Being stuck in this industry is like dying. Corporate yoga chains were popping up. I had to grow. Bigger classes would increase the revenue with the same effort.

Bruce: *Form Yoga* as a true brand began to emerge in the new space. I remember the mirrors.

Mandy: Yes. Right before we opened, I was sitting on the floor looking at these wall-length mirrors. So, I commissioned someone to paint two-foot letters across the length of the room: *YOU ARE BEAUTIFUL.* A lot of people struggle with body image, as I have in the past.

We began to shift from Power Yoga to accepting people as they are. My own acceptance of getting older changed my outlook. Our brand – and our community – offers this pure acceptance. Wherever you are is perfectly fine. If you want to grow, we've got you. If you want to chill, no problem. If you want to stay exactly as you are, great.

The new gift shop. With Shari Fox

I kept my eyes open, and I kept my heart open...

Bruce: I notice how many single people show up at night.

Mandy: They see it as a refuge, a safe space to go and be with their yoga family.

Bruce: Your brand evolved again when you started to offer retreats – Hawaii, Peru, Costa Rica, Mexico, Italy. How did that come about?

Mandy: One day, after class, I sat and talked to two new students, Shari and her fiancé, Adam. We talked in the loft for nearly two hours, like old friends. Over the next few weeks, the universe kept pushing us together. At one point, she said something about having a psycho-spiritual retreat company and I had no idea what that was. Yet soon we joined forces.

Bruce: Expanding from yoga to retreats is a brand extension – *Arm and Hammer* stands for baking soda and suddenly becomes toothpaste. Similar?

Mandy: Yes. *Soul Nourish Retreats* has transformed our business. It's one thing to spend sixty minutes with a student in a class, and another to spend seven days. It was impactful and powerful. It grew our community by leaps and bounds and continues to do so. With the retreats, we offer a culture – it's becoming a lifestyle brand.

Bruce: You have grown to become one of the most successful yoga studios in Atlanta. It's a cliche, but what's the secret of your success? Your path has been so improbable. How many single moms are handed a failing business, told: *"go run with it,"* and make it happen?

Mandy: I listened to my heart and followed what was there without focusing on my personal gain. It was more about what can I give?

and I looked for opportunity and possibility.

I probably wouldn't have given that answer a year ago, but it was there. It was already there; I just don't think I was aware of it. I was already doing it, but I don't think I was cognitively present with what I was doing. I was guided, but I didn't understand.

Bruce: What didn't you understand?

Mandy: I kept my eyes open, and I kept my heart open, and I looked for opportunity and possibility. Then I would try it. If it failed, okay, let me try over here. It was and still is an ever-evolving process of trying and failing and recalibrating. If I focus solely on the numbers, then I'm failing. Because I'm never going to have enough revenue; it will never be enough. Yes, you keep climbing and climbing, but I don't want to be that way. I don't want to live my life that way.

Bruce: (laughing) I was hoping business professors would take an interest in this book. Now I'm not so sure.

Mandy: I couldn't tell you what my margins are. My accountant emails me every month with my profit and loss. Sometimes I look at it; sometimes I don't. This month was good, so I'll take a look!

If you're visiting Atlanta and want to take a class, or are interested in a soulful vacation, visit *Form Yoga* at *formyoga.com*

Photos of Todos Santos Soul Nourish Retreat by 2TPHOTO

YOU ARE BEAUTIFUL

Sara Anderson

How a stay-at-home mom built a brand for women exploring the sensual side of sophistication.

Sara Anderson doesn't import container loads of coffee, nor has she built a major yoga business. But her story fits my favorite demographic – empty nesters seeking to reinvent themselves.

With no venture money or major capital, no board of directors or hired team, Sara has marshalled sheer tenacity to build her dream. In the spirit of Martha Stewart, Donna Karan, and Coco Chanel, Sara created a brand from her namesake. *Sara Anderson* leverages her background as an artist and her love of the natural world. I have been helping Sara make the leap from school mom to designer brand.

Bruce: Thank you, Sara for sharing your story. You offer designer scarves, kimonos, domestic linens, and more – all created from your original patterns. Your tagline is *"Feed Your Heart with Design."* Do I have it right?

Sara: Yes, I call it wearable art.

Bruce: Cool brand concept. What's your background? Were you a *wunderkind* artist as a child?

Sara: From a young age knew I was going to be an artist. When people asked, I would say I wanted to be a nurse, an artist, and a ballerina. I handily dispatched two of the three. With nursing, I realized I only had a three-day tolerance caring for people. And ballerina, uh, no. I studied art from an early age, won awards in high school, and went to the Maryland Institute College of Art Design. After graduation, I got married.

Bruce: Straight out of school?

Sara: I was twenty-two and quickly needed a way to make a living, so I worked as a paralegal until I was thirty, and I had my kids.

Bruce: Did you pursue your art while raising a family?

Sara: The kids and I might roll out paper on the floor and paint together. That was my art career.

SARA
anderson
Feed Your Heart with Design

> **Bruce:** No studio space?

> **Sara:** No, no. That part of my heart was starving. I kept saying to myself, "When they get to be a certain age, I'll be able to really do this."

> **Bruce:** When did this shift?

> **Sara:** It didn't happen all at once. When I was in my forties, I went through a huge crisis. My mother sold her home, and nobody wanted her stuff – really beautiful things. At this point, I was creating canvases, watercolors, and piling it up. Then I recognized the big I was making for my kids to deal with. Suddenly, I felt there was no point in doing this. So, I made a choice to stop. That's when my therapist said, "Oh, I didn't realize you had a choice."

> **Bruce:** How did you switch from painting with the kids to starting a business?

> **Sara:** When I was in art school, several teachers said to me, "You need to go into textile arts." I didn't take this seriously back then, but flash forward when my middle-aged self was gestating my next move, my sister said, "Look at this website, *Spoonflower*. They offer on-demand, digital printing of fabric." Immediately I felt, "Oh my gosh, this is the vehicle!"

> **Bruce:** Pay heed when inspiration arrives out-of-the-blue!

> **Sara:** My sister is almost always that person.
> I have learned to listen to those moments."

> **Bruce:** And this was when, three or four years ago?

"I made a choice to stop. That's when my therapist said, "Oh, I didn't realize you had a choice."

Sara: Yes. Our empty nest was emerging. So, I experimented making napkins and dish towels and sending them off to be printed. After ordering samples for some friends, I thought how can I make money doing this?

Bruce: No big business plan?

Sara: I was curious to see if people liked them. It wasn't slam dunk. Even if I sold them, I made no money. But at the time, I was in it just for my heart. I probably lost money.

Bruce: So now you're experimenting. What was your breakthrough?

Sara: Philip Verre. He's a friend from my kids' school. He was also the Chief Operating Officer of the High Museum of Art in Atlanta. He approached me and said, "Sara, I saw some of your stuff and I would like to introduce you to our gift shop person. Maybe there's a way you can put something in the shop."

Bruce: Okay, need to stop. Big flashing sign for the reader – Chapter 11, Rule 3: *The most effective touchpoint is YOUR KARASS*, your connections. I've never seen business work any other way. More importantly, Philip approached you. That's one part *Karass*, plus another part unsolicited help.

Sara: Exactly. Phillip said, "Here, get this appointment." I called the gift shop and they scheduled a meeting three weeks out. Then I realized, I have nothing show.

Bruce: Small detail.

> "Chapter 11, Rule 3: *The most effective touchpoint is your karass.*"

Sara: I wasn't sure what to put in a museum shop, so I created a line of printed metal cups, some Kimonos and something else – but everything fell through. The guy printing the cups misplaced the order. The woman making the Kimonos came back with something that looked horrific. I just had my dish towels and my napkins.

Bruce: Your three weeks are up. What did you do?

Sara: The High Museum's magazine had an article about an upcoming show by Ronald Lockett, a young African American who died from AIDS. Lockett juxtaposed wire, metal, rust, and decay with images of wildlife. I went through my entire pile of artwork and found five images that aligned with his show.

Bruce: I call that Reversing Space – aligning your brand to your customer's needs...

Sara: Exactly. I showed my products – the dish towels, blah blah blah – and they said, "These are lovely, but they don't really fit..." I replied, "Well, maybe you should take a look at my portfolio." They took a look and said, "This is perfect."

Bruce: They were able to take your rejected dish towels and marry them to your portfolio?

Sara: What's more, they said, "We have this show coming up by Ronald Lockett who has no product. Could you produce these on silk cashmere scarves?" I said, "Uh sure, of course I can." I had no idea how to do that, or where to buy them. No idea how to do any of it. I figured the worst that could happen would be to return empty-handed and concede, "I couldn't make it happen."

One of Sara's Lockett-aligned designs applied to a scarf.

Bruce:	But you made it happen.
Sara:	I went online to India Mart and found someone willing to print on silk, and I've been working with him ever since.
Bruce:	When we started working together, you had a very different idea for the business.
Sara:	I thought the way forward was intellectual property – creating designs and selling them to manufacturers. I spent $5000 to exhibit at SURTEXT in New York. Four or five buyers approached me and said, "We love what you're doing and would like to buy some pattern." But nothing came of it. A year later, one of the artists contacted me, "How did it go for you?" Turns out, no one made money. No one got a contract. After that I tried to get representation with an agency, and they said, "You're nobody."
Bruce:	Ouch.
Sara:	They explained, "Our customers, like *Bed, Bath, & Beyond*, come to us and say, 'That's nice, but who is she? Where she been? What's she doing? You need to be someplace."
Bruce:	The classic conundrum when starting out.
Sara:	At that point I couldn't see a path forward. In life, if you are given a glimpse of at least the next step, much less the next four or five steps, you see the path forward. That was my hope in getting a rep.
Bruce:	But instead, you approached me, wanting to create a brand. Let's talk about your experience with the Brand Story Workshop. Who did you choose to be part of it?

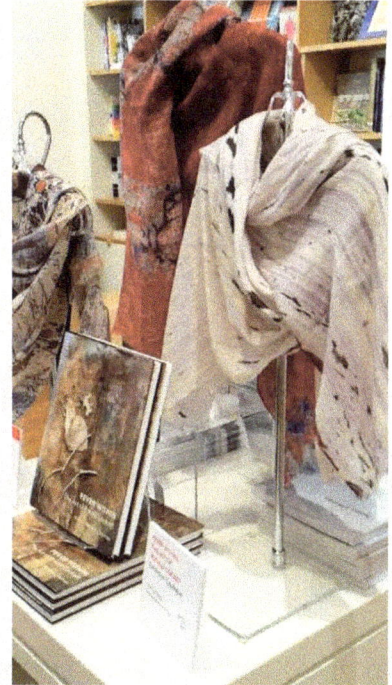

Sara's silk cashmere scarves were displayed with the artist's book at the High Museum Gift Shop, Atlanta.

'That's nice, but who is she? Where she been? What's she doing? You need to be someplace."

"I learned what it means to be 'on-brand.' I've learned to look at the world through my customer's eyes."

Sara: I chose two very candid women – also moms. One had been an interior designer and the other a graphic designer and illustrator. They also had experience with the critique process. If you don't have experience with that, it can be shattering. If you do, you realize that there's tremendous value from honest feedback. And it really points a direction for you. "Don't go there, go here."

Bruce: We identified the target customer and brand position – for the free-spirited, feminine woman who seeks to express her boldness while being true to her sensitive nature. And then, the two moms tossed out half your portfolio – "Not this, not this." What was that like?

Sara: Every piece of my artwork is like my child, like my favorite little puppy." But I also learned what it means to be "on-brand." I've learned to look at the world through my customer's eyes. I'll put together an order of cashmere scarves or kimonos and when I get them back, I can see: "That works, that doesn't work. That was a waste of money. Or, this is going to sell like hotcakes."

Bruce: You hit a lot of roadblocks on your journey, but you were never stymied by them. You're like the *Little Engine that Could*. What's that secret?

Sara: In the same way that you've been my branding advisor, my husband, Jim has been a spiritual advisor. When I say to him, "I don't know what I'm doing. I don't want to waste money. I don't want to waste time." And Jim will say to me,

"Nobody knows what they're doing. And it's okay to not know what you're doing. Just do today."

Bruce: *"Nobody knows what they're doing."* Can we make that into a bumper sticker?

Sara: I'll take it further. Doors close for a reason. Be thankful for the doors that close because you're meant to be doing something else. I really believe all of that, but I forget that. I forget I'm doing Sara and the only thing worthy of hopelessness is if I quit doing Sara.

Bruce: I love your confidence.

Sara: I don't need a certain kind of acknowledgement to feel good about what's happening. The biggest issue I have now is the plate spinning. I will spin a plate and it falls off the little pole up because I can't keep up. Now that I'm growing, I'm going to have to get help, and I've got to figure out about what happens when I outgrow my space. I really like working from home.

Bruce: That's a good problem to have. Congratulations, Sara, and thank you.

> *"Doors close for a reason. Be thankful for the doors that close because you're meant to be doing something else."*

Cooper Harris

From screen stories to brand stories – how Cooper broke out of Hollywood and into Big Tech.

Second careers typically launch after fifty. A middle manager might become a sandwich shop owner, a lawyer might become an innkeeper, or retired teacher a dog walker. Cooper Harris pushed that model to the edge.

In her mid-twenties, Cooper left a successful Hollywood career behind to start a journey into Big Tech – launching *Klickly*, an innovative e-commerce advertising platform. *Klickly* is hardly a shoestring start-up. Cooper raised money from some of the top investors on the West Coast. But Cooper's discipline, perseverance, and iterative process apply to any sized business.

To an outsider, switching horses from acting to software seems improbable. But for Cooper, her transition from dramatic stories to brand stories reignited her lifelong curiosity and passion for problem-solving.

Cooper was signed by an agent straight out of school to perform in *As the World Turns.* Thirty-eight actress credits quickly followed, including a recurring role on *The Young and the Restless.* But as Cooper tells it, she wanted something more:

"After graduating, I signed with one of the best agents in New York, and suddenly I was on a TV show! It was a journey that was exciting and really fulfilling – until it wasn't. Eventually, it didn't fully engage me. My training as an actor was incredibly intense. I learned to wield broadswords and fence, and I am certified in knife-fighting, rapier, and dagger. Even though I had a role on my grandmother's favorite soap, I needed to exit from entertainment. I felt I had different skills to employ."[1]

When a random email announcing a 48-hour hackathon landed in Cooper's inbox, she had no idea that she would soon become hooked on tech.

"A hackathon is not nefarious; it's an app-building competition with teams. It was weird to be in this room of nerdy guys, but they accepted me to be the team leader. At the end of the 48 hours, and without sleep, we had built a product that was pretty legit.

---

1 Matt Hunckler interview on Powderkeg, From Hollywood to Hackathons: How Cooper Harris Launched Her Startup and Built Her Business, November 14, 2016.

"I became intoxicated in these 48-hour tech sprints, where we could run with an idea and create a company in just two days. The scalability and potential for positive impact with tech were so huge for me. I was totally hooked. So, I quit acting and took the leap."[2]

Cooper's big life-pivot occurred when she clicked on an ad.

"I was on *HuffPost* where I saw an ad for shoes. They were cute, attractive – and they were on sale! I clicked the ad and immediately a new browser page launched that took me to another site, which loaded very, very, very slowly. I'm counting one-one-thousand, two-one-thousand, and it took forever. How often do we see a product, but don't buy it because it takes too long? That was the moment, three years ago, when I realized there needs to be a way to make an online purchase directly within the ad, or the email, or the social post, or anywhere."

Cooper assembled the team and financing to build *Klickly*, described by techies as "a data-driven commerce engine that lets people complete entire purchases directly within hard-to-reach digital ecosystems."

I asked Cooper to translate that statement for her mom.

"With my mom, I wouldn't talk about data-driven, machine learning, or the AI technology behind the user experience because she wouldn't care. I would say, 'Mom, suppose you saw some shoes on *MarthaStewart.com*. *Klickly* makes it possible for you to click the ad, choose the size, and confirm your purchase in two to three touches – directly within the ad. We enable commerce directly within the advertising.'"

Unlike Cooper's mom, I was intrigued by the AI, so I asked Cooper to elaborate:

"Every site keeps track of where you are and what you're doing," Cooper explained. "It might sound malicious, but it's not.

2   https://medium.com/thrive-global/the-inspiring-backstory-of-cooper-harris-actress-ceo-and-founder-of-klickly-55bc58908224

"The tracking aims to give you a better online experience. For example, you don't want to see ads for diapers. Right? It's more pleasant to see ads that are relevant to you. But you can't eliminate ads because they pay for the content you're browsing.

USER — VISITS YOUR SITE — LEAVES IT — SEES YOUR ADS

"We track that you like some products and not others, buy some and not others. We use this data to personalize your online experience and make it fast and easy to purchase what you see."

In my interview, Cooper described the step-by-step that built her company:

Bruce: Were you considering the technology from the start?

Cooper: The inspiration for *Klickly* did not come from a tech idea – but rather, from a human pain-point.

Bruce: Steve Jobs is relevant here. Long before iPhones, Jobs described the genius of his method: *Mass-scalable technology must be reverse-engineered from the user experience, and not by building a better mousetrap – and hoping there's a market for it.*

Cooper: Exactly. And for me, even though this pain-point seemed meaningful, I did a ton of market research to determine whether the numbers were there to back the concept. Do other people get annoyed when they're trying to make a purchase or give a donation online, and it takes too long? Are others frustrated by shopping on the phone?

Bruce: What does it mean for the numbers to back it up?

Cooper: I've had ideas before that seemed brilliant, for example, a heated push-up bra.

Bruce: That would make for interesting market research...

Cooper: The reality is that I'm always cold. The bra idea is obviously a very small market. As a VC-funded company in the tech realm, you have to have big ideas that apply to huge numbers of people.

"I did a ton of market research to determine whether the numbers were there to back the concept."

Launching a tech company: Step-by-step:

Bruce: Take us through the step-by-step to launch a tech company.

Cooper: This applies to any start-up idea, but Step One is to take your idea and be excited about it – but also poke holes in it. Try to tear it down, because the biggest trap is to get saddled with an idea that doesn't have a viable market or is too niche. This is why you do your research. I discovered that $5.5 trillion worth of purchases are abandoned in shopping carts each year. By comparison, the entire e-commerce industry was $2.3 trillion last year. A huge number of items aren't being purchased – partly because shopping on your phone is annoyingly hard. An enormous market exists if you can solve that problem.

Step 1. Research

Bruce: What's the second step?

Cooper: Step Two, you model the solution. I brainstormed a massive model on a whiteboard. I went at it from the user experience instead of the technology. Then I asked, how can I make that happen technically? Is there a really cool solution?

Step 2. Model

Bruce: Sounds like Steve Jobs.

Cooper: Yes. Step Three is to build a prototype – to prove your idea is technically possible – even if it's hacked together with third-party apps. You can always pay some guy a couple of thousand bucks to hack it together. For a non-tech example, imagine that you're launching a fantastic camel milk soap (and I honestly don't know if that exists), you need to demonstrate that you can make soap out of camel's milk.

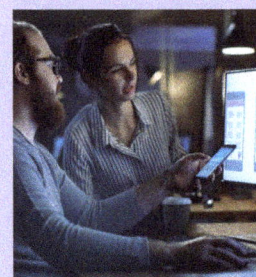
Step 3. Prototype

Bruce: Once you have a tangible prototype in hand, do you go for funding?

Cooper: No. Step Four is to get LOIs – Letters of Intent – from potential customers. Suppose you wanted to make that soap. You go to *Bergdorf Goodman* and see if they are interested. Ask them to give you a Letter of Intent that says, Camel Soap is such a unique product that they could sell four-thousand units. It's not legally binding, so companies will do it for you. With *Klickly*, we got an LOI from *Atom Factory*, the big artist management company founded by Troy Carter, who launched Lady Gaga and other amazing artists. We also received an LOI from *Omaze*, a company that sells celebrity experiences, and a New York radio station to sell their merchandise.

Step 4. LOIs

"Hold off making a formal pitch for as long as possible."

Bruce: So now you're building all this movement around the product. Are you pitching investors?

Cooper: No. You want to hold off making a formal pitch for as long as possible. It's much easier to get money when you have a prototype plus Letters of Intent that say: *"We're going to pay you money when you make this.*

Bruce: Okay. With the LOI's in hand, are you now ready to pitch?

Cooper: No. While all this was going on with my founder's journey, I aggressively sought meetings with potential investors – to gather information, not money – just to learn.

Bruce: Where are we – Step 4.5? How did you find these people?

Cooper: A bubbling tech scene was emerging in Los Angeles, so I went to every tech event I could get my hands on, sometimes three a night. I would approach people and ask, "Hey, do you know experts in the tech industry who'd be willing to have coffee with me in the next two to three weeks?" I like people and get really excited hearing people's stories. I met Rishi, a well-connected VC, at a tech event this way. He had just come to town, and he saw me, thinking, "She knows everyone." He ended up offering incredibly helpful guidance. He now runs innovation at *Bain*. From these contacts, I would schedule two to three meetings every single day. I would buy them coffee and ask questions.

Step 4 ½

Bruce: What did you ask?

Cooper: I had a specific list of questions. I wanted to know what did they think of the idea, what do investors want to hear, and who should I pitch to? Some thought it was a terrible idea; others felt the market was saturated. Of the 700 people I had coffee with, 40 were mildly interested in the concept and the space, and only 10 or 20 thought the idea had legs. After six months of coffee, those were the ones I contacted to pitch.

"A bubbling tech scene was emerging in Los Angeles, so I went to every tech event I could get my hands on."

Bruce: So now we're at Step Five, making the pitch to investors. Is there a standard sequence for valuing the company as you go from angel investors to round one, to round two, and so on?

Cooper: I was literally self-taught, so I had to make all of this up. And I had to be remarkably disciplined since I didn't know what the heck I was doing. But yes, there is a structure. That first funding is the hardest because you don't even have a product – some people call it early angel funding, others call it R&D funding, and still others call it friends and family. I took no family money, but it's often the first funding.

Step 5. The Pitch

Before going for your next round – let's call it pre-seed – you set certain markers. Today, people raise many rounds before they get to their series A, which is the debut of the company. So, your friends and family round gets you started – anywhere from $20 thousand to $100 thousand – super small for a tech company. Then you raise your pre-seed round – anywhere from $250 thousand to a million on the high side. At this point, you still don't have revenue. You're working toward early customer adoption, building a better prototype, and enhancing your numbers.

Eventually, you get to your seed stage, which is still before your series A. Seed-stage funding ranges from $750 K, up to two, three, five million dollars. Investors want to see some traction – small revenues of $5k, $10k to $40k per month.

Bruce: And with each round, your prospectus becomes more detailed and more promising?

COOPER HARRIS

220

Anastasia Simon, of Shadow Ventures (R), chats with Kat Cole COO & President, N. America of FOCUS Brands (L), and Cooper Harris about the future of retail.

"To give away more of your company, you better be making more money."

Cooper: Yes, but you are also giving away pieces of your company at every stage. And, if you're going to give away more of your company, you better be making more money, have better LOIs, and better client contracts.

Bruce: What happens after the seed stage?

Cooper: Now, you're ready to ask for Series A. At this point, you've raised maybe two or three rounds, and even sometimes five. On the West Coast, we see founders raising Series A for anywhere from $3 million at the low end, up to $25 million. It's insane. At this point, you need anywhere from $100 thousand to $300 thousand in monthly recurring revenue.

Bruce: At this point, is it a working company?

Cooper: Yes. You're either making money or building user adoption. A company like *Uber* had to move very fast to build mass scale adoption before there was any profit. For companies into robotics or advanced AI, they are looking at building products that are ten years ahead of the market. If you have the right names behind you, and a lot of patents, you can justify a hundred-million valuation without any revenue.

Bruce: This is a book for shoestring start-ups, so maybe we're getting ahead of ourselves. Let's talk about the moment you first felt that, *yes*, this idea could work.

Cooper: I had already solved that because we built a working prototype.

Bruce: Yes, but when did you sense that customers will respond, and the business will take off?

Cooper: To be honest, it took a while.

Jane King interviews Cooper Harris at the Nasdaq MarketSite.

Bruce: This is where I invoke *Field of Dreams* and the voice in the cornfield, *"If you build it, they will come."* You can't bank on the second part, *"They will come."*

Cooper: I see people building products all the time, doing the whole shebang, raising money, without really testing the product. They built it, but no one *"comes"* – and they lose a lot of money. We were very iterative, spending two years before we thought it would work – one year of R&D, and another year of pilots, including partnerships with *Shopify* and *Magento*. We projected 40 brands in our beta test, and we had around 400. Today, we have well over a thousand customers.

Bruce: That's a lot of customers. Did you have a sales team?

Cooper: Initially, just me and an intern. We went to *Facebook* groups and used other outreach methods. It wasn't so much about selling as getting the word out. What we got right was our core concept, which was: *"We're going to advertise for you. You don't need to pay us unless we make a sale."* Klickly is commissioned-based. It's the easiest sell in the world.

Bruce: So, *Klickly* is buying lots of media space upfront and inviting brands to the platform without needing to pay. Aren't you taking a huge risk?

Cooper: Our investors hated it, but it turned out to be the best piece of *Klickly* – and our intellectual property. Brands can jump on the platform, choose the commission they want to pay and receive exposure based on their commission. Our investors hated the idea that our customers could choose to pay the minimum without any skin in the game. Our investors didn't understand that when advertisers see their priority in our algorithm, they become incentivized to increase their commission. If you give us a 50 percent commission on every sale, we're going to work our butts off for you. If you give us two percent, you will rank lower than other brands.

Klickly dashboard screens.

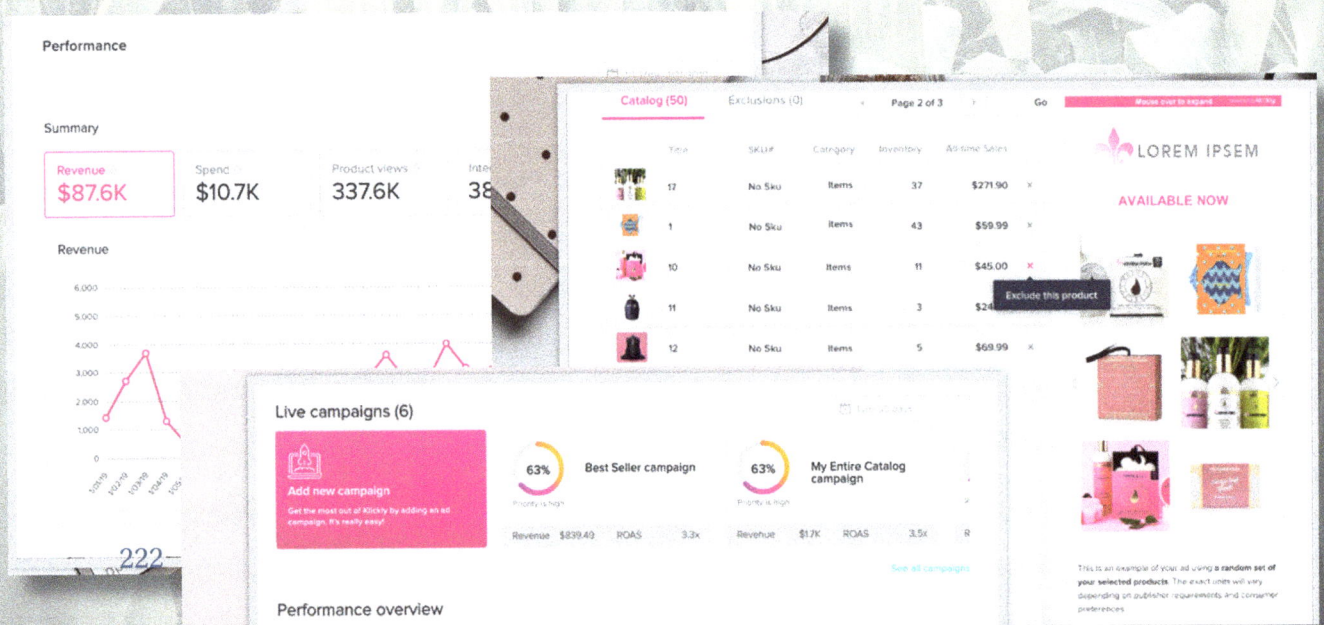

"In Waldorf, you learn to address the holistic problem, not just memorize certain pieces of it."

Bruce: This book encourages start-ups to build a unique brand position. I was surprised at your barebones branding.

Cooper: We have played it very close to the vest. Initially, we didn't want anyone to know what we were doing.

Bruce: That's a novel marketing strategy.

Cooper: We were intentionally vague and intentionally confusing because of competitors. *Klickly* is an invitation-only platform, so we only accept certain brands. Our proposition is very attractive, but to work, our customers must have enough data points to build out predictive modeling. We are very targeted in our customer acquisition. For every brand enrolled in the *Klickly* platform, we turn away five.

Bruce: I want to go back to the beginning. You received your early education in a *Waldorf School.* Our son went to *Waldorf,* and I remember him knitting a pair of socks in fifth grade. I marveled at the planning, visualization, and math involved – counting rows, stitch counts, alternating colors, the gusset, and so on. *Waldorf* gives children this sense of agency – that they can make and do things.

Cooper: That's the reason I'm on the board of the *Emerson Waldorf School* in Chapel Hill, NC now. My parents instilled this sense that with a lot of work and discipline and thoughtfulness, I could solve problems. In *Waldorf,* you learn to address the holistic problem, not just memorize certain pieces of it. Understanding the whole system – or the machine used to solve a problem – allows you to approach problems in a more multi-faceted, well-rounded way.

1	2	3	4
2	4	6	8
3	6	9	12
4	8	12	16
5	10	15	20
6	12	18	24
7	14	21	28
8	16	24	32
9	18	27	36

Bruce: Everyone focuses on your background in acting and how you journeyed from actor to entrepreneur. Can you make a case for entrepreneur to actor? If someone is going into business, should an entrepreneur develop skills in diction, stage presence, and confidence?

Cooper: My training in acting has served me well in business. You don't receive acting training if you're in business, but they give you executive coaching and how to give talks. As an actor, you learn how to empathize and understand the emotional space of another person.

When you're talking to investors, you try to understand their real problems with your pitch versus just what they're saying. You identify on an emotional level. Acting also teaches you to like people and understand them. This is the key in business. You are better working with people when you can empathize with them when you understand their motivations, and sense where they're coming from. Bottom line, you prefer doing business with people you like.

Bruce: Business is so much about communication.

Cooper: Yes, and discipline. I had seven years of vocal training where I learned how to tell a story and express ideas so the audience understands you. It's a discipline. I went to a boarding school for performing arts, and then a conservatory, plus a BA in performing arts. Every day we wore black leotards that stripped any external façade. We worked from 8:00 a.m. and rehearsed until midnight, including weekends. There is a discipline to learn eighty pages of lines a day. These skills translate into business, and they help handle the stress from getting in front of a lot of people.

Bruce: To close, I want to go to a quote from Goethe that you shared, a passage that inspires that sense of "just do it."

224

> Lose this day loitering—
>   'twill be the same story
> To-morrow–and the next
>   more dilatory;
> Then indecision brings its
>   own delays,
> And days are lost lamenting
>   o'er lost days.
>
> Are you in earnest?
>   Seize this very minute-
> What you can do, or dream
>   you can, begin it,
> Boldness has genius, power,
>   and magic in it,
> Only engage, and then the
>   mind grows heated—
> Begin it, and the work will
>   be completed!
>
> - Goethe, *Faust*

Cooper: Goethe is challenging us. So many people feel they can't do big things. But when does the galvanizing moment arrive where the world gives you permission to do your thing? Everyone is waiting for that moment, or for the message, or the sign, where the world gives you permission to act on your dream. But that moment, that permission, has been granted by virtue of you being here and having the idea.

Bruce: The resistance to being bold is built into our wiring.

Cooper: Yes, but if you simply start, putting one foot in front of the other, I firmly now believe that the forces of nature will collaborate to get you where you need to go. Goethe is saying, "Don't sit back and wait for permission. Step boldly in the direction of your dreams. Boldness has genius, power, and magic in it."

Bruce: That's so beautiful. Thank you.

Cooper: No, this is awesome. I love what you're doing.

Bruce: The feeling is mutual.

THE ROLLER-COASTER OF RISK.

"The thrill is gone... The thrill is gone, baby..."

B.B. King's plaintive lyric triggered a dark funk as Donnie pushed his eco-friendly lawnmower across the perfectly manicured tiny lawn.

Yep. The thrill was gone.

Donnie was a committed environmentalist, but the fun was gone. With fewer people attending his Saturday demos, Donnie learned something new about his target customer: hip, urban, climate-savvy homeowners with tiny lawns represented a too-small universe.

Carbon-Free Lawns was a great business idea for a college student, but no longer felt viable as a career path at age 23. Yes, Donnie could shift his business model to gas power, but that would cast his brand into a sea of landscaping competition. More importantly, he realized that the real thrill was the creativity that comes with being an entrepreneur.

A few days later, the Ace Hardware manager asked Donnie if he would demo a new tumbling composter alongside the *Fiskars* mower as a package deal.

Donnie took the composter home to learn how it worked. He experimented with kitchen scraps, yard waste, water, and starter. Donnie loved the idea of converting his garbage into garden soil, but turning and tending the drum was tedious. His first batch smelled like rotten eggs; plus, the process took a month. When he realized he would need two units — $180 each — to handle a normal kitchen, he dismissed the whole exercise.

The next day, still feeling morose, Donnie raked leaves while streaming Sam Cooke:

"It's been a long, long time coming. But I know a change gonna come, oh yes it will."

While Donnie bagged leaves, an idea popped in — outsourcing your compost! If a sack of good compost cost $20 at the store, there must be a market for fresh, living compost – like probiotics but for the garden.

Within minutes the picture came together: Donnie would pick-up his customers' kitchen scraps each week in a 5-gallon pail for $36 per month and swap it out with fresh delivered compost or donate their finished compost for local use. Donnie would give the donated compost to Ace Hardware's Garden Center in exchange for a spot behind the store to rotate his composting barrels. His lawn-raking would provide the "brown matter."

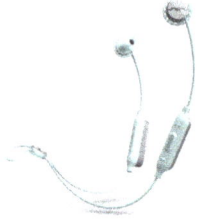

Donnie now had a new business card to hand out: "Carbon Free Compost." To pay one worker, Donnie calculated he would need to collect 12 pails per day. Twenty-four pails would net $25,000 per year in gross profit per route. Four routes in a large city would net $100,000 per year — not enough to retire in five years, but an exciting goal for a twenty-three-year-old. The grand vision would be to franchise the concept. He even trademarked his tagline: *"Turn Garbage into Gardens."*

I tell this story to illustrate the trajectories possible with owning a business: What works one day will stop working the next. A trendy product or service might suddenly lose steam after a maddeningly short shelf-life. Whether the feeling comes from a song, or from not making payroll, one day, you might realize that a shift in direction is needed.

Major life shifts appear innocently from out of the blue:

"Donnie, could you promote this new composter at the Saturday demo?"

"Sure. Can I take it home and play with it?"

Entrepreneurial Thinking — Successful entrepreneurs respond to leads and openings like a hound on a scent. They pursue hunches, watch for trends, and keep their creative fires lit. Entrepreneurs also grow stuck in their ways, comfortable in the tried-and-true, and resistant to change. Most people look at life – and at building a business – like a bricklayer. In the bricklayer model, you lay down a starter row and keep adding rows until you either build your way to the top or tire of laying bricks.

The "brick-by-brick" model goes back to Dale Carnegie (1888 - 1955), whose Depression-era blockbuster, *"How to Win Friends and Influence People,"* launched today's craze for self-development. Fresh off the farm, Carnegie's first job was selling correspondence courses to ranchers. Later, he sold bacon, soap, and lard for the meat-packer, *Armour & Company.*

As the company's number one salesman, Carnegie demonstrated a knack for selling and connecting to people, a skill that he built into a mini-empire of self-improvement training. He is remembered for brick-laying quotes like this:

"Most of the important things in the world have been accomplished by people who have kept on trying when there seemed to be no hope at all. If you want to conquer fear... go out and get busy."

This principle was famously reinvented by Nike to *"Just do it."*

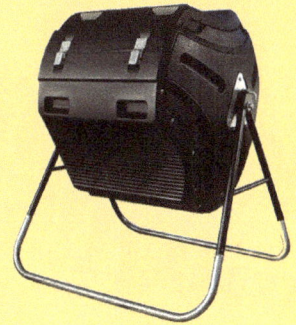

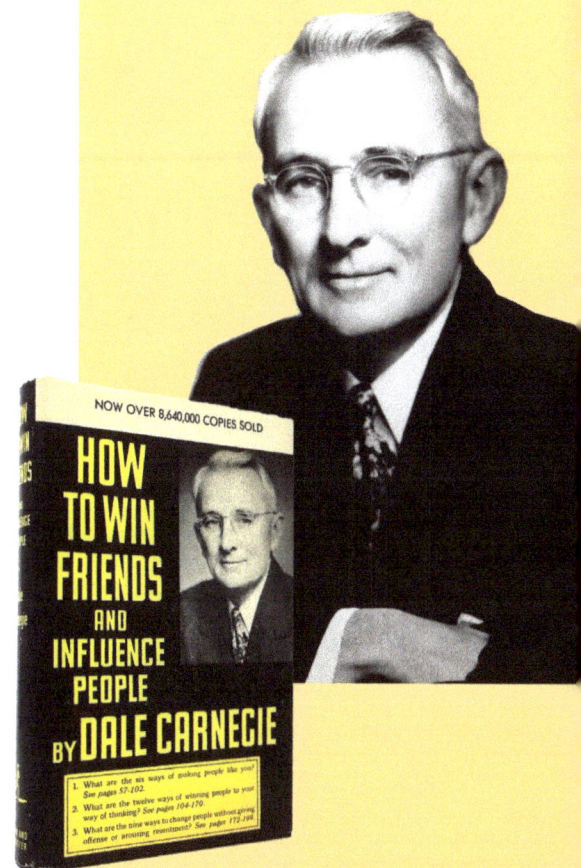

"If you want to conquer fear... go out and get busy."

HOW TO WIN FRIENDS AND INFLUENCE PEOPLE

Carnegie's *"keep on trying"* works for some, but for others, it brings to mind the famous aphorism for *"definition of insanity."*

My preferred Carnegie quote acknowledged the rollercoaster trajectory of all human endeavors:

"Develop success from failures. Discouragement and failure are two of the surest stepping stones to success."

Dale Carnegie's approach to business success still rules the day, but his actual story was more complicated.

Hoping to steal some luster from the industrial titan of steel (Andrew Carnegie), Dale changed his name from Carnagey to Carnegie.

Dale successfully applied his *get-busy* approach to business, but his personal life was more complicated. Dale and his first wife divorced after his affair with a married woman produced a daughter out of wedlock — a girl he supported without ever acknowledging paternity. It was an era when one's public life and private life rarely intersected, so why should we care today?

As an aspiring entrepreneur, you will seek role models and mentors to counsel your hopes and dreams. Discernment and discrimination should guide your way.

Norman Vincent Peale's *"Power of Positive Thinking"* forms a guiding philosophy for many entrepreneurs. Peale claimed that one could achieve a *permanent* optimistic attitude through unending positive, conscious thought. Critics of Peale warned he was peddling a form of auto-suggestion or self-hypnosis that defeats an individual's self-motivation, sense of reality, and ability to think critically.[4]

That takes us to Tony Robbins, born Anthony J. Mahavoric, who added jet fuel to Carnegie and Peale's message and claimed the mantle of *"the nation's #1 Life and Business Strategist."* Tony Robbins' brand position is to have *"dedicated his life to helping people discover their true purpose and leverage their unique gifts to achieve massive success – to make their life a true masterpiece."*[5]

Yes, I want that for you too. But, realistically, you will paint over your canvas many times on the rollercoaster of risk — never achieving "massive success" nor reaching the summit of your "masterpiece." One day you will realize that, like *Hansel & Gretel* following the breadcrumbs, your business journey is inseparable from the ups and downs of personal suffering, self-discovery, and inner growth. Success corresponds directly to your ability to find comfort in the Unknown.

Your business journey is inseparable from the ups and downs of personal suffering, self-discovery, and inner growth.

4 Murphy, R. C. "Reverend Peale's Panacea." Nation. 180: 398–400, via Wikipedia: https://en.wikipedia.org/wiki/The_Power_of_Positive_Thinking

5 The official Website of Tony Robbins: https://www.tonyrobbins.com

Riding the Rollercoaster

Being an entrepreneur feels less like painting a masterpiece and more like strapping your butt into the rollercoaster. Most entrepreneurs take this plunge willingly by leaving careers and paychecks behind. They may also launch a second act to reinvent themselves in retirement — often with a short supply of capital, self-confidence, experience, or luck.

The Principle of Hazard

John G. Bennett, a British author, philosopher, and industrial researcher (1897-1974), saw how the rollercoaster of risk reflects something bigger: a universal principle of *Hazard* that governs our individual affairs. It's the same principle that governs the evolution of a species, the appearance of life on earth, and the formation of the universe.

Bennett saw *Hazard*, not as mechanical chance or luck, but as the larger force that moves the cosmic drama forward. As a principle, *Hazard* is not the chance that a tree will hit your house or that you will win the lottery. *Hazard* comes into play as an energizing force when you invite significant risk into a situation of importance — for example, starting a business.[6] Suddenly, the right people become attracted to this force and want to participate.

"If man sees Hazard as a misfortune rather than an opportunity, he will seek to close the door to freedom rather than keep it open." – J.G. Bennett

Hazard carries risk. When an Olympics skier jumps out the slalom gate, she puts years of training on the line. No matter how skilled and practiced, Hazard and the unknown always play a role in the outcome.

---

6 J.G. Bennett. *Hazard: The Risk of Realization*. Bennett Books.

The opera singer who hits the high note, the gymnast who sticks the landing, the potter who finesses the clay, and the slugger who swings for the fences all push their practice to the edge of failure.

Hazard ceases to be a place of looming danger, but instead, the source of creativity and change.

Hazard is not a blind bet or over-confidence. It's a creative force that upends the status quo. Your ability to find comfort with *Hazard* might draw from a dad who encouraged you to paddle through the rapids, or from a mom who taught you to express your feelings. In either case, *Hazard* ceases to be a place of looming danger, but instead, the source of creativity, dynamism, and change.

In our brand strategy work, I would often size up a client by looking for cracks in their corporate culture, asking:

"How can the creative force enter this business? Is this a closed system run by an autocrat, a fearful flock of corporate sheep, or an open culture that invites many points of view?"

Because the client hired us, I assumed they outsourced the "sorcerer role" to us for a reason — specifically to invoke *Hazard* — but more often not. Corporations are tightly-wired to protect against a creatively-aimed "spanner" from landing in the works.

"Forget your perfect offering
There is a crack in everything
That's how the light gets in."

– Leonard Cohen

233

Successful Entrepreneurs Reveal How Risk-Taking Propelled Their Careers.

Arianna Huffington, the founder of *The Huffington Post*, made a prescient bet that a new type of media platform could play an essential role in the digital age. She also gripped the rope of *Hazard* when she leaped from prominent Republican to prominent Progressive. In her words: "Failure is not the opposite of success — it is the stepping stone to success. For anyone who is an entrepreneur, that is perhaps the most important lesson."

Mark Cuban, a founder of many tech companies, espoused a healthy fear of *Hazard*: "I hate risk," he told CreativeLive. "I'm terrified of it." He understood that Hazard played a catalytic role, but he also mitigated the risk through relentless market research and learning.

Jeff Bezos sacrificed his well-paying job in finance to launch an online bookstore out of his garage. He didn't leave Wall Street to retire from Hazard, but quite the opposite — he chose to push at Hazard's creative edge: "I had to project myself forward to age 80. I don't want to be 80 years old, cataloging a bunch of major regrets of my life."

And then, there is *Mic*, the high-hopes news site for millennials, started in 2010 by two 23-year-olds — high-school friends, Chris Altchek and Jake Horowitz — who, understandably, had little work experience or journalism know-how, but did display remarkable comfort with *Hazard*. Having rolled the dice with $60 million in funding, 160 staffers, offices on the 82nd floor of One World Trade Center, and a $500,000 domain name, *Mic's* grandiose venture overlooked one critical fact: they never developed a sustainable business model. [4]

---

4 Inc.com. 5 Wildly Successful Entrepreneurs Reveal How Risk Taking Propelled Their Careers

If you accept OPM (other people's money), it's easy to send it down a hole – the startup's "burn rate." With a shoestring start-up, you stay closer to the ground, sensing *Hazard's* pulse to keep you frugal and honest. Evidence of what's working (or not) appears quite quickly — often before you open the doors. Pouring money down the Hazard hole obscures that realization and prolongs the day of reckoning. "We didn't really know what we were doing," one of *Mic's* founders said in 2014.

"So we took a startup, entrepreneurial approach, which was to try a bunch of different things and see what worked and what resonated."[5] It took seven years for Mic to burn through its funding. If *Mic* had a viable brand position, they would not have tried to compete with *Vice* and *HuffPost*. "*Millennial audience*" is not a brand position – it's a demographic. Yoga detox stories for 23-year-olds are no different than detox stories for 55-year-olds.

5. *"Hope, Change and Venture Capital,"* Observer, 9-11-2014

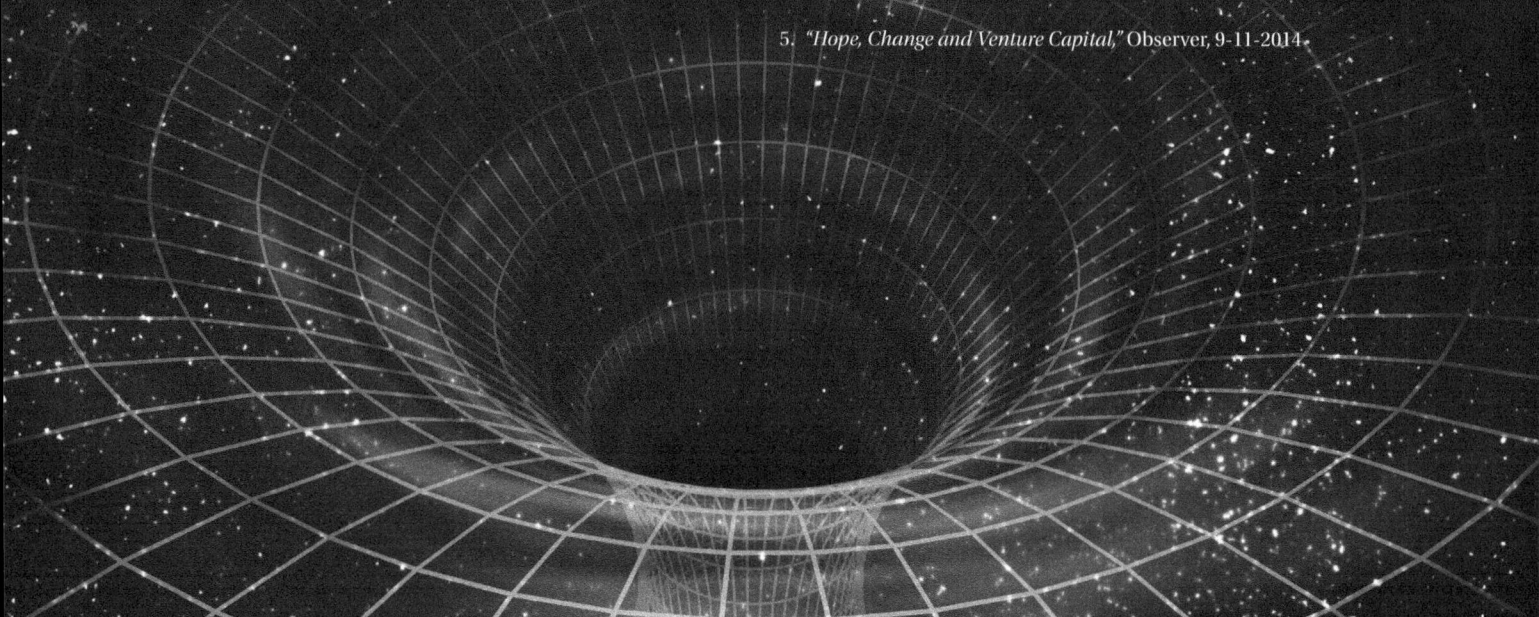

Engaging Hazard — So how do you engage *Hazard* without getting burnt, and without getting out over your skis?

The Sorcerer's Apprentice offers an object lesson. You're tired of lugging water pail by pail, paycheck to paycheck, so you start a business. You enchant a broom to do the work for you (the power of leverage), using capital, scalability, creativity, and labor to perform the magic. Since you're reading this book, you're an apprentice. You recognize the risk a young business faces, but you can't presume that an elder sorcerer will bail you out. That's because the Sorcerer also screwed up as an apprentice.

235

The elder Sorcerer learned from life – just like you.

The Sorcerer learned how to invoke *Hazard* — how to ride the crest where the rolling sea and a turbulent surf meet as an unending, unfolding curl. As a startup Sorcerer, you're learning to ride this wave as well.

This may be more philosophy than you expected – you just want to sell CBD oil.

But since you've chosen to don the Sorcerer's hat, all bets are off.

My advice is to start each day attending to *Hazard* — recognizing that the wave of the *Unknown* (and not just your business smarts) is propelling your journey.

Here is the method:

Hazard and the Three Balls — When you shake hands, sign the agreement, clink glasses, snip the ribbon, or turn the spade of dirt, the startup clock starts running. You have plucked the harp string to awaken the angels — the people, materials, vendors, contractors, city officials, and strategies that must align like musical harmonics to launch your business. By announcing, "I'm starting a business," you activate a timeline *with a life of its own* — so be patient and vigilant.

To keep on track, you must sense where you're at each day in the process. Imagine keeping three balls aloft representing the beginning, middle, and completion of your project:

- **Ball Number One**
  represents the moment you decided to start the business — full of promise and purpose, but nothing to show yet. Can you remember when you decided, "I'm starting a business." This moment might have ocurred two months ago, or in a dream as a child.

- **Ball Number Two**
  reflects the present moment – where you're at right now. Is this a happy moment watching materials get delivered, a perfect vendor appearing, or a partner joining? Or are you stuck in a delay, a funding issue, or a process failure?

- **Ball Number Three**
  lives in the future. It's the day when you open your doors. Ball Number Three is neither a vague fantasy, nor grounded in reality. Yet, it's steering the whole enterprise.

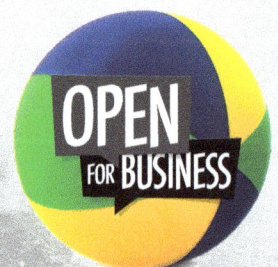

Keeping on Course

With Ball Two hijacking your feelings, there are always problems to fix, fires to put out, and doubts to allay. But, if you don't attend to Balls One and Three, the train can fall off the tracks. You, the budding Sorcerer, must maintain the presence of mind to juggle all three balls. Here's how:

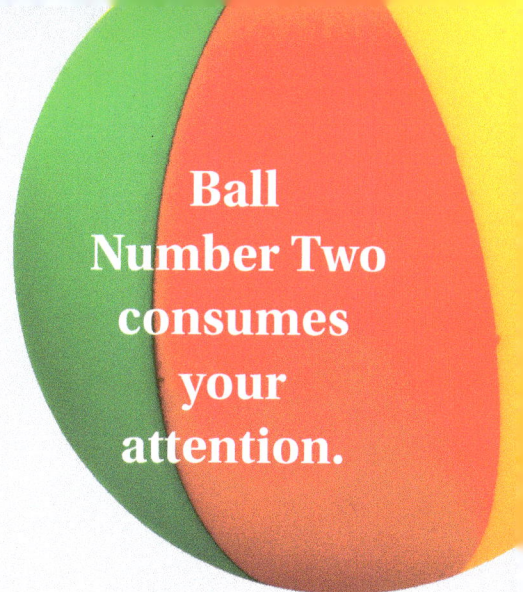

Ball Number Two consumes your attention.

2. The Present Moment

1. Decision to Commence

3. Open for Business

1. Sense the decision to commence.
Remember the day you started with a blank page of promise. Now, acknowledge the distance you have traveled (woohoo!). *Even if the project stalls, complications mount, or you become frustrated in the present moment, acknowledging your progress keeps your momentum alive.*

2. Sense your destination.
Where are you right now? As problems arise, they can pull you off course and force you to make a bad decision. Now sense Ball Three. *Keeping your destination in focus will guide you to make the right course corrections, even in the heat of the battle.*

3. Don't be afraid to adjust your course.
The quality of the present moment – *Ball Two* – is your compass. Progress that leaps and then stalls is normal.

Up-up-up is unlikely. But, if Ball Two keeps heading **down-down-down**, you need to make a course correction.

The *Mic* magazine guys waited too long to rethink their strategy and were forced to liquidate their dream.

When the wind shifts, don't be afraid to adjust your course. Constant course correction defines what it means to be in business.

The Rollercoaster of Risk

Our brand agency, *Design Coup*, went through a rollercoaster of its own. We enjoyed a fairy tale launch investing just $250 each.

Over the next decade, we grew organically to reach nearly a million in revenue. A big chunk of that revenue came from printing direct mail for *Matria Healthcare*.

Matria Healthcare was sold, and our work began to move in a digital direction. There's far less profit in emails. More importantly, by placing ever more attention on our car-selling product, we failed to re-tool our brand, build a digital skill-set, and pivot to compete in an e-marketing world.

With *AutoTrader* and *Lowe's* floating our hopes, we burnt through lots of OPM (other people's money). The money pressures and the Recession exacerbated cracks in our partnership. Could we have redefined our goals and brand position? Maybe, but the *Design Coup* rollercoaster seemed to have a life of its own.

Brands Drift

Fuzzy brand positions, trying to do it all, failing to correct course, and a lack of direction all contribute to drift. Even worse, the smaller the business, the bigger the drift. In a big company, tight corporate standards keep the brand on track. In a shoestring startup, you have to keep Ball Three aloft yourself.

The NASA brand manual of 1975 specified branding rules for each spacecraft.

How cool is that?

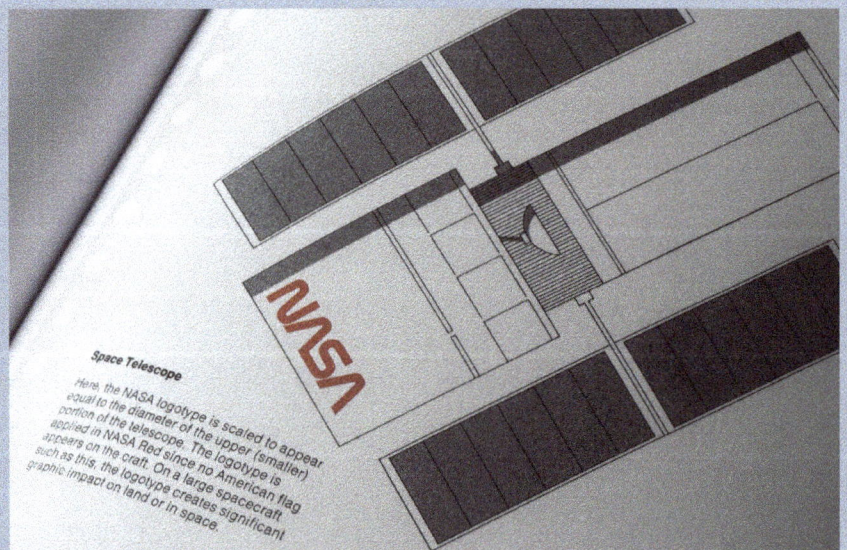

Space Telescope

Here, the NASA logotype is scaled to appear equal to the diameter of the telescope. The logotype (smaller) portion of the telescope. The logotype is applied in NASA Red since no American flag appears on the craft. On a large spacecraft such as this, the logotype creates significant graphic impact on land or in space.

A free-styling NASA employee would never go rogue with the Space Shuttle's markings, but it's highly *likely* that you will present slide decks with different looks, hand out promo items with squished logos, or more likely, create ads that fail to voice the brand position.

Big companies recalibrate their brands all the time: *When Federal Express* became *FedEx,* it transformed its brand from a business with airplanes and trucks to one with neighborhood print shops.

The big guys know how to do this. Smaller brands and startups tend to drift.

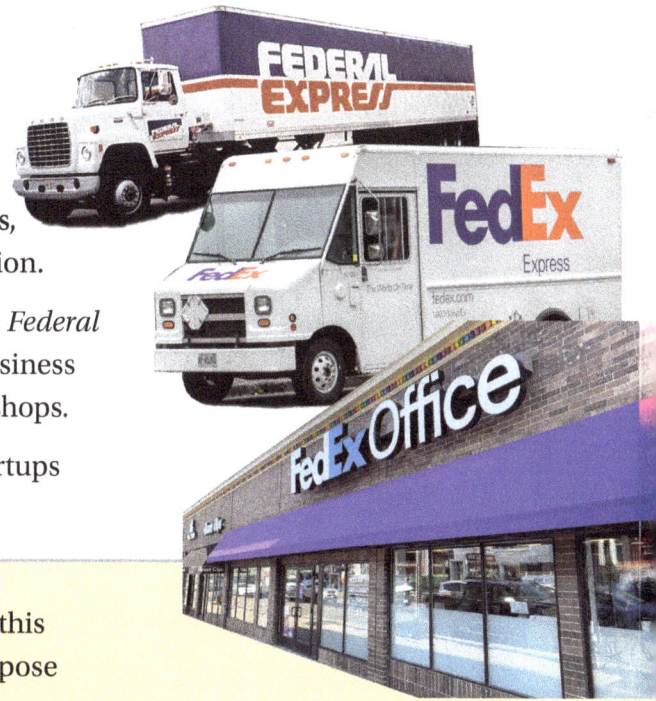

Is this on-brand? — Now, it's your turn to recite this mantra every day: *"Is this on-brand?"* Every time you compose an email, make a pitch, design a display, create a promotion, or shoot a video, four words should come to mind:

"Is this on-brand?"

During the 1992 Presidential election, campaign strategist, James Carville helped elect a little-known governor from Arkansas, Bill Clinton, by famously rebranding the campaign. Carville hung a whiteboard in the campaign war room that listed three rules. One ultimately became the campaign mantra and brand position:

"The Economy. Stupid"

Yes, you can hang your diploma above your leather chair, but you will get more mileage by hanging your brand story in your conference room.

If you're not working with a big agency (and you're not), <u>you</u> are the Brand Police. It's hard work to maintain brand vigilance, but you will reap big rewards from a consistent and effective Brand Story.

Thanks for putting in the hard work.

Now, follow your dream.

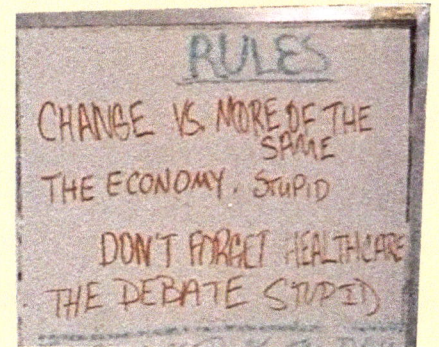

ACKNOWLEDGEMENTS.

FM MULTIPLEX STEREO BROADCAST MAKES HISTORY

CHICAGO, Ill.—Station WKFM made the world's first FM stereo multiplex broadcast simultaneous with their usual background music programming. Equipment used was designed, constructed, and installed by Sherwood Electronic Laboratories. Another World's "first" was achieved by Sherwood's sponsoring the FM Stereocast.

Edward S. Miller, Gen. Mgr. of Sherwood cues Frank Kovas, WKFM Pres., to start the pioneer stereocast.

My mom (rest her soul) grabbed all the attention in my Introduction, so I would be remiss not to acknowledge my dad.

Edward Miller was a legendary audio engineer whose Chicago startup, *Sherwood Electronics*, grew to become one of the largest AV receiver manufacturers in the world (now based in South Korea).

Ed founded the company in 1953 at age 32 with a simple brand concept: *High fidelity sound from elegant gear.* As a kid, I grew up with sine waves and stereo effects ping-ponging across our living room in our namesake, *Sherwood Forest* neighborhood.

My dad made two major contributions to the industry: the world's first FM stereo broadcast (using his technology on WKFM in 1961) and the first 100% solid-state audio receiver (in 1967).

Neither friends nor family were truly aware of Ed's accomplishments. That's because at dinner parties, with his love of garden design, my dad would likely grab a shovel from the host's garage and dig new borders in the backyard while the other guests mingled inside.

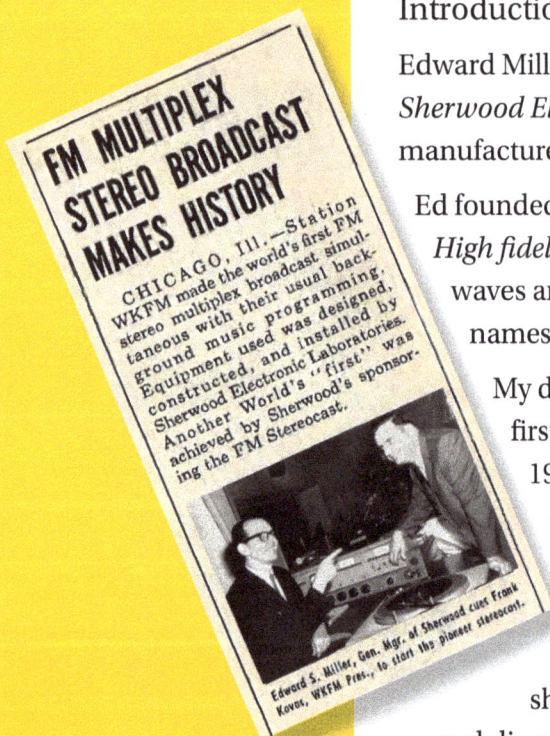

My dad understood the inseparability of form and function. His sense of engineering and aesthetics has manifested in my work over the years as "structure meets character."

Ed's elegant receivers still stand apart for their slim designs, sleek escutcheons, walnut surrounds, and muted glowing dials.

While Ogilvy, Trout, Ries, and Strowitz were creating legendary ads, my dad was also adding to the oeuvre of sixties advertising – except he had the gumption to break the molds of *Radio Electronics* and *Audio Magazine*. What kind of engineer abandons promoting with technical specs and goes straight to the customer's desire: *"SO, Who Needs a Ticket?"*

I also want to give big thanks to the protagonists in my brand stories: Michael Jones and Kenneth Lander of *Thrive Farmers*, my good friend, Sara Anderson, Mandy Roberts of *Form Yoga*, and Cooper Harris of *Klickly*.

Also, thanks to Cindi Johnson of *Side by Side*, and Hugh Huntington and Scott Tower of the *Meher Archives* for their non-profit stories. And to my good friend, Bill Green, Managing Director at *Climate Adaptive Infrastructure Fund*.

A special thanks to my generous neighbor, a corporate trademark lawyer who asked to remain anonymous. Her *Spectrum of Trademarkability* will help you avoid much grief.

I want to thank my wife, Karen, who manages to appear in each of my books, and my sons, Nathaniel and Jacob and girlfriend, Hilary, for their millennial insights.

Finally, a big shout out to Michael Higgins, my former business partner. We came to our craft as writer and designer, but emerged as brand strategists, primarily by trial and fire.

You can debate strategy all day, but a 5:00 pm deadline forces a special kind of clarity. "Eventually, we gotta put ink on paper," was our call to arms. Either the idea gets customers to pick up the phone – or it doesn't. If it works, there's your brand strategy.

Many thanks to our clients who let us develop these insights – on their nickel! And a bigger thanks to the clients (not many) who were willing to go down the path of Brand Story with us.

And thanks to you, the reader, for taking the plunge. To quote Goethe one more time: *Begin it, and the work will be completed!*

1999 – Starting our agency in the back of my house.

Credits

About the Author

Bruce Miller has more than 30 years of experience in marketing, media production, and brand development for Fortune 500 corporations, mid-sized companies, non-profits, and shoestring startups.

While working with clients, Bruce realized that few companies followed a coherent brand strategy, so he developed the Brand Story® approach. In the process, he discovered:

- A wealth of brand knowledge exists in most companies, but it is not properly leveraged.

- Team ownership is necessary to implement a brand. For this reason, Brand Story workshops work best when they are collaborative.

- The lack of positioning makes a brand ineffective. Small companies only look small because they lack a brand position.

- The best way to engage customers is by building a Brand Story that aligns to their needs.

Bruce is a graduate of the UCLA Department of Motion Pictures and Television. He is also an author and screenwriter. Previously, he was a creative partner at *Design Coup, Inc.* and before that, Senior Writer at *CheckFree Corp.* (now *Fiserv*).

Bruce is an avid sailor, political junkie, and yoga enthusiast. He and his wife Karen, a chaplain educator, live in a 120-year-old house in Decatur, Georgia.

A few years ago, Bruce used his startup methodology to launch *The Learning Tribe,* an alternative approach to high school education.

As an author, Bruce has written, *"FORTUNE, Our Deep Dive into the Mysteries of Love, Healing, and Success,"* and *"RUMI Comes to America."*